HOW TO BE A JEWISH PARENT

A Practical Handbook
for Family Life

Anita Diamant
with Karen Kushner

SCHOCKEN BOOKS

New York

Grateful acknowledgment is made to the following for permission to reprint previously
published material: *Janet Berkenfield:* Translation of "Modeh Ani," by Janet Berkenfield,
from *Siddur Birkhat Shalom* (1993, Havurat Shalom Siddur Project, Somerville, Mass).
Reprinted by permission of the author. • *Marcia Falk:* "Blessing of the Children"
from *The Book of Blessings: New Jewish Prayers for Daily Life, the Sabbath, and the
New Moon Festival* by Marcia Falk (1996, HarperCollins; 1999 paperback edition,
Beacon Press). Copyright © 1996 by Marcia Lee Falk. Reprinted by permission of the
author. • *The Reconstructionist Press:* "Blessing for the Family," from *Kol Haneshama
Shirim Uvrahot* (1998, The Reconstructionist Press, 7804 Montgomery Ave.,
Elkins Park, PA 19027). Reprinted by permission of the publisher.

Library of Congress Cataloging-in-Publication Data

Diamant, Anita.
How to be a Jewish parent / Anita Diamant with Karen Kushner.
p.   cm.
Includes index.
ISBN 0-8052-4170-1 (hc); 0-8052-1116-0 (pb)
1. Child rearing—Religious aspects—Judaism.   2. Parenting—Religious
aspects—Judaism.   3. Jewish religious education of children.
4. Jewish families—Religious life.   5. Fasts and feasts—Judaism.
I. Kushner, Karen, 1946- II. Title.

HG769.3 .D53 2000   649'.1'089924—dc21   00-026574

www.schocken.com

Book design by Deborah Kerner

Printed in the United States of America
First Edition
2 4 6 8 9 7 5 3 1

For our children,
who continue to teach us the important stuff

Emilia Ball Diamant
Noa Rachel Kushner
Zachary Kushner
Lev Yakov Kushner

Contents

CONTENTS

Acknowledgments

A book about parenting owes everything to parents—especially our own mothers and fathers, who did everything they could for us.

This book also owes an enormous debt to our partners in parenting and life, Jim Ball and Larry Kushner, whose wisdom, humor, love, and tech support are a wonder.

Thanks to all of these parents, teachers, rabbis, cantors, and friends for their time and expertise; we are especially indebted to the generous folks who read and commented on draft chapters when they might have been working or playing or sleeping: Steven Chervin, Barbara Davis, Rabbi Joshua Elkin, Merle Feld, Sheila Goldberg, Becca Hornstein, Carolyn Keller, Dr. Sam Kunin, Rabbi Daniel Lehmann, Cantor Riki Lippitz, Rabbi Daniel J. Margolis, Edward Myers, Rabbi Simcha Pearl, Amy Sales, Rabbi Sandy Eisenberg Sasso, Carol Sheingold, Rabbi John Schechter, Sara Rubinow Simon, Rabbi Liza Stern, Sallie Randolph, Serene Victor, Rabbi David Wolfman, Cantor Lorel Zar-Kessler, Arnold Zar-Kessler.

Thanks to Arthur Samuelson, Jennifer Turvey, Susan Ralston, and Dassi Zeidel at Schocken Books, who still care to make beautiful books.

Rabbi Barbara Penzner has been a sounding board, source, hand-holder, and thoughtful commentator on every-last-chapter for all of Anita's books. *Todah rabah,* Barbara.

Preface

The day-to-day realities of raising children are delightful, frustrating, exhausting, transforming, fulfilling, and humbling. We do the best that we can. We make mistakes. We try again. We learn and grow together. They teach us more than we teach them.

Parenting is a wholly human practice, and a holy one. Making babies and raising them to be adults capable of loving and learning is not only the way we get to "play God," it is also how many of us find God and connect with what is most sacred in life.

How to Be a Jewish Parent is a book of strategies and tools for the greatest adventure life offers. But even more than that, *How to Be a Jewish Parent* is a celebration of Jewish life.

Dire statistics about the demise of the Jewish people (sometimes discussed under the code word "continuity") tend to make discussions of Jewish parenting seem like a last-ditch effort to preserve an endangered way of life, a hedge against assimilation and intermarriage.

For us, Jewish parenting is not about building a wall to keep your children from abandoning Judaism; it is about raising healthy, joyful human beings within our rich, diverse, life-giving tradition. Jewish parenting is about giving your children a gift that will help them become the wisest, strongest, happiest people they can be.

This notion is rooted deep in Jewish tradition. "Be fruitful and multiply" is the first *mitzvah* in the Torah, the first Jewish obligation. Childlessness is treated as a tragedy in the Hebrew Bible in part because raising up the next generation provides the mysterious, elemental joy of creation itself. The Talmud says, "With every child the world begins anew."

The ideas and suggestions in these pages are offered as means to serve the wishes, dreams, hopes, and prayers you hold for the lives entrusted to you during the all-too-brief span of childhood. These are years of countless miracles. First smile, first tooth, first step, first book, first date. Enjoy them all.

Anita Diamant
Karen Kushner
Newton and Sudbury, Massachusetts
September, 1999/Tishrei 5760

Introduction

Every day, parents make hundreds of decisions for their children. Does she need an extra sweater? What should we hang on the nursery walls? Is this a safe neighborhood for children? What kind of preschool would be best for our child?

Every choice a parent makes—even a sweater-sized one—is a model to young eyes. Every decision is a life lesson. For Jewish parents, many choices—even the little ones—can have Jewish content and impact.

How to Be a Jewish Parent was written to help you turn some of the big and small choices of raising children into opportunities for expressing and imparting Jewish values and traditions.

How to Be a Jewish Parent is a unique guide to Jewish family life. Both a parenting manual and a guide to Jewish customs and beliefs, this book combines contemporary developmental understanding of how children learn and grow, respect for traditional Jewish wisdom, faith in the vitality of the diverse constellations that comprise today's Jewish families, and a belief that you are the real expert about your own children.

In these pages, you'll find answers to straightforward questions: Where do I find a Hebrew name for my baby? How can I make the Passover seder interesting to my four-year-old? What are the blessings for the Sabbath table? How can we make this bar mitzvah meaningful?

You'll also find discussions of the long-term implications of choices you make when children are little: why choosing a Jewish preschool or summer camp is more important than selecting a college. How sending a child to a Jewish day school can have an impact on the whole family's religious observance.

How to Be a Jewish Parent also provides guidance for giving growing children age-appropriate choices: What do I tell my three-year-old who feels cheated out of Christmas? How do we negotiate plans for a bat mitzvah with an emotionally erratic thirteen-year-old? What do I do when my teenager announces she wants to keep kosher?

How to Be a Jewish Parent answers these questions with insights collected from many sources: the rabbis who wrote the Talmud, child psychologists, Jewish educators, and lots of experienced moms and dads. Even so, you will find very few "shoulds" and "shouldn'ts" in these pages. This is a book of choices—your choices.

No two families do things the same way. We all season our soups with different spices. We paint our walls different colors. We play different games and different kinds of music.

Similarly, no two Jewish families provide their children with precisely the same combination of Jewish history, spirituality, culture, and community. Contemporary Jews tend to believe that in the past all Jews did things the same "orthodox" way, but that is not true. Judaism has always been a pluralistic tradition, deep and wide enough to carry many kinds of vessels on many different journeys.

Nonetheless, and in the interest of full disclosure, *How to Be a Jewish Parent* does have an "agenda." The goal of this book is to help you raise healthy, happy children by providing you a window into Judaism's rich, varied, and life-affirming traditions and values.

You don't have to know how to read Hebrew, or be able to quote from the Bible, or bake your own challah to make this goal your own. Parenthood makes beginners of us all.

But regardless of your Jewish background, only you can provide your children with a Jewish childhood. Giving your child a Jewish education, and seeing him or her through bar or bat mitzvah is not enough. Healthy Jewish parenting isn't something you "provide for" your children, it requires sharing a Jewish life *with* your children.

Although children do not come with guarantees, people who grow up to be proud of and positive about their Jewishness tend to have parents who are connected to a Jewish community, engaged in Jewish learning, and perhaps most importantly, find pleasure in their own ongoing, life-long Jewish "journey." *How to Be a Jewish Parent* is the atlas to help guide you on your family's Jewish journey.

WHO IS THIS BOOK FOR?

How to Be a Jewish Parent is for Jews who grew up in homes rich in ritual and tradition, and for Jews who were raised without any religious education or observance. It is for Jews by choice, who may feel overwhelmed by the prospect of providing children with an identity that is still new to them. And this book is for non-Jewish parents who are committed to raising Jewish children.

How to Be a Jewish Parent is for new mothers and fathers, just starting to make choices for infants and toddlers. It is for parents with preschool and school-age children, and for parents of adolescents.

How to Be a Jewish Parent is also for grandparents who want to provide grandchildren with warm Jewish memories, for non-Jewish grandparents who want to understand their grandchildren's religious upbringing, and for rabbis, cantors, and educators who teach Jewish parents.

This book is for members of Reform, Conservative, or Reconstructionist synagogues, members of secular Jewish organizations, and participants in smaller, less formal study and/or prayer groups called *havurot* or *minyanim*.

How to Be a Jewish Parent is also for people who are still searching for their place in the Jewish world. In other words, it's for the entire liberal Jewish community—the majority of American Jews—for whom Jewish law (*halachah*) is not *the* unifying arbiter of all Jewish life but a venerable authority and important source of values and standards.

Part I ("Parents As Teachers") is an introduction and guide to Jewish family practice. This section gives you a chance to consider and shape a connection to Judaism you can model and teach. Since children are exquisitely sensitive to dishonesty and hypocrisy, this connection must be genuine and fulfilling—something that goes beyond an effort just "for the sake of the children."

Chapter 1 ("Values and Goals") invites you to consider the basic Jewish values, goals, and expectations summarized in the prayer recited for

Jewish babies: "May he/she grow into a life of Torah, marriage, and right-eous deeds." Here you'll find how to translate these ideals into loving objectives for yourself as a parent.

Chapter 2 ("Creating a Jewish Space") explains the idea of the Jewish home as a "little sanctuary." Since all people learn the meaning of "comfort" and "peace" within the walls of their childhood homes, a household suffused with Jewish images, smells, and tastes imparts a bred-in-the-bone affinity for Jewish modes of thought, behavior, and happiness. This chapter also addresses the importance of food and eating for Jews, including the range of ways Jewish families interpret the laws and customs of keeping kosher.

Chapter 3 ("Making Community") spells out ways to connect with organizations, institutions, and networks that can foster your goals as parents and provide your children with other important Jewish models and teachers. This section also describes the global Jewish "village," which includes Jewish vacationing and connecting to the land of Israel.

Chapter 4 ("Defining Jewish Time") describes the moment-to-moment, week-to-week, and year-to-year cycles of Jewish life, and how to bring them home with an introduction to the Sabbath and a holiday-by-holiday guide to family celebration.

Chapter 5 ("Conflict") takes an honest look at the inevitable frictions in Jewish family life: between spouses, between siblings, between parent and child.

Part II ("Ages and Stages") covers life-cycle moments, major developmental issues, and choices Jewish parents confront, from the crib to college.

Part III (Modern Life) recognizes that although the Jewish community has always included special-needs children and adopted children, the community has only recently begun to respond to the particular needs of these two increasingly visible groups. Chapter 10 ("Special-Needs Families") reviews support available to special families and Chapter 11 focuses on needs and services for adoptive families. Finally, children deserve honest answers to questions about death and dying, but since this is an area most parents find difficult to address, we included some suggestions in Chapter 12 ("Talking to Children about Death").

Most chapters end with a brief list of books and other resources that the authors consider useful and inspirational.

A FEW WORDS OF ADVICE
ON USING THIS BOOK

How to Be a Jewish Parent is filled with suggestions, ideas, and strategies. Try only what makes sense to you, what seems right for you and your family. As in all aspects of parenting, there is no faking Jewish commitment. You can't teach what you don't love. Ultimately, you have to discover your own Jewish way if you want your children to find theirs.

And please, read ahead. Although it seems incomprehensible today, the baby in your arms will be setting off to school someday. Your Jewish choices—even some of those seemingly sweater-sized ones—can make a difference in your family's life in the years to come.

PART I

Parents
As Teachers

Parents spend lots of time teaching their children facts and skills: The stove is hot. The sky is blue. Use soap when you wash your hands. Say "thank you."

But this kind of instruction is only a small part of what and how parents teach. Parents teach children what is delicious by putting food in their own mouths and whispering, "Yum"; what smells good by putting flowers to their noses and sighing, "Ahh." Parents define kindness, generosity, and love with kisses and hugs, smiles and frowns, questions and answers. Unconsciously, parents teach their children complicated cultural constructions such as manners, grammar, and gender roles.

We do most of this simply by being there in the morning when our children wake up and in the evening when they go to sleep, by living under the same roof. Just being ourselves, we teach them how to be human.

Which is why it comes as no surprise when the children of physicians apply to medical school, or when the sons and daughters of music-lovers take up musical instruments. In those families children learn that medicine or music is what grown-ups talk about, study, practice, and love.

Children not only follow in parents' professional footsteps, they also mimic their mannerisms and absorb their tastes. During adolescence, teenagers notice these patterns with an unpleasant shock and often do what they can to remake themselves by noisily rejecting their parents' fondest wishes while unconsciously duplicating their gestures and values. There are exceptions galore, but by and large, Democratic-party activists beget Democrats, music-lovers beget season-ticket holders, and Jews who care about Judaism beget children who embrace Judaism.

"Cares about Judaism" counts for much more than your family background or even years of Jewish education. In this sense, Judaism is not inherited like brown eyes or freckles.[1] It is transmitted, parent-to-child, by example as well as instruction, in countless ways.

3

The following four "principles" may help you find your way to be an effective Jewish model for your children.

1. Model Jewish Learning   You do not have to know "everything." In fact, whenever a child asks a question that goes beyond your ability to answer, you have an opportunity to teach one of Judaism's great lessons: learning is for everyone. When you tell your child, "I don't know. Let's look it up together," you demonstrate that Jewish learning is a life-long endeavor—and if you do it with a smile, one of life's pleasures. Learning together with a child gives him or her a sense of shared purpose with the adults they love, which makes them feel grown-up, powerful, and good about themselves.

You don't have to speak Hebrew, or cook chicken soup, or keep Yiddish folk songs on the CD player to be an effective Jewish role model. You don't necessarily have to be Jewish—although an unambiguous Jewish identity provides a solid foundation. But in order to be an effective Jewish parent, it is essential to become, in some way, shape, or form, a student of Judaism for yourself.

There are many things parents learn "for the children": which car seat is safest, how to mediate between siblings, how to solve algebra problems all over again. Similarly, many parents start to learn about Judaism "for the children." But if exposing your children to their tradition remains the only reason for your connection to Judaism, if holiday celebrations are centered solely around children and have no adult content, if you find no reason to enter a temple apart from walking your kids into Sunday school, and your only Jewish commitment is a car pool, your kids will probably come to share your view that Judaism is for children only. They will learn that Judaism is something children outgrow.

But when sons and daughters see mothers and fathers reading Jewish books, taking Jewish courses, bringing Jewish questions and enthusiasms to the dinner table, they absorb the idea that Jewish study is something grown-ups do. And they will want to do it, too.

2. Identify Jewish Teachable Moments   Everyday life is filled with what educators call "teachable moments," opportunities to tease out a fact, practice a skill, encourage appreciation, introduce a new word, explore a moral dilemma. Parents tend to do this automatically. Driving in the car you might say, "See that sign? It says, 'Merge.' Do you know what that word means?" Walking in the park you might stop and say, "Do you hear that sound? It's a robin singing."

Connecting Jewish moments—or words or objects or values—with your child's natural curiosity is a simple extension of this process. Many Jewish teachable moments are embedded in the holidays, Shabbat, and life-cycle rituals. Judaism's entire ritual structure might be seen as a way to insure that such moments happen to every Jewish child. "Look at the special challah I got for Rosh Hashanah." "How many candles in the menorah tonight?"

Nowhere is this more obvious than during Passover. The seder, most beloved of all Jewish rituals, was actually structured to beguile little children, to provoke their questions, to create a whole evening of teachable moments.

But Jewish teachable moments don't have to be limited to "Jewish time." Parents can introduce Hebrew words into everyday speech: *boker tov* and *leila tov* (good morning and good night), *Ima* (Mommy) and *Abba* (Daddy). Shopping for food can be a time to teach about *tzedakah* (righteous giving): "Would you like to pick out a can of soup for *tzedakah* to bring to the temple's food drive?" Vacationing in a new city or country, put some Jewish "sights" on your itinerary: "How is this synagogue different from ours?"

3. Create Positive Jewish Memories Most Jewish adults will tell you that their happiest and most meaningful Jewish childhood memories are connected to family celebrations, and associated with meals and good times. Or else they are connected to summer camping or youth groups. Providing your children with these memories requires planning: inviting guests to your holiday table, saving for camp, choosing a synagogue with a strong youth program.

Another kind of cherished memory is created in the rhythms of the day and the week, reading Jewish storybooks at bedtime, visiting the bakery for challah and cupcakes every Friday, making origami frogs for the family seder.

4. Make Room for Holy Moments Children are curious about God. They ask what God looks like, where God lives, what God wants. The best way to answer is by asking your child what she thinks God looks like, where he thinks God lives, and what he believes God wants. Avoid telling a child that she is "wrong." Be honest and say, "Nobody knows what God looks like." Or "Everyone spends their life trying to figure out what God wants."

It may help to put aside the "G word" and its unfortunate association with a bearded old man in the sky. If your child asks about God, share the "holy moments" in your life: the birth of a baby or the first sight of an adopted child, the glow of Shabbat candles on your children's faces. Jewish life provides many openings for such "holy moments." Take advantage of them; point out the beauty of your holidays, the peace of your Sabbath table, acknowledge and name these holy moments.

Whenever you say a prayer—any prayer—you help your child frame a moment of wonder or peace as an expression or acknowledgment of holiness. And whenever or however your child expresses awe or reverence, applaud their sensitivity.

Chapter 1

Values
and Goals

Jewish parents celebrate the birth of children with delight, with food, and with an ancient promise called *brit*—covenant. *Brit* is the way Jews conceive of their relationship with God: it is a contract renewed in every generation when parents gather family, friends, and community to say, "This child is now part of the Jewish people."

This covenant is "sealed" with rituals and celebrations (explained in Chapter 6). But the ceremonies are only the beginning of this "bargain." At virtually every *brit milah* (covenant of circumcision) or *brit bat* (covenant for a daughter), parents and friends recite a prayer/wish/promise that constitutes the "fine print" of the *brit:*

> As he/she has been brought into the covenant, so may he/she enter into Torah, *huppah* [the wedding canopy] and *ma'asim tovim* [good deeds].

This ancient three-fold wish[1] gives voice to the dreams and hopes of Jewish parents. Generations understand and interpret these terms differently, but the fundamental principles transcend history, because they express universal wishes that children reach their full potential—intellectually, emotionally, morally, and spiritually.

Torah, *huppah, ma'asim tovim.* Each of these ideas is both metaphor and goal, each implies traditional values and demands authentic standards. And though they may seem like nouns, they are really imperative verbs.

Torah means "Learn." *Huppah* means "Love." *Ma'asim tovim* means "Live righteously."

These principles are not abstractions, because each of them is a *mitzvah*. *Mitzvah* is the Hebrew word for "commandment" or "good deed," or "Jewish obligation." There really is no English term that captures the complexity of this concept. *Mitzvah* is simultaneously value *and* goal, concept *and* action. *Mitzvah* is praxis—it is how you "do" Judaism, which is an activist tradition, passionately concerned with the details of how life should be lived. Matters of faith are, by comparison, left unspoken, which is why it's no accident that the three-fold prayer for babies does not mention God.

Of course, for many Jews, "commandments" imply a divine Commander, which means that *mitzvot* (the plural of *mitzvah*), laid out in the revealed scripture, called Torah, must be obeyed. But there are other ways to understand *mitzvot* and to feel commanded or directed by Jewish tradition.

The Hasidic teacher Rabbi Yehuda Aryeh-Lieb of Ger discerned a relationship between the Hebrew *mitzvah* and an Aramaic word that means "together," and taught that a *mitzvah* could be seen as an act that unites people, and connects people with the divine.[2] Thus, teaching and modeling *mitzvot* to your children becomes a way to unite them with the Jewish people throughout history and around the world, and also to unite their lives with such sacred purposes as *shalom* (peace) and *tzedek* (justice).

Merle Feld, a contemporary Jewish feminist, recasts the word in a different light. "I can't honestly say we are 'commanded' to rest—it's not my language—I don't think I've ever felt 'commanded' to observe Shabbat or anything else for that matter. 'Invited' feels like a more accurate verb for me."[3]

Being a Jewish parent means forging your own understanding of and connection to these *mitzvot,* and then teaching and showing your children how to learn, love, and do good—as Jews.

Torah   Torah is a complicated word. "The Torah" refers to the first five books of the Hebrew Bible*, also called the Pentateuch, or the Five Books of Moses.

---

* The word for "Bible" comes from the Greek *biblia,* meaning "books." The Hebrew Bible includes the Five Books of Moses, the Prophets, and the Writings. This is what Christians call the "Old Testament," believing that Jesus announced a new covenant between God and humanity, which was spelled out in a "New Testament."

"A Torah" is the handwritten scroll from which Jews read in an annual cycle of Genesis, Exodus, Leviticus, Numbers, and Deuteronomy.

"Torah" means "teaching," and can refer to much more than the Five Books of Moses. It may be applied to the entire Bible—as well as to Jewish commentaries, starting with the Talmud and embracing contemporary theology.

Finally, since every person is unique and every person has something to contribute to the on-going conversation about Jewish texts and Jewish life, everyone can be said to be in possession of his or her own "Torah."

The Talmud, the great collection of Jewish thought compiled between 200 B.C.E. and 500 C.E, places Torah study at the apex of all human endeavor:

> These are the obligations without measure, whose reward, too, is without measure: To honor mother and father, to perform acts of lovingkindness, to attend the house of study daily, to welcome the stranger, to visit the sick, to rejoice with the bride and bridegroom, to comfort the bereaved, to pray with sincerity, to make peace when there is strife.
> And the study of Torah is equal to them all.[4]

Torah study is considered a delight and one of life's great pleasures, yet it is not entirely its own reward. As the Talmud points out, it is meant to lead to all forms of righteous behavior: offering hospitality, making peace where there is strife, participating in all of life's pleasures (weddings) and sorrows (funerals)—in other words, Torah study is the path to doing *mitzvot.*

A life of Torah may also be understood as an on-going engagement with others in a lively reading and re-reading of Jewish texts. Torah study is not accomplished through memorization and recitation, nor can it ever be "mastered," since Torah is an on-going, dynamic, and essentially creative process.

Nevertheless, the process of Jewish learning does yield intellectual rewards. The back-and-forth dialectic that is the essence of classical Torah study, encourages curiosity, diligence, intellectual precision. It rewards hard questions and honors new ideas. Students of Torah are expected to disagree with each other and even with their teachers—respectfully but forcefully.

Torah celebrates context—the warmth of community—as well as content—the light of insight. Or, in more traditional language:

> It is a tree of life to those who hold fast to it
> And all of its supporters are happy.[5]

Teaching "Torah" Universal literacy among Jews is a long-standing tradition. Even in times and places when reading and writing were the privilege of aristocracies and their minions, Jews taught their sons to read. The most sought-after groom was not a rich man but a promising scholar. And even though literacy was considered less important for women, fathers in every generation saw to it that their daughters learned to read, though often in a vernacular, such as Yiddish, rather than the sacred language of Hebrew.

The American Jewish community is famous for academic attainment. In any given year, 20 to 40 percent of students at Ivy League schools are Jewish[6], as are nearly 40 percent of America's recent Nobel laureates.[7] But Jewish literacy is another matter. While most American Jews are familiar with the works of Shakespeare, the writings of Maimonides are known to a much smaller number. Only a minority can read Hebrew.

Jewish parents are becoming less tolerant of this discrepancy between general and Judaic knowledge and are working to provide their children with a solid understanding of Jewish concepts, languages, values, and texts.

No two Jews will agree on what belongs on a list of the fundamentals of Jewish literacy, but for the sake of a worthwhile argument, here is one attempt at an outline of the Jewish Basics that will guide you as you consider what you want your own child to learn:

• *A Jewish Vocabulary* English, Yiddish, and Hebrew terms that give the speaker a sense of membership and mastery of some basic Jewish concepts: synagogue, Israel, rabbi, cantor, *chutzpah, kippah, mitzvah, schlep, shalom, Shema,* Shabbat, Torah, *tzedakah.*

• *Familiarity with Jewish Holidays* The annual cycle of major celebrations: Rosh Hashanah, Yom Kippur, Sukkot, Simchat Torah, Hanukkah, Purim, Passover, Shavuot. Also, Tu B'Shvat, Holocaust Remembrance Day, Israel Independence Day, Tisha B'Av.

• *Biblical Characters and Bible Stories*   The stories we've been telling our children from the beginning: Adam and Eve, Noah and the Flood, Abraham and Sarah, Isaac and Rachel, Jacob and Leah and Rebecca, Joseph and his brothers, Moses, Aaron, Miriam and the Exodus, Ruth the convert, Isaiah the prophet.

• *Famous Jews*   Names that are a source of identity and pride: the Baal Shem Tov, Bruria, Martin Buber, Albert Einstein, Anne Frank, Abraham Joshua Heschel, Emma Lazarus, Maimonides, Golda Meir, Rashi, Yitzhak and Leah Rabin, Jonas Salk, Henrietta Szold.

• *Jewish Geography*   Finding ourselves around the world: Jerusalem, Babylonia, Barcelona, Warsaw, Chelm, Borough Park, Tel Aviv.

• *Jewish History*   From Ancient Israel to the State of Israel, the 4,000-year saga includes the Golden Age in medieval Spain, the Holocaust, and the story of the Jews in America.

• *Modern Jewish Culture*   High and low: the stories of Sholom Aleichem and the humor of Mel Brooks, the klezmer stylings of Mickey Katz and the symphonies of Leonard Bernstein, the show tunes of George and Ira Gershwin and the pop tunes of Paul Simon, the fiction of Cynthia Ozick and Allegra Goodman.

• *Teaching Tools*   Children's books are a great resource for teaching the "basics," and since the 1980s, there has been a renaissance in Jewish children's literature—from picture books to young-adult fare. Browsing in a Jewish bookstore or through a Jewish book catalogue, parents can encourage their kids' interests by saying yes when they are intrigued by a title or topic.

Ultimately, Jewish literacy requires some kind of formal Jewish education. Unfortunately, many adults recall Hebrew school as a miserable or irrelevant experience that may have even alienated them from Judaism and Jewish life. To instill a love of Torah—a lasting commitment to Jewish learning that can be a source of meaning and connection—means insisting on excellence in whatever Jewish educational institution you select for your children.

Parents must apply the same standards to Hebrew school curricula and teaching as we do for public or private school. Parents also have to hold their children to the same standards in terms of attendance, getting homework done, and respect for teachers. Kids need to know that their Jewish studies are not on a par with "extracurricular activities" such as dance lessons, gymnastics, or soccer.

One of the best ways to do this is by modeling Jewish learning yourself. If you are taking an adult education class, make sure your children know about it: "The baby-sitter is here so Mommy can go to her Hebrew class." Or "I'll be in the temple library reading a Jewish book while you're in Sunday school."

But Jewish learning is not just a matter of classrooms and books. Taking the family to Jewish book fairs, children's music and storytelling concerts, Israel Independence Day parades, Jewish craft fairs, synagogue Purim fairs, and Hanukkah parties are also ways to impart Jewish basics. Participating in community and/or synagogue-sponsored social-action projects brings Jewish values to life. Summer camps and youth groups give children new sets of Jewish peers and Jewish communities in addition to and separate from their families.

Huppah   When the word *huppah* is used at a baby's *brit* ceremony, it is usually translated as "marriage," an image that seems both a little silly (she can't even lift her head yet!) and melancholy (before you know it . . .). But *huppah* is as complex a word as *Torah*. It means "that which covers or floats above," making the marriage canopy a beautiful and multifaceted symbol that hovers over the ineffable power of human love.[8]

On the most basic level, the *huppah* symbolizes bedclothes. In Talmudic times, a groom's father would set up a purple tent in his courtyard and the couple consummated the marriage within it. The canopy has not been used as a bedroom for centuries, but it remains as a kind of public affirmation and celebration of sexuality.

Judaism frowns on celibacy, and encourages marriage and parenthood for everyone in the community. Many contemporary Jews read *huppah* as an umbrella term that covers all committed relationships, including those between gay and lesbian couples. The *huppah* proclaims that physical love can be holy.

Huppah also stands for the new home being established by the wedding couple. It is a unique model of home. Nothing like a fortress, but open on all four sides like Abraham's tent, it is always ready to welcome strangers who may turn out to be emissaries from God. Indeed, even during the wedding ceremony, the *huppah* is "inhabited," not only by the bride and groom. Depending on local custom, there may be a rabbi (or two), a cantor (or two), both sets of parents, and other witnesses. The *huppah* is not only a bedroom, it is a living room.

The *huppah* is also a symbol of community and the relationship between individual families and the larger "family" of Israel. Most *huppot* (the plural of *huppah*) are held aloft on poles by four honored relatives or friends. The four faces surrounding the couple are the pillars of the "house" and represent the community. Their presence reassures the couple that their relationship will have the support and fellowship it needs to thrive.

The *huppah* is a symbol of the Jewish future, the place where the first *mitzvah*, "Be fruitful and multiply,"[9] will be fulfilled, where Jewish children will be conceived and nurtured.

In the Jewish mystical tradition, the *huppah* is a sign of God's presence. The Bible uses the metaphors of bride and groom to describe the relationship between the people of Israel and God, and the *Zohar* compares the tabernacle built by the Israelites in the desert to a bridal canopy.[10] According to one legend, the divine Name floats above the *huppah*, making the space spiritually charged. At some weddings, after the ceremony, people come forward to pray under it and couples who have been married for a long time come forward to reconnect with the feelings that brought them to their own *huppah*.

While any piece of fabric can serve as the canopy at a wedding, many couples marry under a *tallit*, a prayer shawl. The ritual fringes and knots on the four corners of the *tallit*—called *tzitzit*—are reminders of the *mitzvot* or connections between the Jewish people, to the dream of peace (*shalom*) and justice (*tzedek*), and to God.

Finally, a *huppah* can be raised anywhere, testifying to the mobility and flexibility of Jewish tradition. The portability of the *huppah* also shows that human beings can transform any place on earth into a Jewish space, into a holy place, into an occasion for rejoicing.

Teaching "Huppah" A prayer that your child be "entered into *huppah*" is a prayer that he grow up to be an adult capable of love and commitment to another human being. It is also a prayer that your child will love and marry as a Jew.

There are no guarantees in parenting, especially when it comes to such mysterious matters as our children's love lives. We can only provide the best Jewish examples we can—and hope. The examples are, however, crucial.

Parents "teach *huppah*" in all the ways they treat one another. Children learn about loving relationships and develop expectations about marriage and commitment by watching what their parents do and say. The best lessons are taught by affectionate and respectful partners who take time for one another. It also helps to avoid jokes that belittle marriage and to voice disapproval of negative stereotypes that populate much of the mass media.

The image of the *huppah* as a welcoming Jewish home means extending family feeling beyond the confines of the nuclear family. In this sense, teaching *huppah* means being a model of hospitality: supporting family and friends through bad times and celebrating with them during good times, making sure there's a comfortable sofa bed for guests, inviting guests to the Friday-night Shabbat table—and the Tuesday lunch table, too.

Ma'asim Tovim   There are countless kinds of good deeds: giving money to the local Jewish federation, volunteering in a Jewish agency, becoming a physician, visiting the sick, membership in Amnesty International, running for Congress, organizing a food drive, cooking for a grieving member of your temple. According to the Talmud, "Though it is not your duty to complete the work, neither are you free to desist from it."[11]

Teaching "Ma'asim Tovim"   This entails showing children that Jews are supposed to behave as though everything we do in life can make the world a better place.

Judaism does not leave good deeds to the vicissitudes of human kindness or generosity. For Jews, feeding the hungry, clothing the naked, and housing the homeless are not voluntary acts of charity. The word "charity" derives from the Latin *caritas,* and means "Christian love"; the Hebrew word that underlies the Jewish obligation to do good (*tzedakah*) is *tzedek,* which means justice. The Jewish community as a whole is obligated to organize on behalf of the poor and the needy, but every individual must assume the responsibility, too.

Ma'asim tovim—good deeds—include three kinds of actions: *tzedakah, gemilut hassadim,* and *tikkun olam.*

Tzedakah, "righteous giving," basically means donating money to the poor. It is a value of paramount importance; according to the Talmud, "*Tzedakah* is as important as all the other commandments put together."[12]

There is no notion of the "undeserving" poor in Judaism; the *mitzvah* of giving to anyone in need is based upon a belief that all human beings deserve help. And giving is not only a responsibility; it is also seen as a privilege, an expression of dignity and one of the activities that defines a *mensch,* a good and honorable person. Thus, Jewish law requires that the poor give to those less fortunate than themselves—even if their gift comes directly from someone else's *tzedakah.*[13]

Gemilut hassadim, "acts of lovingkindness," are the kinds of activities Americans associate with voluntarism, such as reading to the blind or working in a soup kitchen. Money cannot assuage some kinds of pain, thus *gemilut hassadim* calls for a face-to-face encounter with need. Its traditional forms include providing clothes for the naked, visiting the sick, comforting mourners, accompanying the dead to the grave, providing for brides, and offering hospitality to strangers. A contemporary definition might also include helping people find jobs, teaching people to read, providing shelter for the homeless, saving animals from suffering, planting trees, and lifting the spirits of the depressed.

Tikkun olam, "the repair of the world," is the religious obligation to work for peace, freedom, equality, justice for all people, and the protection of the natural world. The distinctions between religious duties and social obligations are blurred in Jewish life. The notion of redemption articulated by the biblical prophets calls for an end to poverty, bigotry, and all forms of oppression.[14] *Tikkun olam* assumes that the world is not perfect, but that it is perfectible, and in our hands.

Teaching Righteousness Providing children with models and age-appropriate experiences of charitable giving, kindness, and repairing the world, teaches them not only about the problems and needs around them, but also that it is in their power to make things better.

Make *tzedakah* a part of your child's weekly allowance. Open your checkbook and show them how much you give to charity, and what organizations you support. Support school *tzedakah* and volunteer projects. Ask if the bar and bat mitzvah curriculum has a social-justice or charitable component.

If you do volunteer work, let your children know what you are doing and why, and provide appropriate opportunities for them to volunteer, too. Teaching children about *tikkun olam* can include suggesting they write e-mail letters to Congress about topics discussed in social studies classes, taking them to rallies, supporting local recycling efforts, and engaging them in discussion of the political issues of the day—injecting a Jewish perspective wherever it applies. (For more about *tzedakah*, see Chapter 4.)

BOOKS FOR CHILDREN

What Is God? by Etan Boritzer (Firefly Books, 1990).

God's Paintbrush; In God's Name; and other books by Rabbi Sandy Eisenberg Sasso (Jewish Lights Publishing).

Because Nothing Looks Like God by Karen Kushner (Jewish Lights Publishing).

BOOKS FOR PARENTS

Living a Jewish Life, by Anita Diamant and Howard Cooper (Harper-Collins, 1991).

When Children Ask about God, by Rabbi Harold Kushner (Schocken Books, 1995).

Jewish Literacy, by Rabbi Joseph Telushkin (William Morrow, 1991).

Chapter 2

Creating a
Jewish Space

Home is where the heart is, where tastes are shaped, where the eye first focuses, where identity is forged. Home is the place where children learn life's most intimate and powerful lessons about love, respect, beauty, sanctity, and community. Most people think of their homes as a haven, a refuge from the rest of the world. In Jewish tradition, the home is called a "little sanctuary," *mikdash ma'at*. Making your little sanctuary into a Jewish space is more a matter of what your family does inside it (celebrating holidays, welcoming guests, learning and teaching) than what it looks like.

But physical surroundings are not incidental. There are countless ways to identify your home as a Jewish space and to make it a beautiful setting for Jewish living: a *mezuzah* on the doorway, candlesticks and a kiddush cup on the mantle, Jewish books on the shelves, a Jewish calendar and kosher cookbooks in the kitchen, a *tzedakah* box in the dining room, a Chagall print in the living room.

Whatever your tastes or interests, if you make your Jewishness visible, the implicit lesson for children is pride in the family's identity and traditions. You also teach—without saying a word—that Judaism is not something to pull out of a cupboard three times a year, but a beautiful part of everyday life.

DOORS AND WALLS

The Mezuzah   The little box on the doorways of a Jewish home tells the outside world: "Jews live here." But its main function is to remind the Jews inside: "Jews live here."

Inside each *mezuzah*, there is a handwritten parchment scroll called a *klaf*, which is inscribed with the *Shema*, the affirmation of God's oneness, and the commandments to love God everywhere, "When you sit in your home, when you walk by the way, when you lie down, and when you rise up." The *klaf* also contains the words "and you shall write them upon the doorposts of your house."

A *mezuzah* is a signal that the space within is a place where special, holy things can happen. In traditional language, the goal for what happens inside a Jewish home is *shalom bayit*—"peace in (or of) the house." Shalom/peace here does not mean the absence of conflict: no family is stress-free or problem-free. *Shalom bayit* is what happens when people act respectfully toward one another, parents toward children as well as children toward parents. The *mezuzah* thus serves as a reminder to leave "garbage" outside when you enter, and to take *shalom bayit* with you when you leave.

The practice of hanging *mezuzot* (the plural of *mezuzah*) dates back to biblical times and has been part of the Jewish landscape ever since. Containers can be made of any material—wood, ceramic, silver, glass—and are available at Judaica shops and from catalogues in a wide variety of styles and prices. There are colorful, fun designs made especially for children's rooms, decorated with balloons, Noah's ark animals, or teddy bears.

Mezuzah cases and their scrolls are usually sold separately. Since the scrolls are handwritten by a trained scribe (*sofer* in Hebrew), the parchment may cost more than the case.

Mezuzot are usually hung within thirty days of moving into a new house, but a "naked" doorway may be dressed at any time. A *mezuzah* is hung on the front door of a home and may also go on every doorway inside, except for doors to closets and bathrooms. It goes on the right-hand side as you enter, on the upper third of the doorway. A *mezuzah* is hung at an angle, with the top facing inward.

Two simple blessings are said when you hang a *mezuzah:*

Baruch Ata Adonai Eloheynu Melech Ha-olam asher kid'shanu b'mitzvotav vitsivanu likboa mezuzah.

Blessed be the Eternal One, Source of Life, by Whose power we sanctify life with the *mitzvah* of affixing this *mezuzah.*

Baruch Ata Adonai Eloheynu Melech Ha-olam shehechiyanu v'keyamanu v'higianu lazman hazeh.

Blessed be the Eternal One, Source of Life, Who has given us life, helped us to grow, and enabled us to reach this moment.

Make sure your children are with you as you hang the *mezuzah,* or make it an occasion—a house-warming party called a *Hanukkat HaBayit,* "dedication of the home." You can ask your guests to gather outside the door while the family says the blessings and hangs the *mezuzah.* Then, as each person enters the newly dedicated home, he or she offers a blessing or wish for the family: that the house should always be filled with laughter, that the company gather soon and often for happy occasions, that squirrels never nest in the attic.

What It Says Inside the Mezuzah

Listen, Israel, Adonai the Eternal, Adonai is One.

You shall love your God with all your heart, with all your soul, and with all your might. And these words, which I command you this day, shall be upon your heart. You shall teach them diligently to your children, and shall speak of them when you sit in your home, when you walk by the way, when you lie down, and when you rise up. You shall bind them as a sign upon your hand, and they shall be for frontlets between your eyes. You shall write them upon the doorposts of your home and upon your gates.

And it will come to pass, if you will listen diligently to My commandments which I command you this day, to love your God and to serve Me with all your heart and with all your soul, that I will bring rain to the land in its season, rain in autumn and rain in spring and harvest rich in grain and wine and oil. And there will be grass in the fields for the cattle and abundant food to eat. But you must take care not to be lured away to serve gods of luxury and fashion, turning away from Me. For I will turn My face from you, and I will close the heavens and hold back the rain and the earth will bear no fruit and you will soon perish from the good land that I am giving you. Therefore impress My words upon your heart and upon your soul; bind them as a sign upon your hand, let them serve as frontlets between your eyes. Teach them to your children and talk about them when you are at home and when you are away, in the evening and the morning. Write them on the doorposts of your home and upon your gates. Then will your days be multiplied and the days of your children, upon the land which I promised to give to your ancestors, as the days of the heavens above the earth.[1]

Home Decoration   Your home says a lot about you. The art on the walls, the bookshelves, the presence of religious images and ritual items express your values as well as your tastes. Your home also provides your children with an aesthetic benchmark and a visual vocabulary. There are many ways to incorporate Jewish elements into your home decoration, not only for its own sake but also to inspire your children.

The rabbinic principal of *hiddur mitzvah* holds that whenever Jews need a physical object to fulfill a commandment, the object should be beautiful. Thus, while you can say the blessing over wine using a chipped coffee mug, it's better to use a fine china kiddush cup, which enhances enjoyment of the *mitzvah*.

Of course, what one woman calls art is another woman's vision of tacky kitsch. Fortunately, there has never been a greater choice of Jewish art objects or ritual items, which means that there is no reason to "settle" for a pair of candlesticks or a kiddush cup you don't love.

Living a Jewish life usually entails the purchase of ritual and seasonal objects, from Shabbat candlesticks to Rosh Hashanah greeting cards. The Jewish life cycle comes with a whole set of accoutrements as well: a *ketubah* (marriage certificate), birth announcements, photographs from the bar mitzvah, and so on. Displaying such items rather than keeping them in a cupboard or drawer gives family and friends occasion to revisit good times.

Jewish ritual objects are decorative elements, too. A particularly handsome *hanukkiah* (Hanukkah menorah) can stay on the mantle all year round. Some people start a collection of a favorite ritual object, such as spice boxes, and display them. And many couples frame and hang their *ketubah*.

There are lots of creative ways to incorporate personal, Jewish images in your decor; for example, family heirlooms such as a challah cover hand-embroidered in the old country, or a great-grandparent's passport, can be framed and displayed. Depending on your interests, you can hang photographs of Israel, Hebrew calligraphy, posters from the Jewish Museum, illustrated Jewish calendars, prints or posters by such well-known Jewish artists as Marc Chagall, Ben Shahn, Chaim Gross, and Agam.

The Jewish holidays provide opportunities to fill your home with beautiful touches your children will enjoy and remember. In addition to displaying your child's Rosh Hashanah artwork and livening up the Hanukkah table with colorful paper goods, the holidays can be occasions for buying fresh flowers, creating vivid centerpieces out of recyclables and toys, rearranging the art on the walls, hanging a banner on the front door. (Chapter 4, "Defining Jewish Time," contains specific suggestions for celebrating holidays.)

Creating Jewish Space for Children

- If your child's room lacks a *mezuzah,* let him or her select one or make one, and celebrate with a family party when you hang it.
- Teach your children the traditional gesture of touching the *mezuzah* and then kissing their fingers.
- Make a *mezuzah* for the doll's house.
- Put your child's name on his or her door in Hebrew and English.
- Decorate your child's room with colorful posters of the Hebrew alphabet, Israel, the Jewish holidays.
- Post drawings or paintings from Hebrew school on the refrigerator.
- Put magnetic Hebrew letters on the refrigerator.
- When your child creates a real "masterpiece" of Jewish art, have it framed and hang it in a prominent place.

- As each holiday approaches, put the Jewish books about the up-coming celebration face out on the child's bookcase.

THE LIBRARY

Jews have long been called "the people of the book." In fact, we are the people of the library. Given the levels of educational achievement among American Jews, it's no surprise that most Jewish homes contain bookcases filled with everything from college textbooks to popular novels, encyclope-dias and dictionaries, and lots of magazines and newspapers.

By example as well as by expectation, Jewish parents tend to encour-age a real love of reading in their children. One way we do this is by giving books as gifts, and, indeed, most Jewish children own libraries of their own at an early age. There are good Jewish books for all children: Hebrew letter books for toddlers, picture books for pre-readers, colorful reference books and novels for grade-school readers, mysteries and fiction for junior high and high school students.

Fostering Jewish Literacy

- Never settle for anything but first-rate writing and illustration in your child's Jewish books.
- When shopping at a Jewish bookstore with your child, say yes to their requests for a new book.
- Give every child his or her own bookcase and dedicate the top shelf for favorites and Jewish titles.
- Take your kids to story hour at the temple library; go to Jewish storytelling concerts.
- When making selections for bedtime read-aloud time, include Jewish books every week.
- Let your children see you reading Jewish books.

- Subscribe to Jewish periodicals.
- Display your Jewish books prominently.
- Make sure you have good reference books to help answer your children's questions and to enhance holiday celebrations.
- Purchase and use Jewish cookbooks.

THE GUEST ROOM

For Jews, hospitality is more than good manners, it is the *mitzvah* called *hachnasat orchim*, "the bringing in of guests." This *mitzvah* is not only about doing the good deed of hosting friends and relatives, it also speaks to the idea that Jews should open our homes to strangers and people in need. Abraham is the biblical exemplar of *hachnasat orchim*; it was said that his tent opened on all four sides so that strangers would always know they were welcome. For much of history, when Jewish travelers were unwelcome and at risk, this *mitzvah* was crucial to their survival.

Although Jewish travelers tend to find their own way these days, there are still ways to offer hospitality to strangers, such as inviting college students or military personnel from a local base for a Friday night meal or a Passover seder. Nor is *hachnasat orchim* limited to Jews; volunteering at a shelter for the homeless can be an expression of this *mitzvah*, too.

The prophet Elijah, the legendary harbinger of the messiah, is often portrayed as a beggar who tests the practical morality of people who offer him—or don't—food and shelter. Jewish folk literature abounds with tales about people who were richly rewarded for providing shelter and sharing their meager meals with beggars.

Parents who open their home to friends and neighbors—welcoming people for meals and conversation, keeping a cot or foldout couch for out-of-town visitors—are teaching their children a vital lesson in Jewish living. Not only do children learn the skills and pleasures of hosting by watching their parents, they also absorb a sense of Jewish communal responsibility. Learning to function as a member of the give-and-take dynamic of a community is part of learning how to be Jewish—a part best learned at home.

THE KITCHEN

The kitchen is the heart of every household. Childhood's first sensual experiences and earliest memories are of taste and smell, which explains the power of food to evoke the past. For Jews, the kitchen is the "holy of holies" of the "little sanctuary," the *mikdash ma'at*.

Beloved memories of holidays and Sabbath observance are vividly connected to the kitchen and the palate. Apples dripping honey signal the start of the Jewish year. Hanukkah tastes like potato pancakes. Another name for Passover is the Feast of Unleavened Bread. The food cycle creates a taste for the holiday cycle, which connects us to the cycles of the natural world, too. The Jewish holidays, rooted in the ancient calendar, reconnect us to the seasonal harvests and rebirths that are nearly lost in a global economy that puts exotic fruits on our tables all year round.

But food is more than a cultural artifact. For Jews, the preparation and consumption of food is regulated by an elaborate code called *kashrut,* which is really an attempt to transform the most basic of all human needs into an opportunity for holiness.

Understanding Kashrut   The system of rules and laws regulating what Jews eat and how Jews prepare food elaborates a few biblical verses into a way of life. *Kashrut* has never been an end in itself, nor was it ever a health code to protect Jews against trichinosis or other food-borne illness. *Kashrut*'s apparent obsession with the details of the kitchen and table is not about food at all but about the place of humanity in the universe.

According to some interpreters, God's original plan was for humans to be vegetarians. As expressed in Genesis: "I give you every seed-bearing plant that is upon the earth, and every tree that has seed-bearing fruit, they shall be yours for food."[2] Elsewhere, however, the Bible acknowledges the human taste for meat, but seeks to limit pain to any living thing (*tsa'ar ba'alei chayim.*) The rabbis codified an elaborate system of ritual slaughter (*sh'chitah*) that implies Jews can kill for food but only by divine sanction and in a humane fashion.

Kashrut was also a kind of fence that served to keep Jews separate from their neighbors. Prohibitions against eating non-kosher foods limited contact between Jews and non-Jews, and thus helped prevent assimilation.

Most important, *kashrut* is understood as a way of staying connected to God in one of the mundane aspects of life. Being conscious of every bite we put into our mouths—mindful and grateful for sustenance and health —is a spiritual practice. Adding blessings to family mealtimes acknowledges the power and sanctity of the daily, taken-for-granted miracles of food and love.

What's Kosher, What's Not   *Kashrut* divides food into two basic categories: kosher ("fit" or "proper" for human consumption), and *trafe* ("torn" or "damaged" and unfit for people to eat). The primary source for the dietary laws is the Torah, which lists animals, birds, fish, and insects that may and may not be consumed by the people of Israel.[3] The laws that regulate food preparation were laid out in the Talmud and subsequent law codes.[4]

Kosher foods include everything that grows from the earth: herbs, weeds, grains, mosses, fungi, ferns, flowers, seeds, roots, nuts, fruits, and vegetables.

Kosher fish have both fins and scales, for example: anchovies, bluefish, carp, flounder, grouper, halibut, mackerel, perch, salmon, tuna, trout, and yellowtail.

Meat from all domesticated birds (chicken, turkey, goose, duck) and animals that both chew a cud and have a split hoof (antelope, buffalo, cattle, deer, goat, moose, sheep, and yak) are potentially kosher. To become kosher, however, these animals and fowl must be slaughtered according to the laws of *sh'chitah* by a trained Jewish butcher called a *shochet* and then washed and salted to remove any trace of blood.

Eggs from domestic birds are kosher, unless they contain even a single spot of blood.

Dairy products.

All alcoholic beverages including beer, grain, and fruit liquors. "Kosher wine" is made under rabbinical supervision.[5]

Among kosher foods, there are three categories: dairy (*milchig*), meat (*flayshig*), which includes fowl, and neutral (*pareve*), which includes all fruits and vegetables, fish, eggs, and alcoholic beverages. Dairy and meat are not eaten together, but neutral foods can be prepared with and eaten with either.

Trafe food includes meat from animals that do not both chew a cud and have a split hoof: camels, donkeys, pigs, horses, and rodents.

Non-kosher fish have neither fins nor scales and include crustaceans such as crab, lobster, mussels, shrimp. Also forbidden are the eel, frog, turtle, octopus, shark, porpoise, whale, and all other sea mammals.

Wild birds and birds of prey are not permitted, a group that includes the eagle, heron, owl, pelican, swan, and vulture. Eggs from non-kosher birds are prohibited.

Ways to Keep Kosher

If you did not grow up in a kosher home, taking on the mitzvah of kashrut can seem overwhelming. However, liberal Jews can honor the spirit of the tradition—and learn from it—in a variety of ways. The following strategies are listed in increasing order of "difficulty." Some people find that one step leads to the next.

- *Biblical kosher:* Avoid all animals and fish prohibited in the Torah. No crustaceans or pork.
- *Separating meat and milk:* No butter on the rolls with a steak dinner. No cream sauces on the chicken. No cheese on the burger. At home, use one set of dishes, cutlery, and pots and pans for milk, another set for meat. Wait to eat dairy after eating meat—one to six hours depending upon your custom. Traditionally, there is no waiting period for serving meat after eating dairy products.
- *Kosher meat only:* Eat no meat that was not prepared by a kosher butcher. In restaurants, order fish or vegetarian meals only.
- *Rabbinic supervision:* Buy only those packaged or prepared foods that bear a *hechsher,* a symbol that declares the product kosher and prepared under rabbinical supervision.[6] For example: Ⓤ, Ⓚ, ⒜.
- *Vegetarian:* Eat no meat, but all *pareve* and dairy foods in any combination.
- *Home vs. away:* Some people who keep strictly kosher at home will eat vegetarian meals in restaurants or other people's homes. Some, who avoid all *trafe* at home, will order pork lo mein at

a restaurant. Depending on your point of view, practicing different levels of *kashrut* at home and on the road is either hypocritical or a simple distinction between what happens inside a Jewish space and what happens in the rest of the world.

Your Kosher Kitchen   Kosher kitchens are set up in a variety of ways. A vegetarian home, or one where biblical *kashrut* is the rule, will have only one set of dishes. For families that buy kosher meat and separate all dairy and meat, the kitchen may have two sets of dishes, cutlery, pots, pans, and cooking utensils. Some people also use different dish towels, dish rags, sponges, potholders, and cutting boards. Dishes and drinking glasses made of glass may be used for any meal. Once any such system is in place, it is not difficult to keep it going. The biggest problem for most families is storage space.

No matter how you define or practice *kashrut,* at some point a dairy pot will be used for reheating chicken soup. (Or halfway through a restaurant salad, you'll find bacon bits.) The Talmud acknowledges the inevitability of mistakes by providing ways to correct them through some form of ritual cleansing. The point is not cleaning so much as reordering.[7]

Stocking food in a kosher kitchen is an increasingly easy task since health concerns have eliminated lard (rendered, non-kosher animal fat) from most packaged goods and the number of products bearing a *hechsher* (a stamp indicating that an item is kosher) has soared. Regular supermarkets can supply most necessities, and supermarkets that serve a sizeable Jewish clientele even stock kosher meats. Most cities of any size support at least one kosher butcher; people living in smaller communities either shop by mail or commute to larger Jewish centers to buy meat.

Jewish Food, Kosher Cooking   Jewish food is much more than bagels and kugel; it embraces potato latkes and rose water, herring and felafel, chicken soup and egg-lemon soup. The variety of culinary traditions reflects the diversity of cultures from which Jewish communities have borrowed. Dozens of excellent Jewish and kosher cookbooks make this point. But recipes and cookbooks of almost any description can be useful to the kosher cook. Italian, Middle Eastern, many Asian, and all vegetarian cookbooks are great resources, but it is easy to adapt and change virtually any recipe by using non-dairy margarine instead of butter, or substituting vegetable stock for beef or chicken bouillon. Jews-by-choice raised in African-American homes or Chinese homes or Swedish homes find they can translate most of their childhood favorites into a kosher idiom.

KASHRUT IN AGES AND STAGES

Unfortunately, the stereotype lingers that anyone who keeps kosher is rigid, strict, and unforgiving. It is possible to be both flexible and kosher at the same time if you remember that *kashrut* is not an end in itself but a means for imparting Jewish identity and encouraging a sense of holiness or mindfulness in daily life.

To get this notion across, parents need to be consistent models, not only in what they eat, but also in the ways they talk about choices in keeping kosher. Remember your goal of creating positive Jewish memories at mealtimes. Never shout at children about mistakes, such as buttered toast on a "meat" dish. If you accept the idea that mistakes are bound to happen, children will see *kashrut* as a natural part of Jewish life.

Infancy Through Preschool   If your children are born into a kosher home, they will learn your systems and rules as effortlessly as they learn your native tongue. *Kashrut* will be the "grammar" of their food language.

Food tastes are acquired, not inborn. A child who never ate a cheeseburger or pepperoni pizza probably won't want or like them—at least not until s/he gets older, at which point his/her habits will be well-established.

Whenever possible, make food a source of fun rather than restriction. Let your children help bake and cook. When food shopping, let your children play detective in search of the kosher cookies and then let them select which kind to buy.

Correct "mistakes" without anger. Be clear about your system for reestablishing the *kashrut* of the spoon or cup so that your child can correct his error swiftly and without guilt.

School-age Children   As children get older and eat outside the house more often, they discover that your family's food rules and habits differ from most of the world's—including, perhaps, some of their Jewish friends'. School-age children may ask why they can't eat hamburgers at

McDonald's, or why you eat non-kosher meat outside the house, or why Mrs. Feinberg served milk with hot dogs.

Explain why you keep kosher in terms your children will understand. For example, "This is how Jews have eaten for thousands of years and it's a way of connecting us to our history and of reminding ourselves of who we are." Or, "*Kashrut* is a way to stay connected to God even when we are eating."

Older children may be struck by the differences among Jews in observance—why some Jewish kids eat cheeseburgers and others won't eat at your house because it isn't "kosher enough." One possible response is, "Our family is trying to take this *mitzvah* seriously. We respond to the commandment by not eating pork or shellfish. The Cohens have separate dishes for meat and milk. I'm not sure what the Feinbergs do about *kashrut*. But I think we're all trying to be good Jews."

As children grow, they invariably find themselves in situations—in restaurants or at friends' homes—where they will have to decide whether or not to follow your family's rules. While you can express your wishes that they keep kosher, there is no way to police or enforce this. Let go of the idea that you can control these situations. Consider them early practice in making Jewish choices.

Adolescents Teenagers tend to challenge family habits and systems about all kinds of things—including food. A great many teenagers decide to become vegetarians. Some adolescents reject the whole notion of *kashrut*, while others want to become far more observant than their parents.

First, listen to your teen's opinions. Do not dismiss or belittle the ideas they express. Making thoughtful Jewish decisions is what you want them to do. Hear them out respectfully, and ask questions that encourage a considered response: "How do you see your choice fitting in with our family? Are you willing to get involved in your own food preparation? Is it fair to ask us to change the way we eat to accommodate you?"

JEWS AND ALCOHOL

Jewish children grow up around wine, which is part of virtually every Jewish celebration and observance. At home and in the synagogue, on Shabbat, holidays, and at life-cycle events, children see that drinking is not about getting wild or violent but is a part of adult and communal life.

Different parents make very different decisions about whether, when, and how much to let children taste from the Shabbat kiddush cup or at the seder table. But children who are allowed to sip discover the effects of wine in the safest of settings. The use of wine at holy moments links the transformative power of alcohol with spiritual expression and communal or family closeness. And the lesson that alcohol can make you feel sleepy, or silly, or even sick is best learned at home.

BOOKS FOR CHILDREN

The Children's Jewish Holiday Kitchen: 70 Ways to Have Fun with Your Kids and Make Your Family's Celebrations Special, by Joan Nathan (Schocken Books, 1995).

BOOKS FOR PARENTS

Vegetarian Judaism, by Roberta Kalechofsky (Micah Publications, 1998).
The World of Jewish Entertaining, by Gil Marks (Simon and Schuster, 1998).
The Jewish Holiday Kitchen, by Joan Nathan (Schocken Books, 1988).
The Book of Jewish Food, by Claudia Roden (Knopf, 1996).

Chapter 3

Making
Community

Community is one of the core values of the Jewish people. While personal responsibility is a cornerstone of Jewish thought, radical individualism runs against the grain of Judaism, which views community obligations as necessary and binding. Both as individuals and as families, we are required to connect with other Jews—to pray with them, to celebrate births and mourn deaths with them, to pool resources and establish schools, synagogues, and cemeteries, to make sure that no Jew is hungry, to pursue peace and justice for all people. "Do not separate yourself from the community," says the Talmud.[1]

This idea is a great gift to parents who want their children to grow up proud and happy to be Jewish. Because Jewish identity cannot be entirely "homegrown." No matter how committed and active parents may be, Jewish identity needs to be nurtured outside the family, too.

Jewish communal life cannot substitute for family models or memories, but it does supplement and reinforce parental values and beliefs in crucial ways. In a society where geographical mobility and smaller households are the rule, community connections function as extended family—as they always have—providing advice and support and a variety of models of how to live a Jewish life. Communal experiences are part of how children build a storehouse of positive memories, and discover spaces for sacred moments.

Being part of the larger Jewish community provides a whole range of Jewish teachers and role models for children to study and emulate. As in the family, much of the teaching and learning is informal and intergenerational. Children at the temple or the Jewish community center see an array of Jewish role models (athletes, artists, Israelis, grandmothers), which expands the repertoire of ways to be Jewish. This process is ongoing in children, who watch older kids in particular for cues about how to behave.

In a multigenerational community, almost everyone is both expert and novice. Young parents with toddlers can discuss their Jewish naming choices with expectant mothers and fathers. Families with bar and bat mitzvah–age children serve as models for those whose children are just starting Hebrew school. Parents routinely trade information about the quality of Jewish summer camps, about ways to liven up a Passover seder for little kids, about how to find a Hebrew teacher for a child with a reading disability.

Connecting to the community also reinforces and refreshes your family's Jewish choices. If Jewish practice is new to you, holiday celebrations can seem overwhelming. Becoming part of a group of learners is a good way to lighten the load. But even if you've always observed Shabbat and the holidays, communal input and support can add energy and inspire you to try new things.

"Life is with people," says the Yiddish proverb. In other words, you can't live a Jewish life in isolation. It takes a community to raise Jewish children: friends, acquaintances, rabbis, cantors, the other car-pool drivers, the secretaries in the temple office, the lifeguards at the Jewish community center pool.

For Jews, the value of community is embedded in religious practice at key moments in liturgy and life cycle. The presence of a *minyan,* a prayer quorum of ten adult Jews, is required to recite *Kaddish* (the prayer for the dead) or to say the seven wedding blessings. This idea—that community is part of the Jewish model of the sacred—is something children learn not only by studying the Jewish life cycle in class, but also by attending weddings and funerals, by taking part and storing up memories of communal warmth, joy, and comfort.

JOINING A SYNAGOGUE

It really does take a whole community to raise a Jewish child and to sustain a Jewish family. Finding the Jewish community that's right for your family often takes time and effort, but the rewards are incalculable.

The center of Jewish community life for American families is the synagogue. Most Jews do join a congregation at some point in their lives—almost always when they become parents. Seeking a place where children can get a formal religious education and eventually become bar or bat mitzvah is a perfectly reasonable motivation for affiliation. But in order for synagogue membership to be a positive experience for children, it must also support your goals as a Jewish adult. The temple you select should be a good fit for the entire family.

Finding the right congregation requires a certain amount of shopping. Each synagogue in every denomination has a unique culture or climate, and each has its own strengths and weaknesses. Some synagogues specialize in social-action programs, some focus on lifelong learning, others devote a great deal of attention to worship and spirituality. Some temples have a more formal ethos, others emphasize member participation. The only way to find out what is going on inside any particular temple is to take the time to visit.

Call a few synagogues and ask for membership materials. You may receive a brochure, a copy of the temple newsletter or bulletin, and perhaps a phone call from the rabbi or someone on the membership committee. Some congregations hold coffees or open houses for prospective members. If you like what you read and how your questions were answered on the phone, plan to visit, both with your children and without them, too.

Attend regular Shabbat services a few times. If you plan to bring children, call ahead to find out about children's programming and whether there are rules regarding food or certain kinds of toys on Shabbat. Do not go synagogue shopping immediately before or during the High Holy Days; not only are the crowds atypical, it is an impossibly busy time of year for rabbis and temple staff.

Perhaps the most important consideration in selecting a congregation is meeting the members. Don't rule out a synagogue strictly on the basis of its denomination or the rabbi; meet the people and find out if you share common interests and values.

What's in a Name?

Temple Beth Am. Beth Am Synagogue. Congregation Beth Am. Beth Am Hebrew Center.

The word "synagogue" comes from a Greek translation for *beit k'nesset*, "house of assembly." Until the eighteenth century, Jews used "temple" to refer to the ancient temple in Jerusalem, which could be rebuilt only by divine command. In the nineteenth century, the Reform movement rejected the idea of a rebuilt temple in Jerusalem and reclaimed the word as a synonym for "synagogue."

The less "ethnic"-sounding titles "congregation" or "Hebrew center" came into use in America during the 1940s and fifties. Today, liberal Jews often refer to their synagogue as *shul*, once an Orthodox-only and ethnic Yiddish term, from the German *schule*, or "school."

You can't tell a liberal congregation's denomination by reading the words chiseled over the front door. "Synagogue," "temple," "congregation," and "*shul*" are used interchangeably in this book—as they are in casual conversation in the Jewish community.

Shopping for a Congregation   Here are some basic considerations and questions to keep in mind as you search for your family's communal home.

Rabbi   Although synagogues are complex organizations filled with personalities and programs, and despite lay participation in all aspects of temple life, rabbis still shape their congregations in important ways. The duties of congregational rabbis include teaching, preaching, and counseling congregants. They officiate at religious ceremonies and rituals, visit the sick, and represent the Jewish community at interfaith meetings and secular events. Rabbis represent—indeed, they embody—Jewish tradition on the pulpit and in the community.

No rabbi can excel at every part of such a job. To get a sense of him/her in different roles, try to attend classes or meetings as well as services. If possible, schedule a private meeting, and be prepared to spell out your own needs and aspirations as well as ask about how your family might fit into the congregation. Many temples hold coffee hours at which new members can meet the rabbi in an informal setting.

Location   There are obvious benefits to joining a temple that is close to home. Apart from convenience, proximity makes it easier for everyone in the family to take classes or volunteer or just "hang out" at the temple. Children who live nearby are likely to have overlapping groups of friends from the neighborhood, from public school, and from the temple's supplementary school.

However, geography should not be the sole determining factor. If the temple across the street does not have what your family needs (for example, a preschool or an active youth group) driving across town to one that does is worth the time and mileage.

Making the effort to commute to a place that's right for you implicitly demonstrates your commitment and seriousness to your children. And even car pools can have their benefits; time in the car is time to talk to your children, and to connect with other parents and children in the congregation. Even having a different peer group at temple can be a benefit. During adolescence, when social pressures at school tend to heat up, the synagogue school community provides a separate stage and different players for your teenager.

Size   Synagogues range from smaller than fifty members to larger than three thousand households. Small congregations tend to foster intimacy and warmth; however, they can seem cliquish and may be unable to provide some of the basic programs and services that parents want, such as a religious school. Small (and new) synagogues also tend to require more time and effort from members.

Larger temples can seem corporate, and hierarchical. But bigger communities can provide a wide array of services, including religious school, youth groups, and adult programming with "something for everyone." Large congregations sometimes address a potential "warmth deficit" by fostering *havurot*, small groups of members who meet for study and holiday celebration, and often function as extended families.

Religious School   If you expect the temple to provide your child's formal Jewish education, meet with the principal or director of education and make sure that your goals jibe with the school's philosophy. Ask how teachers are hired and how much they are paid. Are parents involved through a school committee or as volunteers in the classroom? Is there a temple preschool? Who tutors students for bar and bat mitzvah? What percentage of students drop out of the religious school after bar or bat mitzvah? Does the temple run a high school program? Take time to visit several classrooms to see if the little ones are having fun and whether the older kids are engaged or bored. (These issues will be discussed in more depth in Chapter 7.)

Adult Learning   Don't make the mistake of focusing entirely on your children's education; check out the opportunities for yourself as well. Are there "family education" programs, geared for parents with young children? Do the adult education lecture topics and course offerings appeal to you?

Synagogue "Style"   Every congregation has a culture, which consists of many tangible elements such as a connection to the larger denomination, and not-so-tangible elements such as the background noise level at services. There is no right or wrong style; the idea is to find a place that matches your family's personality and preference. Here are a few criteria to consider:

- Generational makeup: Is it mostly seniors? Does it seem everyone has very young children? Are single parents welcome? What about gay and lesbian families?
- Music: Is there an organ or does the cantor use a guitar? Is the singing participatory or left to the professionals? Is there a choir?
- Welcome: Do people approach and introduce themselves at services?
- Formality: Is there an emphasis on solemn ritual and quiet devotion or casual storytelling and emotional expression? Does the rabbi make jokes from the *bimah* (the dais)? Do congregants dress in business suits or running suits? Are children expected to sit still at all times during services?
- Bar and Bat Mitzvah: Do children read or chant their Torah portions? Do most families hold their receptions in the temple social hall or at elegant downtown hotels?

Tzedakah and Social Justice   Does the bulletin list opportunities to volunteer for community service? Is the synagogue "a Mazon congregation," whose members donate 3 percent of food costs associated with Jewish celebrations (bar/bat mitzvah, baby namings, and so on) to that organization, which is "a Jewish Response to Hunger."[2]

Dues Most synagogue expenses are met by annual membership dues, which can range from a few hundred to several thousand dollars. There may also be other financial expectations, such as a building fund assessment and school fees. Some congregations have sliding scales based on income and many have fund-raising events to supplement dues. No synagogue will turn people away because of inability to pay, indeed, most handle financial need with tact and confidentiality.

Policies on Intermarried Families If your family includes a non-Jewish member, ask if there is a written policy on the role of the non-Jew in the congregation. Some temples extend full membership to non-Jewish spouses or partners; elsewhere, non-Jewish partners are nonvoting members.

Are there any policies regarding the children of non-Jewish mothers? In some Conservative synagogues, the child may not enroll in the Hebrew school unless he or she has undergone formal conversion. This is not the case in Reform or Reconstructionist temples; however, they may have guidelines that discourage enrollment of children who also attend Christian religious classes.

Find out if there is an active Outreach Committee (Reform) or Keruv Committee (Conservative); if possible, speak to the committee chair.

Denominations Most liberal synagogues are affiliated with one of three major movements or denominations. The Conservative, Reform, and Reconstructionist movements each train rabbis and publish books, magazines, and teaching materials.[3] All three ordain women as rabbis, engage in interfaith and intermovement dialogues, and actively support the State of Israel. All three train cantors and sponsor national youth groups, summer camps, and Israel programs.

Depending on your memories and associations, you may gravitate to the denomination of your youth or try to avoid your parents' movement. However, it is best to put aside all preconceptions, since even your childhood synagogue may now be a very different place from the one you recall. Policies and practices change over time, and while the three denominations differ in important ways, the differences are sometimes more theoretical than practical. The self-governing congregational model of synagogue life means that every temple has customs and traditions that may vary from the denominational "rule." For example, the use of instrumental music—especially the organ—is not widely associated with Conservative practice; however, there are Conservative congregations where organ accompaniment is part of the worship service.

There are only a few broad generalizations that hold: Reform services tend to be conducted mostly in English; Conservative services are longer and emphasize the use of Hebrew; Reconstructionist services run the widest gamut, some emphasizing traditional Hebrew singing while others write their own creative services. Reform and Reconstructionist congregations place fewer restrictions on the participation of non-Jewish members than Conservative synagogues. *Tallit* and *kippah* are generally mandatory for men in Conservative congregations, where women may be required to wear a head-covering on the bimah. Reform and Reconstructionist temples rarely require any of these; then again, in many congregations women and men wear prayer shawls and *kippot* as a matter of course.

> For more information about the movements, contact:
> Union of American Hebrew Congregations (Reform)
> 633 Third Avenue
> New York, NY 10017
> 212-650-4000
> www.uahc.org
>
> United Synagogue of Conservative Judaism
> 155 Fifth Avenue
> New York, NY 10010
> 212-544-7800
> www.uscj.org
>
> Jewish Reconstructionist Federation
> c/o Beit Devora
> 7894 Montgomery Avenue (Suite 9)
> Elkins Park, PA 19027
> 215-782-8500
> www.jrf.org

Alternatives   The following three organizations function as support networks for independent groups, which may be called synagogues, *havurot,* or just "communities."

Aleph: Alliance for Jewish Renewal is an organization of *havurot* and independent synagogues. Dedicated to creating a "spiritually meaningful Judaism for our time," Aleph groups sometimes incorporate ideas and practices from other cultures into their Jewish renewal services and events. It also publishes a quarterly journal, sponsors a retreat center, and runs an alternative process for the ordination of rabbis.

Aleph: Alliance for Jewish Renewal
7318 Germantown Avenue
Philadelphia, PA 19119
215-247-9700.
www.aleph.org

The National Havurah Committee is an umbrella organization supporting *havurot:* small, egalitarian, transdenominational communities that meet for lay-led Jewish study, celebration, and ritual observance. The NHC is best known for its annual week-long Summer Institutes, and also sponsors regional retreats, maintains an active e-mail network, and publishes a newsletter and occasional publications.

National Havurah Committee
7135 Germantown Avenue
Philadelphia, PA 19119
215-248-1335
www.havurah.org

The Society for Humanistic Judaism is based on a nontheistic philosophy that combines humanistic values with a celebration of Jewish values and identity. SHJ publishes educational materials and sponsors programs for its member groups, which run schools and celebrate Jewish holidays and life-cycle events.

Society for Humanistic Judaism
28611 West 12 Mile Road
Farmingham Hills, MI 48334
248-478-3159
www.shj.org

BOOKS FOR ADULTS

Explaining Reform Judaism, by Eugene B. Borowitz and Naomi Patz (Behrman House, 1985).

Conservative Judaism: Our Ancestors to Our Descendents, by Elliot Dorff (United Synagogue of America, 1977).

Exploring Judaism: A Reconstructionist Approach, by Rebecca Alpert and Jacob Staub (Reconstructionist Press, 1985).

YOUR JEWISH NEIGHBORHOOD

Living among other Jews makes it easier to find Jewish schools and peers for your children and a community for yourself. However, finding your place is not so much a matter of neighborhood as of affiliation. You can live in a town that's 80 percent Jewish and still remain aloof from the life of the community; on the other hand, you can live miles from the next house down a dirt road and be part of a close-knit synagogue or *havurah.*

Finding or creating Jewish community is possible in all kinds of settings—city or town, suburb or exurb, island or mountaintop. In our highly mobile and networked world, it is also possible to expand your "neighborhood" in a variety of ways.

Yet wherever you choose to live is bound to have consequences for your Jewish life and your Jewish parenting. When buying or renting a home, Jewish parents have an extra set of criteria to consider: if you plan to send your child to public school, will she be the only Jew in her class? If there are only a handful of Jewish kids in the school system, you need to know how it handles religious differences. For example, is the December choral performance called the Christmas Concert or the Winter Concert? Are Jewish students given flexibility regarding tests and assignments on Rosh Hashanah and Yom Kippur?

Parents who have decided to make Jewish day school a priority generally do not move to areas where that is not an option. Nevertheless, Jewish day school families need to consider neighborhoods, too. Your child may feel cut off from the life of the block where public school children play. If there are absolutely no other Jewish families nearby, there will be no car pool. Play dates with school friends will require planning, extra phone calls and driving.

A few other questions to keep in mind when considering where to move: Are there any synagogues in the vicinity or in a range you consider reasonable for commuting? Is there a Jewish community center? A Jewish preschool? If you keep kosher, are there kosher butcher shops nearby? Will there be a place to buy *matzah* during Passover? Is there a Jewish bookstore?

Wherever you live, you can expand your Jewish "neighborhood" in a variety of ways. Build a great Jewish library of books, videotapes, CDs, and CD-ROMs. Encourage your children to write or e-mail Jewish pen pals around the world. Expose kids to the diversity of Jewish culture and community by taking them to concerts of Jewish music and storytelling, art exhibits, Israeli films, Israel Day parades and celebrations; make a big Hanukkah or Purim party an annual event at your house.

Connect secular interests and hobbies to the Jewish world as well. Jewish community centers offer everything from karate to theater arts classes for kids; athletic children might be encouraged to compete in the local Jewish community center's Maccabi Games, a Jewish amateur sports organization for kids ages thirteen to sixteen, which sponsors a biennial North American competition.

As always, parents' actions are the most powerful models for children. If you are musical, join a Jewish choral society or band; if you are a political activist, get involved in the Jewish Community Relations Council, the Anti-Defamation League, or your temple's social-action committee. And make sure you tell your children about your Jewish commitments and activities. Don't disappear to meetings without explaining where you are going and why.

Jewish Life in Far-flung Places   Jewish families find themselves outside of Jewish population centers for all kinds of reasons: jobs, military postings, family obligations, or the attractions of country living. While living on an island in Puget Sound or on a hilltop in Vermont or on a military base in Asia does not mean you can't be a good Jewish parent, it does call for a different kind of resourcefulness, creativity, and commitment than settings filled with Jewish institutions and services.

If you find yourself far from organized Jewish life, the first thing to do is find out if there are other Jews in the vicinity. Check the phone book under "Jewish" for agencies and synagogues, or contact national movement offices or Web sites. If there is no temple and you can't locate any informal groups, place a personals ad in the local paper seeking other Jews who want to get together for study or holiday celebrations; you may be surprised at the number of replies. This is how many *havurot*, synagogues, and Jewish schools get off the ground.

For Jewish kids in relatively isolated places, parents can provide additional Jewish communal experiences, such as Jewish family camp, sending children to a Jewish summer camp, incorporating Jewish elements into vacations, and planning a trip to Israel (see the section on "Traveling Jewish," immediately below). Encourage your kids to visit Jewish Web sites and chat-rooms and give them a generous allowance for Jewish books and tapes. Cheerfully pay for youth-group trips and phone calls to Jewish friends made at these events and at camp.

If you find a compatible temple within driving distance and decide to join, be consistent and cheerful about your commitment. If you complain about the hours it takes to get to and from Hebrew school, services, or other events, your children will get the message that being Jewish is a drag.

Books for children
Mrs. Katz and Tush, by Patricia Polacco (Bantam, 1992). A beautiful story
about the importance of community and the blessings of reaching out
to others.

TRAVELING JEWISH

There is no better way to teach your children that they are part of a global community than by seeking out Jewish experiences while on the road. Before heading to a family reunion in Milwaukee or for a cruise in the Caribbean, do a little research to add a Jewish dimension to your trip. In Venice, visit the first "ghetto," stop in at the Tenement Museum on the Lower East Side of Manhattan, visit the Jewish Museum in Paris, tour the oldest synagogues in the United States.[4]

Do not turn every vacation into an extended Jewish field trip, however. Too much of any kind of sightseeing wears thin with children. But hunting up a kosher restaurant in a strange city can be a way to engineer an unusual travel experience that allows you to make a personal connection off the beaten tourist track. Likewise, attending a Shabbat service in Mexico City, Montreal, or Orlando, Florida, is sure to create a unique Jewish memory.

Whatever your family's regular Jewish practice, bring it with you wherever you go. Think about keeping kosher or having Shabbat as ways to turn your trip into an extra-special family adventure. You're sure to come home with stories that add a Jewish flavor to the memories.

Visiting Israel for the first time can be a life-transforming experience. Seeing and touching artifacts, buildings, and monuments described in the Bible is sure to change the way you and your children view your connection to Jewish history, culture, and religion. In Israel, the Torah seems part of the hills and paving stones. The commandment to love Jerusalem, one of the world's loveliest cities, is not an abstraction but a joy.

Israel inspires Jews in a variety of ways. Your connection to "the Jewish people" may take on a whole different meaning in a place where there are Jews as far as the eye can see. It is a revelation to live, even for a week, in a country that sets its clock and calendar according to Jewish time— where everyone, religiously observant or not, slows down for Shabbat. Where Passover melodies can be heard from every window on seder nights.

A trip to Israel is also living proof that Jewish civilization is not frozen in the past. Israel is a sophisticated and modern country, complete with computers, rock music, high fashion, fine art, and movies—all expressed in the language of the Bible. In a thousand subtle ways, Israel reconnects Jews to ideas and endeavors that are discontinuous in the Diaspora: mass media, fine art, professional sports, business. (Also dirty politics, corruption, and pollution.) Israel is a model of Jewish integration that is not really available to liberal Jews anywhere else.[5]

There are countless ways to experience Israel. In addition to the various package deals available from travel agencies specializing in Israel tours, many synagogues run trips for members, accompanied by the rabbi and/or cantor. Local Jewish federations sponsor "missions" of all kinds geared to the interests of singles, seniors, young leaders, and families. Some communities provide matching funds for parents who make an annual commitment to a savings account for a child's trip to Israel.

43

Israel with Children   As with any kind of trip, parents must take their children's ages and abilities into account in planning an itinerary. Children get bored in museums and at ancient ruins, and if kids are resentful and unhappy, they can ruin a trip for everyone in the family.

You can avoid this problem by limiting your sightseeing goals. While you may be frustrated by being "so near yet so far" from so many museums and archaeological sites, don't think about tailoring your trip to suit your children's ages and stages as a hedge against whining; it can turn out to be rewarding in its own right. As you relax at the beach in Tel Aviv, hike the Judean hills, play Frisbee at a Haifa playground, or shop at the *shuk* in Jerusalem, you may find that, in addition to enjoying a somewhat slower pace, you may get a chance to meet and talk to Israeli families (many speak English) and get a taste of what their lives are like.

Some families go to Israel in order to celebrate a bar or bat mitzvah. In addition to travel-agency package trips, some local federations run family missions that subsidize the cost of the bar/bat mitzvah child.[6] (See Chapter 8.)

Israel trips for older teenagers and college students are often a watershed experience. Jewish educators and demographers report that an independent (i.e., nonfamily) trip to Israel can be a powerful factor in fostering a lasting Jewish identity. Programs for high school and college students run the gamut: general tours of the country, archaeological digs, movement youth missions, work/Hebrew study on a kibbutz, Israeli/Palestinian youth dialogues, internships at social-service agencies, advanced Jewish studies, arts programs, and the list goes on. For information on denomination-sponsored programs, check the Web sites of the Reform and Conservative movements listed above and click on "Israel" and "Youth."[7] (Also see Chapter 9.)

BOOKS FOR CHILDREN
A Kids' Catalog of Israel, by Chaya M. Burstein (Jewish Publication Society, 1988). Encyclopedic and thus mostly for bookish kids. Still, there are lots of read-aloud stories in the back.

Kids Love Israel, Israel Loves Kids, by Barbara Sofer (Kar-Ben Copies, 1996). For updates and changes, go to www.karben.com.

BOOKS FOR PARENTS:
Israel: A Spiritual Travel Guide, by Lawrence A. Hoffman (Jewish Lights, 1998).

The Jewish Traveler, edited by Alan M. Tigay, (Doubleday, 1987). A collection of articles about forty-eight cities (Atlanta to Tel Aviv) from the pages of *Hadassah Magazine.*

TZEDAKAH

When a baby is born, the Jewish community prays that s/he will grow up to a life of *ma'asim tovim*—a life of good works. Parents make this prayer into a reality by teaching their children about *tzedakah.*

Usually translated as "charity," *tzedakah* is not an abstraction but a *mitzvah* that can permeate family life with opportunities to model and teach Jewish ethics, and to create formative memories that connect family with doing good in the world. Teaching children that *tzedakah* is a privilege and a joy begins simply, by slipping coins into a *tzedakah* box so that even toddlers can experience the pleasure of doing good. It continues by demonstrating that the Jewish mandate to repair the world (*tikkun olam*)— to address hunger, poverty, loneliness, injustice, the destruction of national resources—requires a collective, communal response as well as individual action.

Jewish parents face the challenge of imparting a message that runs counter to America's culture of acquisition, which constantly creates dissatisfaction by reminding us of all the consumer goods we lack. *Tzedakah* is a way to focus on the real needs of others, especially as compared with the extraordinary comfort most of us enjoy.

As always, parents who are *tzedakah* models are the most effective teachers. There are many ways to do this: by talking about the politics of poverty at the dinner table, by giving money to panhandlers on the street, by volunteering at a homeless shelter, by chairing the temple social-action committee, by attending rallies in support of human rights, by raising funds for the local Jewish federation, by participating in the cancer society walk-a-thon.

In whatever ways parents express the *mitzvah* of *tzedakah*, they embody the idea that every individual can make a difference and that every voice counts.

TZEDAKAH IN AGES AND STAGES

Toddlers and Preschoolers Use the word *tzedakah* rather than "charity" when talking to little kids about donations and doing good; this builds a child's basic vocabulary of Hebrew terms and Jewish concepts and also connects the idea of doing good with Jewishness.

If your family custom is to put money in a *tzedakah* box before lighting candles on Friday night, your child will associate the pleasure of giving with the sweetness of the Shabbat table. Preschoolers can make a family *tzedakah* box in several ways; tape your child's drawing over a tin can, or line a milk carton with aluminum foil and prick it with a pin to form a decorative pattern.

Since young children are concrete thinkers, it helps to explain the "whys" of the *tzedakah* box in terms they can understand. "There are children who do not have enough food to eat. We are putting in enough money to buy a loaf of bread for a poor child's family."

You can make *tzedakah* more literal by having a child select a can of soup or a box of pasta from the supermarket shelf. Then let him put his donation in the collection bin at the temple. Around Hanukkah, when many Jewish organizations collect toys for needy children, parents can take their children shopping to pick out a *tzedakah* present. Small acts of generosity and kindness such as these are lessons in belief and values, and about a child's responsibility and ability to change the world.

In simple language, explain how you understand the importance of *tzedakah:* "There are people who aren't as lucky as us, and as Jews it's our responsibility to help them."

"All the people in the world are connected, like a big family. If some people are too poor to eat, we need to help them by getting them food and money."

School-age Children Practice in doing *tzedakah* is part of the classroom experience for children in all Jewish schools. This may include community service (visiting a nursing home) as well as fund-raising projects (collecting money in the aftermath of a natural disaster). Sometimes, children are given the opportunity to make collective decisions about where to send their *tzedakah*—also a great exercise in the give-and-take of community life.

Parents can foster a child's impulse to be "part of the solution" in a number of ways. As always, what children see you do is the most important lesson. So if you stay abreast of the news and talk about the events of the day at the dinner table, children will come to see themselves as part of a global community.

Talk about your own charitable activities. Tell your children how much and to whom you give money. Explain how you decide where to send charitable dollars. Use concrete examples to explain why it's crucial for Jews to support Jewish causes ("If we don't donate *matzah* to the Jewish food pantry on Passover, who will?"), and why as Jews you support nonsectarian groups, too ("Donating to groups that work to keep the air clean helps everyone, including us").

Children who grow up in affluent towns and suburbs tend to be attuned to "who has more stuff than me" rather than who has less. Make a chart to show your child where your family falls in the economic spectrum of your community, the country, and the world. Help her understand that she really is in a position to help others. If you give your children a weekly allowance, tell them you expect some portion to be set aside for *tzedakah* and let them decide where to send it. If they go trick-or-treating at Halloween, encourage them to collect money for UNICEF. Find a project for the whole family, such as serving Christmas dinner to shut-ins, or weeding an elderly neighbor's garden.

Adolescents   Doing *tzedakah* has become part of the bar and bat mitzvah curriculum in synagogues, as a way to mark the beginning of adult Jewish responsibility. The bar/bat mitzvah can earmark a percentage of the money received in gifts for a specific charity, or ask guests to bring canned goods for donation to a food pantry. Parents can take the lead in this by suggesting the family make a donation with money that might otherwise have paid for floral centerpieces, and by making a contribution to the organization Mazon: A Jewish Response to Hunger,[8] which suggests donating 3 percent of food costs from all Jewish celebrations.

Jewish high school and youth groups provide many opportunities to link Judaism with social justice through hands-on *tzedakah* projects and Jewish text study,[9] which can provide wonderful debates about the role of the individual in society, a topic of keen interest to adolescents.

At home, Jewish teens should be encouraged to use their own money for *tzedakah* and to participate in volunteer efforts they find compelling:

tutoring children, renovating an old synagogue or a women's shelter; serving meals at a soup kitchen. Parents can provide material support for these increasingly independent efforts by writing a check for the high school dance-a-thon for AIDS research, by driving a group of kids to a rally in support of Israel, by paying for a trip to repair housing for the poor.

BOOKS FOR CHILDREN

Partners, by Deborah Shayne Syme (UAHC Press, 1990). How kids can be "partners" with God, in making the world a better place.

BOOKS FOR PARENTS

Three titles by Danny Siegel: *Gym Shoes and Irises: Personalized Tzedakah; Gym Shoes and Irises: Book Two;* and *Munbaz II and Other Mitzvah Heroes* (The Town House Press, 1982, 1987, and 1988).[10] These *tzedakah* resource books are filled with inspirational essays, practical guides for children and adults, quotations from the Talmud, poetry, and more.

Chapter 4

Defining
Jewish Time

"Jewish ritual may be characterized as the art of significant forms in time, as architecture of time," wrote Rabbi Abraham Joshua Heschel.[1]

It's a beautiful image, but puzzling. How can something as solid and three-dimensional as architecture be compared to anything as ephemeral as time? After all, time flies, runs through our fingers, waits for no man . . .

But Jewish ritual—from daily prayer to weekly Sabbath observance to annual holiday celebration—builds islands in time that encourage us to stop and savor. Differentiated from the rest of the pell-mell week-month-year, the various Jewish "forms in time" slow things down and infuse the fleeting days-hours-minutes with deliberation and sweetness. Judaism's ritual structures help us see that, although we are subject to clock and calendar, our days do belong to us when we remember to stop and pay attention.

The Jewish sanctification of time—through blessings and holidays—is a call to live in the present, to open our eyes, to give thanks, to be here now. Judaism provides the means to wake up to the wonders of life and of the universe on every possible timetable: moment to moment, day to day, week to week, month to month, year to year, and generation to generation.

This is a special gift to parents watching their children change from week to week, milestone to milestone. The Jewish calendar is full of ways to stay in touch with and to teach this "mindfulness of the moment," this sense of the holiness of time.

Children seem to have a natural affinity for marking time in regular patterns. From bath time to birthdays, young children depend upon routines to help them organize and master a world full of new ideas, sensations, and challenges. They thrive on predictability—which should not be confused with rigidity or inflexibility.

Thus, kids take to the pleasures of Jewish routines as effortlessly as they take to the taste of sweet grape juice and challah. Natural masters of pretend and playfulness, possessed of an uncritical sense of wonder, they are eager pupils of Judaism's tangible practices, which transform the passing of time into "significant forms" with songs and tastes and smells of their own.

MOMENT TO MOMENT:
BLESSINGS FOR EVERY DAY

בָּרוּךְ אַתָּה יְיָ, אֱלֹהֵינוּ מֶלֶךְ הָעוֹלָם,

Baruch Ata Adonai, Eloheynu Melech Ha-olam . . .

You are blessed, Adonai, You are our God, Ruler of eternity . . .

This is the phrase, variously translated, that begins every Hebrew blessing, or *b'racha.** *B'rachot* (the plural of *b'racha*) do not so much bless or praise God as declare God the source of all blessing. They serve as reminders to us to stop, appreciate, and sanctify the moments of our lives.

B'rachot are recited in a variety of settings, some clearly "religious," such as when you light Sabbath candles or begin a holiday. But there are *b'rachot* for virtually every moment in life: seeing a rainbow, hearing of a death, eating a piece of fruit newly in season, even after going to the bathroom. According to one tradition, Jews are invited to recite a hundred blessings every day.

B'rachot are Jewish wake-up calls to wonder or, to use the Buddhist term, "mindfulness." Blessings can remind us that we are not the center of the universe (the bread comes from the work of many hands and the mira-

---

* The "old" translation is "Blessed Art Thou, Lord our God, King of the Universe. . . ." You will find a variety of alternatives versions throughout this book.

cle of photosynthesis), that it is good to be alive (and healthy enough to wake, eat, use the bathroom). *B'rachot* give our sense of awe (at the sunrise, mountaintops, rainbows) a specifically Jewish form.

Jewish blessings address God in two "voices": *Ata* ("You") is singular, intimate, and familiar; *Eloheynu* ("our God") is plural and formal, connecting the individual with the larger Jewish community. Together, the two forms of address also hint at the shimmering duality of spiritual experiences: the feeling of great intimacy or oneness with God/creation, and the sense of awe and humility before the enormity and complexity of creation/God.

One of the best-known and most-used Hebrew *b'rachot* is the *Shehechiyanu.*

בָּרוּךְ אַתָּה יְיָ, אֱלֹהֵינוּ מֶלֶךְ הָעוֹלָם, שֶׁהֶחֱיָנוּ וְקִיְּמָנוּ וְהִגִּיעָנוּ לַזְּמַן הַזֶּה.

Baruch Ata Adonai, Eloheynu Melech Ha-olam shehechiyanu v'keyamanu v'higianu lazman hazeh.

Blessed are You, Ruler of the Universe, You have kept us alive, and sustained us, and enabled us to reach this moment.

A blessing of thanksgiving for beginnings and "firsts" of all kinds, it is recited at the Rosh Hashanah table to commemorate the start of the new year. At a bar or bat mitzvah, it stops the clock so that everyone at the celebration will look at the young person on the verge of adulthood, remembering back to his birth, imagining ahead to her wedding.

But *Shehechiyanu* is also a kind of "all-purpose" blessing that can be invoked whenever a person lifts his or her head above the fray of daily life and, remembering how good it is to be alive, sees the world anew. By blessing the moment, *Shehechiyanu* leaves no room to bemoan the passing of time. It stresses the positive, reveals the miraculous, and reminds us that change is the reward as well as the price of being alive. *Shehechiyanu* connects the profound joy of everyday experience to the whole fabric of creation.

It's also short and easy to learn. In a pinch, all you need to do is say the word *shehechiyanu* ("you have kept us alive") and you can sanctify the moment in the grocery store when your five-year-old reads the word "milk" for the first time, or when your teenager thanks you for making breakfast.

When to Say *Shehechiyanu*

Upon eating your first strawberry of spring.

At the birth of a child.

When your baby says "Mama" for the first time.

When your child makes his first soccer goal.

Upon hearing that your daughter has gotten her first menstrual period.

Whenever first-time guests are seated at your Shabbat dinner table.

After you put together the trampoline, just before anyone jumps.

On the morning your child begins kindergarten.

When your child returns to the family Shabbat table after his first semester of college.

With the first bite of an autumn apple.

DAY TO DAY: MORNING AND EVENING

Most good-night and good-morning rituals are automatic and nearly invisible. But even the simple acts of brushing teeth, reading a story, and kissing your child "night-night" give a predictable and comforting shape to the end of the day. By adding a Jewish dimension to these liminal moments in time, parents shape their children's worldview in sweet and subtle ways.

Judaism encourages praying "when you lie down and when you rise up"[2] and provides specific nighttime and morning prayers. Thus, the day starts with a grateful "Thank you" for another morning, and concludes with a hopeful "Please" for another day on earth.

Shema is the nighttime blessing. The best-known line in all of Jewish liturgy, the *Shema* is neither a prayer nor a blessing. It makes no petition and renders no praise. It proclaims God as a unity (*echad*, in Hebrew); it is also an affirmation of Jewish identity and connection. *Shema* is the last thing a Jew is supposed to say before dying, which is why it is recited before going to sleep at night (in case "I should die before I wake"). For a child, the sound of the Hebrew words chanted softly in the dark becomes a melodic mantra associated with the safety and peace of his own bedroom.

שְׁמַע יִשְׂרָאֵל, יְיָ אֱלֹהֵינוּ, יְיָ אֶחָד.

Shema Yisrael, Adonai Eloheynu, Adonai Echad.

Hear O Israel, Adonai is our God, Adonai is One.

The nightly *Shema*—recited while cuddling quietly in the dark—can set the stage for cozy conversation about the day just ended, what went well and what went wrong. It can also be a time to build the spiritual practice of *teshuvah* (literally, "turning," or "repentance"), of thinking of what you might want to do differently tomorrow.

The morning prayer, *Modeh ani,* thanks God for restoring the sleeper's soul upon waking. Sung to an upbeat melody, this can be a lovely way to awaken a sleepy child, and people who grow up with this ritual find it as comforting as the *Shema* at night.

מוֹדֶה אֲנִי לְפָנֶיךָ, מֶלֶךְ חַי וְקַיָּם, שֶׁהֶחֱזַרְתָּ בִּי נִשְׁמָתִי בְּחֶמְלָה, רַבָּה אֱמוּנָתֶךָ.

Modeh ani lifanecha, melech chai vikayam, shehechezarta bi nish-mati bechemlah; raba emunatecha.

I thank you, everlasting Source of life, for in Your compassion
You have given me back my soul; great is Your Faith.[3]

A shorthand version might be "*Modeh ani,*" which means "I am grateful."

Another way to provide a Jewish dimension to evening and morning rituals is simply to use modern Hebrew greetings. Say "*Leila tov,*" (Good night) as you turn off the lights, and "*Boker tov,*" (Good morning) as you greet the new day. Whatever your custom, parents who start and conclude the day in an explicitly Jewish way provide their children with a model of daily Jewish identification, a fond memory, and a gentle acknowledgment of the divine in our lives.

WEEK TO WEEK: SHABBAT

"What is the most important Jewish holiday?" The answer to this old "trick" question is not Yom Kippur or Passover. The most important holiday is not an annual event but the seventh day of every single week.

Shabbat is the polestar of Jewish time, the only day of the week with a Hebrew name; the rest are merely numbered in relation to the Sabbath, thus Tuesday is only *Yom Shelishi*, the "third day."

Rabbi Heschel imagined Shabbat as the cornerstone in his "architecture of time," and referred to the Sabbath as "our great cathedral."[4] The metaphor, while beautiful, is a little forbidding. Cathedrals suggest sobriety, but Shabbat has as much room for levity as for reflection and prayer.

For parents, Shabbat is the perfect Jewish lesson plan. But that image, too, makes Shabbat sound overly formal because the essence and lesson of Shabbat is joy. Shabbat can have many modes and moods. Parts of the day may be contemplative, peaceful, and studious, but it's also okay to be silly and sensual, relaxed and playful on Shabbat.

Shabbat comes every week. But it doesn't just show up in your home; you have to invite it inside. Shabbat does not just happen; it must be remembered and created week by week. The Jewish locution for this is "making Shabbes" (using the Yiddish word for Sabbath), and it starts with little things, like remembering to add challah to the grocery list. Eventually and with practice, Shabbat can grow on you—and in you—until it becomes a high point of the week. The following pages explain how it's done; but first, a little about why.

Origins and Obstacles The first mention of the word comes early in Genesis, in the form of a verb, *shavat*, which means "stopped," or "ceased," or "rested."

> On the seventh day God finished the work that God had made, and God ceased from all the work that God had made.
> God blessed the seventh day and declared it holy, because on it God ceased from all the work of creation that God had made.

In the book of Exodus, God "gives" the Sabbath to the Jews as a token of the relationship between them: "I have given them my Sabbath to be a

sign between Me and them, so they will know that I am the One that sanctifies them."[5]

According to custom and law, Jews honor their part of this covenant
by imitating what God did on the seventh day—by resting and pronounc-
ing the world good, just as God rested and pronounced the world *tov* (Hebrew for "good").

Shabbat was a revolutionary concept in the ancient world, where only
the rich and powerful enjoyed the privilege of leisure. Jews not only took
every seventh day off, they insisted that everyone within their communities—including servants, non-Jewish guests, and even domesticated animals—refrain from work. The Sabbath gave substance to the dream of
universal peace and justice by offering a glimpse of what the world would
be like if all human beings were free. The rabbis of the Talmud understood
the power of Shabbat as ultimately redemptive; they imagined that if all
Jews would fully observe two consecutive Sabbaths, the world would be returned to the state of perfection known only at the beginning of time, as
imagined in Eden.[6]

Celebrating Shabbat set the Jews apart and sometimes got them in
trouble; at several points in Jewish history, temporal authorities forbade its
observance. But even in the best of times, Shabbat can be a difficult mandate.

Today, the obstacles to making Shabbes are mostly self-imposed.
There's the deadline that can't wait, the long commute home, late meetings
on Friday afternoon, soccer games on Saturday. Even setting aside the ex-
ternal pressures, there are other reasons that prevent us from taking a
weekly respite from work: the kids are cranky, the adults are exhausted, the
refrigerator is empty, the prayers are foreign, the ritual seems artificial, the
synagogue is far away.

Even so, the transformational potential of Shabbat has never been
more attractive. The stresses on family life are extreme. We have too little
time to simply enjoy one another. Parents are acutely aware of how hard
it is to impart a sense of continuity and identity in a culture where con-
sumerism is king, to provide a sense of security in a world that seems so
dangerous, to teach moral and ethical lessons that are so far removed from
the daily headlines.

In the modern world, making Shabbes is a radical act of self-
determination. Taking time to replace the noise of the marketplace and the
media with the voices of the people you treasure fulfills our most important

personal promises. Shabbat is the means for translating "values" and "priorities" from words into actions. Shabbat can transform our fondest wishes for our children into hard-wired memories of connection and peace.

Shabbat provides parents with countless opportunities to teach children how and why to be Jewish using all four strategies described in Chapter 1. Shabbat is all about giving parents ways to model both the form and content of Jewish values and life in ways that are authentic and joyful. It can be filled with "teachable moments" of all kinds, starting with the Sabbath table, a primary setting for tastes, smells, sounds, and associations that last a lifetime. In religious terms, Shabbat is time set aside to remember our relationship with the Divine. However you define or see holiness in life (in nature, in your family's eyes, in the Torah), Shabbat provides a glimpse.

Making Shabbat Your Own For some families, Shabbat observance is a twenty-five-hour span that begins just before sunset on Friday night and ends after sunset on Saturday, when three stars appear in the sky.

For some families, Shabbat observance is Friday night dinner, which begins whenever the entire family is gathered at the table and ends with dessert.

For most families, Shabbat changes from one year to the next, as children grow and change, as adults learn how to relax into its rhythm. In every family, Shabbat varies from one week to the next, depending on people's moods, whether there are guests in the house, if the candles are lit in a vacation cabin.

However you "make Shabbes" this year, this season, this week, the goal of Shabbat is always to build a peaceful respite in your family's life. If you find yourself getting angry, resentful, or stressed about Sabbath observance in your home, take a step back, reconsider, and discuss the choices you've made. Shabbat is an ongoing part of creation. Unlike a cathedral made of mortar and brick, Shabbat is a living tradition, and like all living things, it changes.

The key thing to remember is that there is no one right way to make Shabbes. Jews celebrate the Sabbath with different foods, melodies, and customs that vary not only from one country to the next, but from one kitchen to the next. Regardless of the particulars in your home, Shabbat becomes special—and holy—by being set apart from the rest of the week on a consistent basis. How you set it apart is up to you; it can be the day for shedding ties and high heels, or the day for dressing up in your finest. It can be the day you always have guests for lunch, or the day you take an afternoon nap. It can be the day you go out for ice cream together, or the day your children are permitted to drink soda from a wineglass. Whatever choices you make, consistency is central to creating family traditions. Although there will always be exceptions to your practice (you go on vacation, the children are in summer camp, non-Jewish family members are at the table), the "rules" should be clear.

Any talk of "rules" makes some people bristle—especially those who experienced Shabbat as a day of restrictions and self-denial during childhood. But the limits on normal activities are not meant as punishments. For example, Jewish tradition forbids most kinds of work on Shabbat, but the prohibitions against *doing* are really nothing more than a protective fence around a day set aside for simply *being*.[7] Similarly, your Shabbat rules are the tools for creating that longed-for island of rest and peace in your family's life.

Praying, studying, and eating are all permitted on Shabbat, as is teaching children, arranging marriages, and making love. Shabbat is for sleeping, reading, chatting, singing, meditating, visiting with friends, playing with our children, walking through the woods or on the beach, letting go.

Shabbat is also a day for saying yes. Much of the time parents are required to be nay-sayers; it's an important part of the job. "No, you can't have chocolate cake for breakfast." "No, we can't play now, you're late for school." "No, it's too cold to wear shorts today." Shabbat is the day to try and let go of reflexive or automatic "no's" and go out of your way to say yes.

Paradoxically, saying yes to a day of rest is not easy. Shabbat really is a kind of discipline. Saying yes to Shabbat means saying no to other important elements in your life. Liberal Jews struggle with the criteria for what does and does not "belong" on Shabbat, what violates and what fosters the spirit of the day. Traditionally, one does not spend or even handle money on the Sabbath. Some Jews honor that tradition by avoiding all forms of shopping but make an exception for taking the children out for a treat on Shabbat afternoon. Some Jews agree with the idea that playing music—on a compact-disc player or on the violin—are forms of work to be avoided; but for others, Shabbat is a rare opportunity to enjoy the beauty of music in any form.

In Hebrew, there are two versions of the commandment about Shabbat and two verbs associated with how Jews are supposed to observe it: *shamor*, which means "to guard" or "keep," and the verb *zachor*, "to remember," which suggests mindfulness about everything we say and do on the Sabbath. *Zachor* asks us to measure all our choices against the yardstick of Shabbat peace.

Remembering Shabbat from sunset to sunset in a nonstop, multimedia, global culture, can be a formidable discipline. As with any other freely chosen discipline—like studying the clarinet or playing tennis—it takes time to learn the fundamentals and years to master the finer points. So don't worry too much if the kids whine at the Shabbat table sometimes, or if Dad is too late to eat Friday-night dinner with the little ones. Try not to compare your Sabbath with what you think it "ought" to be. If it's not what you're after this week, there's always next week.

Shabbat gets easier over time. It gets sweeter, too.

Making Shabbes   There are three "seasons" within every Sabbath. Friday night, or *erev* (the evening of) Shabbat, is the most home- and family-centered part of the Sabbath. It is a celebration of the five senses that centers around a festive dinner table.

Saturday morning is the most liturgical, formal, and communal part of the day. Saturday morning, which honors the intellect, tends to revolve around synagogue services, where the focus is reading from the Torah.

Saturday afternoon is the most unstructured part of the day, a time for affirming family ties and for simple pleasures. The period from lunchtime until the brief prayers of *Havdalah* (separation) that end the Sabbath, is, ideally, an obligation-free zone.

If you are just starting to celebrate Shabbat, don't try to do it all. Begin with Friday-night table blessings and grow into the next step that's right for your family.

For liberal Jews, Shabbat begins at the dinner table Friday night. Although Jewish law requires candlelighting eighteen minutes prior to sunset, most families start Shabbat when, and only when, everyone gathers for supper—whether that happens to be an hour after sunset or an hour before.

Although the dinner table is the focus for Friday night, and although eating is a Jewish passion, food is only a part of what makes a meal the ritual start of Shabbat. Equally important is *where* you decide to eat (dining room or deck rather than kitchen), and *how* the table is prepared (cloth napkins instead of paper, fresh flowers). Whether you have a roast chicken feast or take-out pizza (it happens), a special challah plate or a simple cutting board, Shabbat candlesticks and wine cups are cues that Shabbes is about to arrive.

Here are suggestions for ways to "set the stage":

Dress Up or Dress Down.   Slip into your jeans or get gussied up, anything to change your appearance to greet the Sabbath. This can be as simple as washing your hands and face or putting a *yarmulke—kippah* in Hebrew—on your head. If you like to wear cologne, put some on. (If your children want to wear some, too, say yes.) Remove your watch.

Empty Your Pockets or Change Purse into a Tzedakah Box.   Like a piggy bank for charity, the *tzedakah* box (also called a *pushke*) is a reminder that other people in the world need help and that Jews share what we have with the poor. (See Chapter 3 for more about *tzedakah.*)

Change the Mood.   Lower the lights. Unplug the phone. Play favorite Jewish music while you set the table. Watch the sunset for a few minutes. Put a centerpiece on the table. If you have fresh flowers, pass them around for everyone to smell. Eat by candlelight.

Sing a Song.   A Shabbat song is great, and if your children attend Jewish preschool, day school, or Hebrew school, they will be glad to teach you one. But almost any song will change the "climate" to a celebratory one.

Make the House Smell like Heaven.   If dinner is on the stove or in the oven, you're already there. For an effective shortcut, warm your challah in the oven for a few minutes. There is nothing like the aroma of bread to evoke a sense of tranquillity and safety.

Greet Everyone at the Table.   Hold hands for a moment before lighting the candles, passing along a squeeze. Suggest that everyone take a deep breath and release it along with tensions from face and shoulders.

After you light the candles, go around the table and have each family member complete the sentence, "This was a great week because . . ."

Now you're ready for the blessings, the magic-working words that bring Shabbat into your house. The core blessings are recited for candles, wine, and bread.

Lighting candles:

בָּרוּךְ אַתָּה יְיָ, אֱלֹהֵינוּ מֶלֶךְ הָעוֹלָם, אֲשֶׁר קִדְּשָׁנוּ בְּמִצְוֹתָיו
וְצִוָּנוּ לְהַדְלִיק נֵר שֶׁל שַׁבָּת.

Baruch Ata Adonai, Eloheynu Melech Ha-olam asher kid'shanu b'mitzvotav vitsivanu l'hadlik ner shel shabbat.

Holy One of Blessing, Your Presence Fills Creation; You make us holy with Your commandments and call us to light the lights of Shabbat.[8]

Every Friday night, Jews around the world participate in this ritual, which was already part of Jewish life by the first century C.E.[9] In earlier times, Shabbat lights were oil lamps; today, candles are customary for most of us—usually short, white, kosher (no animal fat) tapers, sold for ritual use in Jewish stores and in many supermarkets. (It's fun to substitute colored or rainbow candles in honor of a birthday.)

Two candles are traditional, but some families add a light for every child, and in some households, everyone has his or her own pair of candlesticks. Guests can bring candlesticks, too.

According to tradition, the *mitzvah* of lighting candles belongs to the woman of the house, and many women cherish the custom as their own. In some families, however, the honor rotates and includes everyone, regardless of gender.

The tradition is to light the candles first and recite the blessings second.[10] The custom of closing or covering the eyes while saying the blessing enacts the transformation of the world, since, when you reopen your eyes *Abracadabra!* the weekday, workaday world is special, holy, and Shabbat.

To mark the distinction made by the lighting of candles, you can greet everyone at the table all over again with the words, "Shabbat Shalom," or "Good Shabbes." Many families sing "Shabbat Shalom" after candlelighting. In some homes, it is the custom for everyone at the table to exchange a kiss.

Before saying or chanting the blessing, some people circle the flames with their hands three times, a mystical gesture for drawing in the light, which is a universal symbol of God's presence. Many pause for a moment either before lighting or while covering the eyes for a silent prayer or invocation of peace and quiet.

Children are fascinated by the power and beauty of candlelighting, and also by the matches and flames. Blowing out the match is a coveted honor for little ones. As time passes, the matches and candles become milestones: the first time she strikes the match; the first time he leads the blessing; the birthday when she gets her own set of candlesticks; the September he lights them in his college dorm.

The blessing for wine:

בָּרוּךְ אַתָּה יְיָ, אֱלֹהֵינוּ מֶלֶךְ הָעוֹלָם, בּוֹרֵא פְּרִי הַגָּפֶן.

Baruch Ata Adonai, Eloheynu Melech Ha-olam boray p'ree hagafen.

Holy One of Blessing, Your Presence fills Creation, forming the fruit of the vine.

Judaism uses wine to sanctify time. Based on the same Hebrew root as *kadosh,* or "holy," the act of "making kiddush"—saying the blessing over wine—is part of virtually every joyful celebration in Jewish life. Although there are several extended kiddush blessings for holidays and weddings, for Friday night and for Saturday lunch, the core is always the same *boray p'ree hagafen.*[11]

There are many family traditions about how to say kiddush; many people just recite the *boray p'ree hagafen* in unison, but in some homes a leader sings the long kiddush with others joining in at various points.

If you, your family, or guests are not familiar with the words to the kiddush or the other prayers mentioned here, consider getting some *benchers,* little prayer books intended for home use and made by many Jewish organizations. Many *benchers*—from the Yiddish word for "prayer"—contain transliterations in addition to the Hebrew and an English translation. Or you can create your own customized one- or two-page family *bencher.*

In some families, it is the custom for the leader or the whole company to stand during kiddush; but in others everyone stays seated. Some people say the blessing over a single cup, which is then passed or poured into other cups. Elsewhere, everyone drinks from his or her own glass. Some families make a point of using only kosher wine for making kiddush. (See Chapter 3 for an explanation of kosher wine.) Grape juice is a good substitute for wine, since it, too, is "fruit of the vine."

The blessing for bread:

בָּרוּךְ אַתָּה יְיָ, אֱלֹהֵינוּ מֶלֶךְ הָעוֹלָם, הַמּוֹצִיא לֶחֶם מִן־הָאָרֶץ.

Baruch Ata Adonai, Eloheynu Melech Ha-olam hamotzi lechem min ha-aretz.

Holy One of Blessing, Your Presence Fills Creation, bringing forth bread from the earth.

The blessing called *Hamotzi* ("the One Who brings forth") is recited over any loaf of bread at any time, not just Shabbat. But for Jews who don't usually say blessings before eating, *Hamotzi* has become attached to the loaf eaten on Shabbat. Since this is the first *b'racha* many children learn, it is a nice honor to give and share among children at the Shabbat table.

Even with a custom as simple as breaking bread, there are a variety of ways to do it. Traditionally, there are two loaves of challah on the table—symbolizing plenty, and recalling the "double portion" brought by Jews to the Temple in ancient days which in turn symbolized the double portion of manna received on Friday by the Jews during the exodus from Egypt.

In some homes, challah is ripped apart and pieces are handed around the table; the custom is usually explained as a way of avoiding sharp knives—reminders of violence and war—at the Shabbat table. But in other households, the bread is sliced and passed on a platter. Some families all reach to the center of the table to touch the bread or plate during the *Hamotzi.* The custom of salting challah is explained as a reminder of Temple days, when sacrifices to God were salted on the altar.

For American Jews, challah means the beautiful egg-rich, braided loaf served on Friday nights and holidays. In the Torah, challah was special Shabbat bread, and any loaf prepared according to Jewish law for the purpose of saying a blessing may be called by that name.[12] In different cultures, challah took on the flavors and shapes of local breads—though on Shabbat, it was made to look and taste special, to set it apart from the "daily bread" of the week.

Kosher challah is available in Jewish bakeries, and non-kosher challah is sold in many supermarkets. Children look forward to a weekly trip to buy challah and other Shabbat treats—another opportunity to say yes to a child's desire for cookies or cupcakes, and a way to make a sweet connection with the rhythms of Jewish life.

Challah can be purchased frozen and baked at home. It is also one of the easier breads to bake from scratch, and kids love to get involved in punching the dough and braiding it. (For a step-by-step guide to baking challah with children, see *The Children's Jewish Holiday Kitchen*, by Joan Nathan.)

Other Shabbat Blessings   The following *b'rachot* can become traditions in your home after only a few weeks. These blessings are usually added between candlelighting and kiddush; hand-washing usually precedes *Hamotzi*.

Family Blessings   There are three *b'rachot* that allow us to count our most important blessings—the people we love most. Whatever language you use, Hebrew or English, a family blessing can wipe away, at least for a little while, the inevitable misunderstandings and tensions of the previous week.

Blessing for Children   The traditional blessing for sons, which is based on Jacob's blessing of his grandsons, names the relatively obscure Ephraim and Menashe, children of Joseph and his Egyptian wife, Asenath. The fact that these are the sons of a non-Jewish mother can be read as a powerful affirmation of Jewish inclusiveness and of how the Jewish people grows by in-marriage, adoption, and conversion.

The blessing for daughters lists the four biblical matriarchs: Sarah, Rebecca, Rachel, and Leah—strong women, each in her own way.

Either or both parents say the traditional blessing, or substitute whispered words of appreciation and love.

For Boys:

יְשִׂמְךָ אֱלֹהִים כְּאֶפְרַיִם וְכִמְנַשֶּׁה.

Y'simcha Elohim k'Efrayim v'ch'M'nashe.

May God make you as Ephraim and Menashe.

For Girls:

יְשִׂמֵךְ אֱלֹהִים כְּשָׂרָה, רִבְקָה, רָחֵל וְלֵאָה.

Y'simeych Elohim k'Sarah, Rivkah, Rachel v'Leah.

Make God make you as Sarah, Rebecca, Rachel and Leah.

For Both (the priestly blessing):

יְבָרֶכְךָ יְיָ וְיִשְׁמְרֶךָ. יָאֵר יְיָ פָּנָיו אֵלֶיךָ וִיחֻנֶּךָ.
יִשָּׂא יְיָ פָּנָיו אֵלֶיךָ וְיָשֵׂם לְךָ שָׁלוֹם.

Y'varech-e'cha Adonai v'yish-marecha.
Ya'er Adonai panav eylecha vichuneka.
Yisa Adonai panav eylecha v'yasem l'cha shalom.

May Adonai bless you and keep you.
May Adonai shine Adonai's Countenance upon you and be gra-
cious to you.
May Adonai favor you and grant you peace.

Parents sometimes substitute family names: "May you be like Grandma
Bessie and Grammy Ruth." Poet Marcia Falk rewrote the traditional blessings in language that speaks to the individuality of each child;

Blessing of the Children[13]
by Marcia Falk

To a Girl:
_____ (her name)
Hayi asher tihyi—
vahayi brukhah
ba'asher tihyi.
_____ (her name)
Be who you are—
And may you be blessed
In all that you are.

הֲיִי אֲשֶׁר תִּהְיִי —
וַהֲיִי בְּרוּכָה
בַּאֲשֶׁר תִּהְיִי.

64

To a Boy:
____ (his name)
Heyeyh asher tihyeh—
veheyeyh barukh
ba'asher tihyeh.
____ (his name)
Be who you are—
And may you be blessed
In all that you are.

הֱיֵה אֲשֶׁר תִּהְיֶה—
וֶהְיֵה בָּרוּךְ
בַּאֲשֶׁר תִּהְיֶה.

Blessing for a Spouse   According to ancient custom, a husband reads or chants to his wife from the book of Proverbs.[14] The section called *Eshet Chayil* ("a woman of valor") praises a wife's generosity, beauty, business acumen, wisdom, and lovingkindness. Many couples today use this moment just to say "I love you" and kiss—a wonderful way to put an end to the petty squabbles of the week.[15]

An alternative all-family blessing comes from the Reconstructionist home prayer book.

Everyone at the Shabbat table says:

Harachaman Hu yevarech otanu kulanu yachad
Bevirkat shalom.

May the Merciful One bless all of us together
    With the blessing of peace.[16]

Hand-Washing   This ritual is not about cleanliness (although with small children, it never hurts). Taking a moment to purify the hands before eating is a vestige of purification rituals from the days when priests offered sacrifices. Since the destruction of the Temple, however, the family table has replaced the public altar as the "Holy of Holies," and stopping to wash hands and recite the blessing is a way to recall that the sacred can be found in even the most mundane acts—such as eating.

בָּרוּךְ אַתָּה יְיָ, אֱלֹהֵינוּ מֶלֶךְ הָעוֹלָם, אֲשֶׁר קִדְּשָׁנוּ בְּמִצְוֹתָיו וְצִוָּנוּ עַל נְטִילַת יָדָיִם.

Baruch Ata Adonai, Eloheynu Melech Ha-olam asher kid'shanu
b'mitzvotav vitsivanu al netilat yadayim.

65

Holy One of Blessing, Your presence fills Creation, making us holy with your commandments and calls us to wash our hands.

Washing takes place in a special bowl near the table or at a sink; some people use a special two-handled cup called a laver. In some families, the custom is to take turns pouring water over one another's fingers. According to another custom, you refrain from talking between washing and saying the *Hamotzi*. It's easier for children to do this if everyone sings—a wordless melody (*niggun*) works best—while waiting for everyone to return from the sink to the table.

During Dinner   It is never easy to be intentional about the words that come out of our mouths, but the Shabbat table is a place to pay attention to what we say and how we say it. It may help to think of the Shabbat table the way you would a party for an honored guest, where it would seem inappropriate to bring up unfinished homework or unpaid bills.

One of the wonderful reasons for inviting guests for Shabbat dinner is that the presence of other people tends to put everyone on better behavior, elevate the conversation, and lighten the mood. But even if it's only your immediate family, a nicely set table sets the stage for more pleasant talk. Encourage your children to tell stories from their week. Parents can start by recalling something you learned or enjoyed since last Shabbat. But most important is the way you speak; try not to interrupt, scold, or solve problems. Don't gossip or speak ill of people. Hold on to the good feelings of the family blessings and try not to say no.

Blessings After the Meal   Jews give thanks for their meals after eating with an anthology of blessings and prayers called the *Birkat Hamazon* (blessings for food) that is printed in pocket-sized prayer books called *benchers,* described above.

Many people who know the *Birkat Hamazon* learned the words and melodies in Jewish summer camp, youth group, or school, and thus associate the prayer with large, communal meals. The whole *Birkat Hamazon* is several pages long, but there is also a two-page form in Hebrew, as well as various English versions, which may feel more appropriate for a smaller gathering.

For a shorthand version, you can simply say:

בָּרוּךְ אַתָּה יְיָ, הַזָּן אֶת־הַכֹּל.

Baruch Ata Adonai, Hazan et Ha-kol.

Holy One of Blessing, Sustainer of all there is.

After Dinner The traditional entertainment after Shabbat dinner is singing, and most benchers contain the lyrics to many *z'mirot*, or Shabbat songs. The more people at the table, the more lively the singing and the more varied the songs—another reason to invite guests.

Singing is not the only way to stretch out and unwind into Shabbat. Go outside and look at the night sky and say hello to the moon by its Hebrew name. (Check the section "Your Calendar," page 84.)

Read aloud from a book you save for Shabbat. Play a board game. Play musical instruments. Listen to music together and dance. Read an extra story to your children before tucking them in. It is traditional for couples to make love on Friday night.

Synagogue Services on Friday Night Friday-evening worship services are called *Kabbalat Shabbat,* welcoming the Sabbath. Some synagogues bring the table blessings to the *bimah* with a congregational candlelighting, kiddush, and *Hamotzi.*

In some congregations, *Kabbalat Shabbat* services are scheduled early enough for people to go home for dinner afterwards, but in others, the Friday night service takes place after dinner and is followed by a gathering called an *Oneg Shabbat* (joy of the Sabbath)—a time for socializing with friends, meeting new people, eating Shabbat sweets, and enjoying the community.

Many temples schedule a monthly Friday-night service for families with young children; these may include a community Shabbat dinner, which can be a great place to learn songs and pick up ideas for Shabbat at home.

Food on Shabbat

The Sabbath invites us to enjoy three "feasts," with Friday-night dinner serving as the culinary high point of the week. According to Jewish law, the lighting of fires and cooking after sunset on Friday is not permitted, which meant that Jewish homemakers spent most of Friday shopping and cooking for all three meals. (The section about "Food" in Chapter 3 explains *kashrut*, the laws about what Jews do and do not eat, and why food is part of all Jewish observance.)

The challenge for Jewish parents today is to balance the desire for extra-special Shabbat food on the one hand, with feeling stressed (if not oppressed) by all the planning, shopping, and cooking that expectation can entail.

As you consider how to make Shabbes in your house, be true to yourself and the realities of your lives. In single-parent or two-income families, takeout feasts may be a good solution. If you simply don't like to spend time in the kitchen, try new ways to make Shabbat a day that frees you from cooking. But if you love to cook and have the time, Shabbat can include treating your family and guests to old favorites and new recipes.

There is no rule that Friday-night dinner has to center on chicken or brisket. However, one reason that parents serve the same special Shabbat meal every Friday night is not only to keep the planning easy, but also to turn the food into part of the ritual and to create a family tradition. Shabbat thus comes to have a distinctive and evocative smell, whether the aroma is chicken soup or vegetarian lasagna. One little boy was so accustomed to his mother's roast chicken on Friday night that the Shabbat she cooked a brisket as a special treat for a guest, the boy looked at the serving dish and proclaimed. "Wow! Brown chicken!"

Saturday Morning This is the most liturgical part of Shabbat, and thus the most "adult" time. But it can also be the most social segment of the Sabbath, a time for families to connect to the larger Jewish community.

Taking children to Shabbat morning services can be a pleasure or an ordeal, depending on parents' attitudes, synagogue policies and programs, and children's temperaments, personalities, and peers. Little children are developmentally unable to understand the content of services, and most find it nearly impossible to sit quietly and pay attention for a period that runs from two to three and a half hours. To avoid a miserable experience for everyone, focus on helping your children enjoy and learn what they can.

Actually, children get a great deal out of worship services, especially when you remember that the liturgy is only one part of the larger experience. Going to temple includes getting dressed up, walking or driving there with the family (with singing or word games on the way), seeing special temple friends, and bringing special books, toys, and snacks.

Being in synagogue on Shabbat provides children with all kinds of formative Jewish experiences. They see grown-ups engaged in prayer, they absorb melodies, they watch the dramaturgy of the Torah service (described below), they make friends with children they might not otherwise meet, they see how your family's practices are part of a larger Jewish world, and they come to feel at home in the synagogue.

There are practical steps parents can take to make Shabbat services a pleasure for the whole family. Always make sure you have lots of tempting snacks on hand. At some synagogues, parents bring a Shabbat box or backpack filled with playthings (books, crayons, puzzles, etc.) for quiet play. It is, however, important to check the temple policy first so that you can respect the custom (*minhag*) of the congregation; many Conservative synagogues do not permit writing, drawing, or crafts.

Some temples provide weekly activities for young children, interactive-learning services for school-age kids, even childcare for babies. Children are often brought back to the sanctuary to watch the Torah paraded around the room or to rejoin their parents for the final hymn. If such programs do not already exist, you can request, organize, and help staff them.

Shabbat services—like all worship services—vary from one congregation to the next in terms of the amount of Hebrew, duration, formality, music, and programming for children. Different congregations tolerate varying amounts of hubbub from families with infants and toddlers, which is why it's important to find a temple that feels comfortable for you and your family. (See the section on "Joining a Synagogue" in Chapter 3.)

When you do bring a child into the sanctuary, make an honest assessment about how long your child can stay with you. Every family needs to answer this question individually, taking into account the age, temperament, and developmental abilities of the child, and the standards and customs of the congregation. Of course, the answer will change as your child changes—so remember to update and reassess your decisions.

Shabbat Morning Service
Shacharit: An Overview

There are three parts to the Sabbath morning service. The introductory section consists of daily morning blessings, hymns, and psalms. The second section begins with *Barchu*, the call to worship, is followed by the *Shema* and its blessings, and concludes with the anthology of prayers called *Amida* or *Tefila*, which are recited while standing.

The third part of the service—and its liturgical and dramatic high point—is the Torah reading. The Torah is removed from the Ark (*aron*), and paraded around the sanctuary to the sound of joyful song. The decorative coverings on the Torah scroll are then removed to prepare for reading.

The Torah (the first five books of the Hebrew bible) is divided into fifty-four sections (each called a *parasha*, or *sedra*) that are read in an annual cycle.[17] Every portion is further divided into seven parts, each of which is called an *aliyah*, which is also the name of the honor given to the person who recites blessings before and after each reading. The ritual of bar and bat mitzvah celebrates a thirteen-year-old's first *aliyah*. Rabbis often base a sermon (*d'rash* or *d'var Torah*) on the Torah portion of the week.

The Torah service usually includes a supplemental biblical reading called the *Haftarah* (meaning "conclusion" or "completion"), which is drawn from the writings of the Prophets. Once the *parasha* and *Haftarah* are read, the Torah is returned to the Ark, and the service ends with concluding prayers, including the Mourner's Kaddish, and a final hymn.[18]

After services, most congregations are invited to share a kiddush. Everyone gathers to recite the blessings over wine and bread, and a light snack or lunch is shared.

Saturday Afternoon   This is the least structured part of Shabbat. Its only "official" activity is lunch, which is considered the second Shabbat meal (breakfast does not count). Lunch traditionally begins with the blessing over wine[19] and bread.

Shabbat lunch is a good time to enjoy family favorites; this can be the pizza or bagel or taco meal of the week. Easy potlucks are a good idea, too, and having guests at the table encourages lingering, talking, and singing. Encourage your children to invite friends over.[20]

Traditionally, Shabbat afternoon is nap time, walk time, reading and story time. Writing letters or puttering in the garden are less traditional but still in the spirit of rest and mindfulness.

Shabbat is great time for parents and children to play with each other, or for grown-ups to have a "date" at the library or art museum. As the afternoon stretches on, the challenge of staying relaxed can get harder, especially with children of differing ages and a world of obligations and options just outside the door. Whatever you end up doing, try to stay in touch with the primary goal of Shabbat, which is to revel in time and share it with people you love.

Havdalah   Shabbat ends, as it begins, with blessings that distinguish Sabbath time from "normal" time. The ending ritual is called *Havdalah,* which means "separation" or "distinction." Even if you haven't spent much of the day celebrating Shabbat, gathering for *Havdalah* gives you one more opportunity to regroup before the week begins again.

Havdalah is a vivid, short, dramatic service that involves all five senses, which makes it perfect for children. The ceremony consists of four blessings: over wine, over fragrant spices, over fire, and over distinctions, and ends with two simple songs.

How to make *Havdalah:*

- You begin by turning off the lights in preparation for watching the sunlight fade from the sky. It is officially time for *Havdalah* when three stars are visible, or when it's too dim to tell the difference between a dark thread and a white one.
- Light the *Havdalah* candle, which is made of at least two, and often several, multicolored braided wicks. (Since the blessing refers to the "lights of the fire," more than one wick is necessary.) No blessing is said;

by lighting it, Shabbat, with its prohibitions against lighting fire, is officially over. *Havdalah* candles are available in all Judaica shops.

• Next comes the blessing over wine.

בָּרוּךְ אַתָּה יְיָ, אֱלֹהֵינוּ מֶלֶךְ הָעוֹלָם, בּוֹרֵא פְּרִי הַגָּפֶן.

Baruch Ata Adonai, Eloheynu Melech Ha-olam boray p'ree ha-gafen.

Holy One of Blessing, Your Presence Fills Creation, forming the fruit of the vine.

The cup is raised but it is not drunk until after all the blessings.

• The blessing over fragrant spices.

בָּרוּךְ אַתָּה יְיָ, אֱלֹהֵינוּ מֶלֶךְ הָעוֹלָם, בּוֹרֵא מִינֵי בְשָׂמִים.

Baruch Ata Adonai, Eloheynu Melech Ha-olam, boray minay b'samim.

Holy One of Blessing, Your Presence Fills Creation, making fragrant spices.

After the blessing, it is customary to pass around a box filled with sweet-smelling spices such as cloves and cinnamon. However, any fragrant herb, flower, fruit or sweet grass can be used to symbolize the sweetness of Shabbat and the wish for a sweet week to come. Spice boxes run the gamut from antique silver filigree to kindergarten milk-carton art projects. A wide variety of choices are available at Judaica stores in ceramic, tin, and wood.

• The blessing over the burning fire is recited.

בָּרוּךְ אַתָּה יְיָ, אֱלֹהֵינוּ מֶלֶךְ הָעוֹלָם, בּוֹרֵא מְאוֹרֵי הָאֵשׁ.

Baruch Ata Adonai, Eloheynu Melech Ha-olam, boray m'oray ha'eysh.

Holy One of Blessing, Your Presence Fills Creation, forming the lights of fire.

Since Jewish blessings generally require an action of some kind, it is traditional to hold up your hands to feel the warmth of the flame and use the light to distinguish one finger from another. Some people cup their fingers to reflect the light in their fingernails and cast a shadow in their palms.

- The *Havdalah* blessing is recited.

בָּרוּךְ אַתָּה יְיָ, אֱלֹהֵינוּ מֶלֶךְ הָעוֹלָם, הַמַּבְדִּיל בֵּין קֹדֶשׁ לְחֹל, בֵּין אוֹר לְחֹשֶׁךְ,
בֵּין יִשְׂרָאֵל לָעַמִּים, בֵּין יוֹם הַשְּׁבִיעִי לְשֵׁשֶׁת יְמֵי הַמַּעֲשֶׂה.
בָּרוּךְ אַתָּה יְיָ, הַמַּבְדִּיל בֵּין קֹדֶשׁ לְחֹל.

Baruch Ata Adonai, Eloheynu Melech Ha-olam, hamavdil bayn kodesh l'hol, bayn or lo'hoshech, bayn Yisrael l'amim, bayn yom hashvi-i leshayshet y'may hama'aseh. Baruch Ata Adonai, hamavdil bayn kodesh l'hol.

Holy One of Blessing, Your Presence Fills Creation. You separate the holy from the not-yet-holy, light from darkness, Israel from the other peoples, Shabbat from the six other days. Holy One of Blessing, You separate the holy from the everyday.

The blessing thanks God for creation and for the distinctions of our universe.

- The wine is drunk by the leader or shared by the group. (But leave a little wine left over to pour into a saucer.)
- *"Eliyahu Hanavi"* is sung; this song calls for the coming of the prophet Elijah *(Eliyahu)*.

Eliyahu Hanavi
Eliyahu Hatishbi
Eliyahu, Eliyahu
Eliyahu ha-Giladi

Bimheira v'yameinu
yavo eilenu
Im Maschiach ben David
Im Maschiach ben David.

Elijah the prophet
Elijah from Tishba
Elijah from Gilad
Come to us soon
in our days
with the Messiah
child of David.

Elijah is the legendary harbinger of the Messiah—the one whose arrival means that Shabbat will never end.

- The *Havdalah* flame is extinguished in the wine.
- As the flame is extinguished you say, "Shavua tov" ("A good week"), and the new week begins. It is customary to sing the song of the same name.

Shavua tov [eight times]
A good week
A week of peace
May gladness reign
And joy increase . . .

Ideas for Making Shabbat Your Own

Reciprocal Shabbat dinners. Once a month, trade Friday-night meal preparation with one or more families. This is a wonderful way for family and friends to stay connected. It lightens the work of cooking Shabbat meals, and it's also a great way to pick up ideas, songs, and customs for your family's Shabbat observance.

Take the phone off the hook (or let the answering machine pick up) for at least some part of Shabbat—the fifteen minutes of your table rituals, or three hours on Friday night, or all day long. This helps you stay in the "different space" of the Sabbath.

Keep a Shabbat journal. Just before candlelighting or on Saturday afternoon, take a few minutes to write down what's been going on in your life and your family's life. Take photographs of your children on Friday afternoons.

Ask your children to make Shabbat place cards for Friday night— especially if you have guests at the table. These can be saved in a special guest-scrapbook.

Make your own Shabbat bencher. Make a one-page guide to your family's prayers and customs. Encourage your kids to decorate it before you copy and laminate them. These are great for guests at your table. The family bencher can change as your customs change and as your children grow, and make wonderful additions to your family scrapbook. Alternatively, buy *benchers* and customize the covers with your children's artwork.

Make a Shabbat box for young children. Decorate a shoebox for each child and fill it with a *kippah,* kiddush cup, candlesticks, challah cover.

Take Shabbat on vacation. Judaica shops sell traveling cups and candlesticks, but don't worry if you forget to pack them. You can use any glass for the blessing of the wine and make candleholders out of seashells from the beach or stones from the mountains. If you can't find "real" challah in the local store, any whole loaf of bread will do. Wherever and however you do it, making Shabbat on vacation—in a motel room, or in front of your mountainside tent, or in the lakefront cabin—creates a magical, indelible family memory. You will tell and retell the story of how the smoke alarm went off in the hotel, or how the people in the next campsite chimed in when you sang the blessings.

Leave Shabbat behind. If you have to be out of town over Shabbat, make sure childcare-givers—a family member or baby-sitter— can help your children make Shabbes while you are away. Or arrange for your children to spend part of or all of Shabbat with another family that observes the Sabbath. Not only will this provide continuity and comfort in your absence, it's a chance for your children to see that others do Shabbat, too.

Orient the week around Shabbat. Make plans for guests to invite for dinner on Friday night or for lunch on Saturday. Ask your children to help you plan the menu for Shabbat. Set the Shabbat table on Thursday evening.

Shabbat in the Real World   Making Shabbat means making decisions that foster a sense of peace, connection, happiness, and family harmony. Who could pass up an idea this good?

But then Friday night arrives and the baby is colicky, the toddler is cranky, Dad is out of town. Saturday morning turns out to be the biggest soccer game of the year. You've got matinee tickets to the symphony on Saturday afternoon. Your teenager has a Friday-night school dance or a weekend-long scouting trip. Nobody in the house has a single pair of clean socks, and without a trip to the dry cleaners, you won't have a suit to wear to the big meeting on Monday.

Welcome to Shabbat in the real world. Saying yes to Shabbat means a whole new set of choices and changes. As you choose, try to stay mindful of why you are making Shabbes. Remember that the Torah speaks of keeping Shabbat as a joy, not as a punishment.

Build joy into Shabbat however you can. If you cannot avoid chores, try to choose projects that can be shared and enjoyed, like washing the car, or raking leaves, or baking cookies as a family. Put errands off until late in the afternoon.

Parents who feel okay about soccer games on Shabbat (also T-ball, baseball, hockey, piano lessons, dance class) might decide not to just drop their child off, but stay to cheer the team on, or watch the class, and then share an ice cream cone afterward.

Making Shabbat choices is a great topic for discussion among parents, and makes for a great synagogue workshop or panel.

SHABBAT BY AGES AND STAGES

Every family's experience of Shabbat varies with the age of children at home and changes as children grow and develop.

Shabbat with Your Baby   Developmental studies indicate that infants are learning from the moment they leave the womb, which is why parents are urged to play classical music for their babies and speak in full sentences. If Mozart is good for the infant brain and verbal stimulation helps lay down the neural pathways for language, adding Jewish melodies and Hebrew words and ritual rhythms are also part of the preverbal experience that shapes later life. For parents who are new to Jewish living, this is a wonderful time to experiment. There is no "doing it wrong."

Toddlers and Preschoolers   These are great years for sharing and teaching the joys of Shabbat because children at this age want to imitate their parents. Two-year-olds will cover their eyes at candlelighting, if that's what you do. If you use words like "Shabbat" and "*tzedakah* box," your three-year-old will, too. Four-year-olds who see Hebrew letters on their Shabbat place mat will begin to recognize the shapes and sounds. Five-year-olds will spend all week anticipating the trip to the bakery for Shabbat challah and treats.

During these "magic years," children enter the world of pretend wholeheartedly, so get a play set of wooden candlesticks, challah, and wine cup. If you explain that your preparations—playing music on the stereo and dancing around the dining room table—will bring Shabbat to your house, they will believe you, and make it so!

Of course, life with a young child includes periods of sullenness, too. Tired children can't pay attention or even enjoy themselves, so some parents make Shabbes early on Friday evening, with candlelighting, grape juice, and a child-sized challah well before the adults can sit down. In some families, one parent can't be home from work when the children are able to enjoy Shabbat rituals. While this is not ideal—and it certainly doesn't feel as good as when the whole family is gathered—sometimes it's the only way. You might do all the rituals except one, "saving" kiddush for later when Daddy gets home—even if that means the children have already eaten dessert and are getting ready for bed.

Be as consistent as you can. Children thrive on predictable schedules; there is even research that suggests family rituals are protective of a child's resilience in the face of adversity. This is not to say children cannot tolerate change or exceptions to the rule, but it's a good idea to explain the reasons: "Usually we would be making Shabbes right now, but we decided it was important to go to your uncle's birthday party. Next week, we'll have Shabbat at home."

While children can rarely recall the specifics of early childhood experiences, a consistent, joyful family Sabbath practice is one of those indelible "proofs" of love and safety that sustain people for a lifetime.

Creating Shabbat Traditions

- Write letters or phone grandparents or other family members.
- Tune in to nature by keeping a journal of the weather on Shabbat, with notes on the temperature, moon phase, time of sunset, the seasonal changes in the landscape, etc.
- Tell a story from the weekly Torah portion, or read aloud from a Jewish book.
- Make music together with tambourine, drum, recorder, or other instruments that are part of your life.
- Explore a new art medium every Shabbat: crayons one week, watercolor the next, followed by clay, charcoal sketches, mosaics made of torn paper, etc.

School-age Children   Children in school have a full life that is separate from their parents, so the Shabbat table can be a good place to debrief about the week; ask each child to share an experience or teach you something they learned that week. Then listen without interrupting. This not only demonstrates how important they are to you, it is also an introduction to the fine art of conversation.

You can honor your children's Jewish lives by displaying and using the arts and crafts projects they make in their Jewish supplementary or day school classes. They will be so proud when their challah boards and covers, spice boxes, *tzedakah* boxes, place mats, and centerpieces are on the table with your best china.

There are many ways to help your school-age kids engage with Shabbat. Children who like to cook can be encouraged to make food for Shabbat. Children can also take charge of Shabbat rituals.

By fifth grade, however, some children won't want to do "kid stuff" anymore. They may hang around after dinner to listen to the adult conversation or want to be excused from the table as soon as they've finished eating. By age ten or eleven, some girls start thinking of themselves as "preteens," which turns Jewishly active teenagers into very powerful role models. But adult modeling remains very important at this age, and children need to see that Shabbat is central and enjoyable for their parents, and for other grown-ups as well.

Some parents worry about enforcing Shabbat rules for fear that they will eventually cause resentment and rebellion against everything Jewish. But all the choices you make—from your neighborhood to the kind of music lessons your child takes—also impose limits. At some point, your child will have to make her own decisions about where to live, whether to continue with the violin, and how to be Jewish. In the meanwhile, decision-making remains where it belongs: in parental hands.

Still, older children deserve honest responses if they ask about how and why your family makes Shabbat. They also deserve a respectful audience for their perspective on family traditions. Some parents feel children under the age of thirteen are too young to opt out of any family observance; others permit school-age children to make choices that, at least occasionally, mean they will miss Shabbat with the family.

Whenever you give your child such a choice, be prepared to live with a decision that dismays you. Later you can ask, "How did you feel about going to the birthday party instead of staying home for Shabbat dinner? Did you miss being with us?"

Be clear that you are genuinely curious and not trying to make your child feel guilty. This can give her the opportunity to choose differently next time. Talk about your own reactions to her decision and let her know that, even though you missed her, the family celebrated Shabbat anyway.

Adolescents One of the developmental tasks of the teen years is forging an independent self, separate from parents and family. Sometimes, this involves rejecting parts of your family's Jewish practice. Here are a few simple strategies for these transitional years.

First, make it clear that your teenager's friends are always welcome in your home for Friday-night dinner, or to hang out on Saturday. Then, actively encourage your teenager to make Jewish friends by supporting interest in Jewish camps and Jewish youth groups; insist on his/her attendance at a Jewish high school program. These kinds of activities and the relationships they foster can help your teenager develop his/her own Shabbat traditions.

Going to services is usually pretty low on a teenager's "to-do" list. Those who do attend synagogue services generally go only if and because their friends will be there, too. This happens when kids have their own community of peers (from their Hebrew school classes, a "youth congregation," or a youth group) at the family's synagogue.

Many adolescents have competing interests that take them away from Shabbat observance: school sports events, performances, and dances are often scheduled for Friday nights. Parents respond to this issue in a whole range of ways; some require only that their teens be home for Shabbat blessings before going out, others do not sanction any non-Jewish activities on Shabbat.

In the event your teen is away from home on a given Friday night, try to connect with her by phone, wherever she is, to say "*Shabbat shalom*" and "I love you."

Adolescence is time for young people to practice making their own choices. Ask your teenager to make decisions about Shabbat. Remind him that, whatever he is doing (whether you agree with it or not), he is making a Jewish choice.

Many people wander away from their family's traditions on the path to adulthood; this doesn't mean they're going to reject Judaism. Try not to overreact. Have faith in your child and in the Jewish foundation and example you provided when she was little. Remember your own adolescent struggles to be independent from your parents. And read Chapter 5 ("Conflict") and Chapter 9 ("Ages 15 to 18").

BOOKS FOR CHILDREN

Mrs. Moskowitz and the Sabbath Candlesticks, by Amy Schwartz (Jewish Publication Society, 1983).

Joseph Who Loved the Sabbath, by Marilyn Hirsch (Viking Penguin, 1986).
Once upon a Shabbos, by Jacqueline Jules (Kar-Ben Copies, 1998).

Books for parents
The Sabbath, by Rabbi Abraham Joshua Heschel (Noonday, 1996).
Book of Blessings, by Marcia Falk (HarperSanFrancisco, 1995).
Kol Haneshama: Songs, Blessings and Rituals for the Home (The Reconstructionist Press, 1991).

MONTH TO MONTH:
CELEBRATING THE HOLIDAYS

"The calendar of the Jew is his catechism," wrote Rabbi Samson Raphael Hirsch.[21] Although most people associate "catechism" with instruction in the Catholic faith, the word refers specifically to a format: a question-and-answer explanation for religious belief.

The Jewish holiday cycle teaches Judaism's core beliefs by eliciting questions—especially from children. At Passover, getting children to ask questions is the whole point of the teaching-meal called "seder." Indeed, four questions are built into the liturgy of the seder to make sure that children ask "Why?"

But the same process takes place throughout the Jewish year. Exposed to the customs and stories of each holiday, children will ask questions whose answers build a foundation of Jewish knowledge: What are these letters on the sides of my *draydl?* Why do people fast on Yom Kippur? Why did Haman hate the Jews so much? How could God kill all the first-born Egyptian children?

Some answers may come from the teachers in your child's Jewish classroom, and from your rabbi(s). But all Jewish holidays are cultural events as well as religious observances, which means that their lessons are taught and reinforced in a myriad of ways, not only through stories and books and lessons, but also through the senses, with food, song, family gatherings, special clothes and such. Which is why the holiday cycle is one of the most effective forms of Jewish pedagogy. Sharing the holidays— modeling the holidays—is the core lesson plan for Jewish parents.

Young children thrive on regular bedtimes and mealtimes; they need rules about behavior and clear expectations to feel secure and safe. Of course, too much consistency can turn into stifling rigidity. For Jewish parents, the goal is to balance a respect for tradition ("It wouldn't be Rosh Hashanah if the whole family didn't take a walk together after services") with the realities of change ("Now that the kids are in high school, let's spend the first night of Hanukkah wrapping gifts for poor children at the local homeless shelter instead of exchanging gifts at home").

If you want to create warm, lasting Jewish family memories, you will have to do some of the same things year after year, like praying the same prayers, eating the same foods, singing the same songs, visiting the same family members, attending the same temple. But adding and altering practices to reflect changes in your children's development is also crucial. For example, a child's ability to read transforms the seder from one where he may need a baby-sitter to one where he can participate, and eventually to one where he can lead part of it.

Although the holidays are fixed by the calendar, there is enormous variation in the specifics of the celebrations. Just as no two families celebrate any occasion in precisely the same way, Sephardic and Ashkenazic Jews cook different meals and sing different songs. Over time, even the reasons for celebrating have changed in response to the historical situation of the Jews; for instance, when Jews were a persecuted and largely powerless people, Hanukkah was a festival of miraculous deliverance. But after Israel became a state in 1948, there was a new focus on the Maccabees' extraordinary military victory.

Celebrating the full year's worth of Jewish holidays—living the calendar—connects your children and indeed, your whole family, to the rest of the Jewish world and to the sweep of Jewish history. It answers the all-too-common question, "Why don't we celebrate Christmas?" with a compelling answer: "Because we're busy celebrating Hanukkah and Purim and Passover and Shabbat."

One Day or Two?   One of the more confusing aspects of Jewish holiday observance is that some parts of the Jewish community celebrate holidays for two days while other parts observe for only one. Conservative, Orthodox, and many Reconstructionist synagogues celebrate the first and last two days of festivals (Sukkot, Passover, and Shavuot). Reform temples and

Jews living in Israel observe only one day.[22] Likewise, at Passover, some Jews refrain from eating leavened foods for eight days, while others eat bread again after seven days.

The difference dates back to ancient times, when the exact date of the new moon, which is invisible, was not always easy to determine. Since dates for the rest of the month were set by the new moon, rather than risk celebrating on the wrong day, Jews who lived outside of the land of Israel began two-day observances of holidays that required refraining from work and attending services. In Israel, the exact timing could be communicated quickly and one-day observances remained the practice there, except for Rosh Hashanah. Even though mathematically composed calendars and modern communications long ago removed all doubt as to the timing of the new moon, many consider the old practice too enshrined in custom to change.

Greetings "*Gut yontif,*" the Yiddish version of "Good holiday," is based on the Hebrew *yom tov,* which literally means "a good day." *Chag sameach,* is the Hebrew greeting; *chag* means "holiday," *sameach* means "happy" (from the same root as *simcha*). At Rosh Hashanah, the Jewish New Year, you say "*Shanah tovah,*" the Hebrew for "a good year."

Making Memorable Holidays

- Decorate the house. Hang children's art on the fridge; make a centerpiece for the dining room; festoon the front door.
- Read books about the upcoming holiday to young children; pick one that is both age appropriate and a little challenging.
- Attend a class about the meaning of the holidays. Sign up for family programs where parents and children can learn and prepare together.
- Have a family portrait taken on the same holiday every year—at the Passover table, in your Rosh Hashanah finery, in jeans in the Sukkah, or around the Hanukkah lights.
- Make contributions to a charity that seems appropriate for the day: on Yom Kippur, send an amount equivalent to a day's worth

of meals to a local food pantry, and/or participate in the temple's canned-food drive that day.
- Go to a Jewish nursing home to attend services or help lead them for people unable to get to a synagogue.

YOUR CALENDAR

You need a Jewish calendar. Beautiful as it may be, the Sierra Club calendar may not tell you whether December 14 is the night for lighting the first Hanukkah candle or the first full day of the holiday. Your art museum calendar may or may not even mention Sukkot, and it almost certainly won't alert you to the whereabouts of Tu B'Shvat.

In a Jewish calendar, the months and days—which have their own names and numbering systems—are always laid out in relation to the secular calendar, with a page for each of the twelve familiar Gregorian months. There is no discrepancy in this for Jews. The schedule for work weeks, mortgage payments, and taxes is set by the secular calendar, while the Jewish date is used for religious purposes only: in addition to setting out the holidays, it's also used for dating Jewish marriage contracts (*ketubot*), and to determine the anniversary of a death (*yahrzeit*).

The Jewish calendar has no civic function—not even in Israel. It is, however, an active reminder of the holiday cycle and a way to stay in touch with the sacred in time. The artwork on a Jewish calendar, which almost always illustrates the holiday of the month, not only adds a meaningful decorative element to your home, it also orients it toward the up-coming festival, and also to Shabbat. While Saturdays are simply Saturday on a secular calendar (unless New Year's Day or the Fourth of July happens to fall on one) Jewish calendars characterize every Saturday by naming it with the title of the weekly Torah reading.

Jewish calendars begin with September, the month in which the Jewish year starts. The annual discrepancies between non-Jewish and Jewish dates and holidays—sometimes Hanukkah falls near Thanksgiving, sometimes closer to Christmas—illustrate the different bases for the two calendars: the secular year is solar, while the Jewish year is essentially lunar. The Jewish custom of starting holidays in the evening (*erev*) rather than the morning is based on the wording of Genesis 1:5: "And there was evening and there was morning, the first day."

Jewish calendars come in a wide variety of styles, so choosing one can be a way to express your family's tastes and interests. Large bookstores and Judaica shops tend to offer a big selection featuring everything from Jewish art reproductions, to photographs of Israel, food and recipes, and Jewish humor. If you contribute to a local federation or belong to a movement-affiliated synagogue, you may automatically get a free Jewish calendar. Some temples and day schools produce them as fund-raisers, and most funeral homes distribute calendars free of charge.

The Family Calendar

- Choose a Jewish calendar for the main family calendar—the big one that hangs prominently in the kitchen or family room and is used to keep everyone's schedule straight. This is a subtle but persistent reminder that your family lives according to a "Jewish clock."
- Make an annual event out of shopping for the family calendar. Go to a Judaica store and look over the selection together. Let children pick out the one they like best or have a family vote to decide the "winner." (The "losing" candidate might become a gift for a child's room.)
- Every time the month changes, gather the family and let children take turns flipping the page. Since the artwork on most Jewish calendars is somehow keyed to the holiday of the month, this can be a good time to talk about the up-coming festival and how you plan to celebrate. Use colored markers to highlight the up-coming holidays and family birthdays.
- Use the calendar to stay in touch with the cycles of the moon.[23] Jewish months begin on the new moon, on the day called *Rosh Hodesh* or "head of the month." New moons are not visible in the sky, and the moon is full on the fifteenth of every month. You can make each full moon an occasion for taking children outside to greet the moon by name: Tishri (September/October), Heshvan (October/November), Kislev (November/December), Tevet

(December/January), Shvat (January/February), Adar[24] (February/March), Nisan (March/April), Iyar (April/May), Sivan (May/June), Tammuz (June/July), Av (July/August), and Elul (August/September). Keep a journal and track where the moon rises, how it appears through a tree in the backyard, the temperature.

- Make your own Jewish calendar. Software and kits are available in photography and craft stores for producing calendars with family snapshots or children's artwork. Fill in the family birthdays as well as all the Jewish holidays. (To find the secular dates that correspond to Jewish holidays check http://bnaibrith.org/caln.html.)

BOOKS FOR ADULTS:

The brief overview of history, liturgy, and theology in this chapter is only an introduction. The following books can provide more depth.

The Jewish Way: Living the Holidays, by Rabbi Irving Greenberg (Touchstone Books, 1993).

The Jewish Holidays: A Guide and Commentary, by Michael Strassfeld (HarperCollins, 1985).

Seasons of Our Joy: A Modern Guide to the Jewish Holidays, by Arthur Waskow (Beacon, 1991).

FALL

The Jewish year starts with what feels like a deluge of holidays. From the first to the twenty-third of the Hebrew month of Tishri, there are a total of four religious celebrations: Rosh Hashanah, Yom Kippur, Sukkot, and Simchat Torah. Unfortunately, many Jews end their observance of "the holidays" prematurely with the somber notes of Yom Kippur and miss the happier, home-based holidays that launch the Jewish year with sweetness.

The entire cycle travels a broad range of human emotion from remorse to joy: on Rosh Hashanah we rejoice at the creation of the world, on Yom Kippur we atone for failing to live up to the promise of Creation, on Sukkot we give thanks for life on earth, and on Simchat Torah we delight in the pleasures of study and community.

However your family celebrates the fall holidays, they are bound to be among your child's earliest Jewish memories. Even in infancy, children absorb the rhythms and melodies of the services and celebrations, the warmth generated by the gathering of family and friends, the aroma and tastes of special foods. And when children see their parents participating—genuinely sorry for wrongdoing on Yom Kippur, giddily dancing on Simchat Torah—they are learning how to be Jewish adults.

Preparing for the Fall Holidays

- Get a *shofar,* the horn of a ram or other animal that is sounded on Rosh Hashanah and Yom Kippur. Available in Judaica stores and catalogues, this is not a sacred object but something children—and adults—can handle, practice, and play with.
- Buy new clothes to wear on Rosh Hashanah and Yom Kippur. Make appointments for a haircut in preparation for the holiday.
- Make apple-picking an annual pre–Rosh Hashanah family outing.
- Find a local beekeeper, tour the hives, and buy some of his honey.
- Get different kinds of honey—made from clover, apple blossoms, flowers. Have a tasting and see if you can tell the difference.
- Get a copy of the *machzor* (the prayer book for Rosh Hashanah and Yom Kippur) you'll be using and familiarize yourself with the structure and content. In the same spirit, get a tape or CD featuring songs and melodies of the holidays.
- There are a lot of Hebrew words flying around at this season: *Akedah, etrog, kittel, Kol Nidre, lulav, machzor, ne'ila, l'shanah tovah tikatevu, shofar, sukkah,* Sukkot, *Taschlich, teshuva, ushpizin.* Check the glossary at the end of this book; use it to create your own one-page fall holiday glossary.

> - Make Jewish New Year cards to send to family and friends featuring a design created by your child.
> - Count the change in your family's *tzedakah* box, discuss where to send it, and let your children mail the check.
> - Visit the graves of loved ones before the holidays. During a season of intense reflection, you may miss them keenly and this is a way to mourn and to make peace with the fact that life continues, even in their absence.

ROSH HASHANAH AND YOM KIPPUR

The "High Holy Days" include not only Rosh Hashanah and Yom Kippur, but also the days between them. All of these *Yamim Nora'im,* or Days of Awe, are a time of serious soul-searching for adults.

One of the overarching metaphors in the liturgies of both holidays is "The Book of Life." According to this image, on the first day of the year, the names of all righteous people are written in the book and thus assured another year of life. But there is hope for those who are not entirely good or righteous; even the wicked have the ten days from Rosh Hashanah to Yom Kippur in which to turn away (to make *teshuvah*) from their wrongs before the book is sealed during the final minutes of Yom Kippur.

Turning away from the wrongdoings of the previous year is the spiritual "business" of Rosh Hashanah and Yom Kippur. Synagogue services give us time to reflect and resolve, but prayer and meditation are not sufficient to wipe the slate clean. The only way to expunge sins committed against other people is by sincerely apologizing and asking for forgiveness.

Although most of these concepts are beyond the understanding of young children, the holidays do offer parents the opportunity to talk about growing and changing, and about the importance of saying "I'm sorry" to people and to God. And children can certainly relate to the idea of the new year as "the birthday of the world."

Rosh Hashanah (literally, "head of the year") celebrates creation and honors the Creator. The number assigned to the Jewish year, which changes on Rosh Hashanah, is based on an ancient rabbinic reckoning of when the world was created,[25] which is why the Jewish New Year is sometimes referred to as "the birthday of the world."

Home Observance   The focus of home celebration is the evening meal served at the start of Rosh Hashanah. This is one of the culinary high points of the Jewish calendar. Some families have generations-old menus and recipes for the occasion, but it is easy to start brand-new "venerable" customs, since children (and most adults) will treat any meal or special dish served for two consecutive years as "traditional."

Rosh Hashanah menus vary among Jewish subcultures and from household to household, but two customs are pervasive: using a round challah (with or without raisins) as a symbol of the cycle of the year, and starting Rosh Hashanah with apples dipped in honey as a harbinger of a sweet year.

Before the Erev Rosh Hashanah meal, the following blessings are recited (and the blessing for hand-washing—see page 65—may be added before the meal):

For candlelighting:

בָּרוּךְ אַתָּה יְיָ, אֱלֹהֵינוּ מֶלֶךְ הָעוֹלָם, אֲשֶׁר קִדְּשָׁנוּ בְּמִצְוֹתָיו
וְצִוָּנוּ לְהַדְלִיק נֵר שֶׁל (שַׁבָּת וְשֶׁל) יוֹם טוֹב.

Baruch Ata Adonai, Eloheynu Melech Ha-olam, asher kid'shanu b'mitzvotav vitsivanu l'hadlik ner shel yom tov.*

Blessed are You, Eternal One, Sovereign of all worlds, Who makes us holy with your mitzvot, and calls us to light the festival lights.

For wine:

בָּרוּךְ אַתָּה יְיָ, אֱלֹהֵינוּ מֶלֶךְ הָעוֹלָם, בּוֹרֵא פְּרִי הַגָּפֶן.

Baruch Ata Adonai Eloheynu Melech Ha-olam boray p'ree hagafen.

---

* As with any candlelighting, if the holiday falls on Shabbat, the prayer doubles as the Sabbath blessing and concludes with the words "*shel Shabbat v'yom tov*" ("Sabbath and festival lights") instead of "*shel yom tov.*"

Blessed are You, Eternal One, Sovereign of all worlds, who makes the fruit of the vine.

On the occasion of the holiday:

בָּרוּךְ אַתָּה יְיָ, אֱלֹהֵינוּ מֶלֶךְ הָעוֹלָם, שֶׁהֶחֱיָנוּ וְקִיְּמָנוּ וְהִגִּיעָנוּ לַזְּמַן הַזֶּה.

Baruch Ata Adonai, Eloheynu Melech Ha-olam, shehechiyanu v'keyamanu v'higianu lazman hazeh.

Blessed are You, Eternal One, Sovereign of all worlds, Who has kept us alive, Who has sustained us, Who has brought us to this moment.

For the round challah:

בָּרוּךְ אַתָּה יְיָ, אֱלֹהֵינוּ מֶלֶךְ הָעוֹלָם, הַמּוֹצִיא לֶחֶם מִן־הָאָרֶץ.

Baruch Ata Adonai, Eloheynu Melech Ha-olam, hamotzi lechem min ha'aretz.

Blessed are You, Eternal One, Sovereign of all worlds, Who brings forth bread from the earth.

For apple sections dipped in honey:

בָּרוּךְ אַתָּה יְיָ, אֱלֹהֵינוּ מֶלֶךְ הָעוֹלָם, בּוֹרֵא פְּרִי הָעֵץ.
יְהִי רָצוֹן שֶׁתְּחַדֵּשׁ עָלֵינוּ שָׁנָה טוֹבָה וּמְתוּקָה.

Baruch Ata Adonai, Eloheynu Melech Ha-olam, boray p'ree ha'eytz. Y'hi ratzon she'te'chadesh aleynu shana tova umetukah.

Blessed are You, Eternal One, Sovereign of all worlds, Who creates the fruit of the tree.
May it be Your will, Adonai, God of our fathers and mothers, to renew us for a good and sweet year.

Synagogue Observance   Rosh Hashanah is primarily a liturgical or synagogue holiday. It's difficult to generalize about Rosh Hashanah services since every congregation makes choices about the form and content of High Holy Day services, as they do with other services throughout the year. Nevertheless, the holiday liturgy does have a few core elements, including the blowing of a *shofar* (the horn of a ram or other animal) and distinctive holiday melodies, which are reprised over and over during Rosh Hashanah, and again on Yom Kippur.

Rosh Hashanah prayers sound the themes of judgment and repentance, and the recurrent image of God as a father-king is given voice in one of the most memorable prayers and melodies of all the Jewish holidays, *Avinu Malkeynu*, "Our Father, our King."

During the morning service on Rosh Hashanah, the Torah readings, from Genesis 21 and 22, are always a focal point. Among the most powerful and problematic stories in the Torah, Genesis 21 tells of the birth of Isaac, the casting out of Hagar and Ishmael into the desert, and their subsequent deliverance. Genesis 22, which is the Torah reading for the second day, contains the terrible test of Abraham's faith, when he is asked to sacrifice his son, Isaac. This story is referred to as "the binding of Isaac," or the *Akedah*.[26] These Torah portions may be the subject of the rabbi's sermon—another high point of the morning service.

After synagogue, people generally have lunch with family and friends. Then it is traditional to go to a lake, river, or harbor for a ceremony called *Tashlich*, from the Hebrew for "send off" or "cast away." An informal and nonliturgical custom, people symbolically cast off their sins by emptying crumbs from their pockets into the water. Some synagogues and *havurot* (groups that meet for study and prayer) hold a communal *Tashlich*.

Tossing bread to a pond full of quacking ducks is a favorite Rosh Hashanah activity for children, especially after a long morning of sitting. Some families take this time to apologize to one another for unkind words spoken in the year past.

People who celebrate the second day of Rosh Hashanah, light candles at sunset, make kiddush, and serve a festive meal. In order to say the *Shehechiyanu* for the second day in a row, shop for a fruit that you have not eaten for several months.

Second-day services feature different Torah and *Haftarah* readings, and some synagogues use a different liturgy. If the first day of Rosh Hashanah falls on Shabbat, *Tashlich* is performed on the second day.

Between the Holidays   The Shabbat between Rosh Hashanah and Yom Kippur is called *Shabbat Shuvah,* the "Sabbath of turning." The ten-day period between the holidays is considered a period of reflection, thus a good time to reconnect with estranged friends and family members with a call or a card. Some congregations offer a workshop on writing an ethical will, a statement of beliefs and insights you want to leave as a legacy to loved ones—especially children. (See Appendix: Writing a Will.)

Yom Kippur, the most somber day of the year is called *Shabbat Shabbaton,* the "Sabbath of Sabbaths" in the Bible. On this day devoted to reflection and repentance, healthy adults fast from all food and drink from sunset to sunset.

Home Observance   Although this is probably the least home-based of all holidays, it begins and ends with a family meal. The evening meal is cooked with a mind to the fast ahead, so generally it is neither too heavy nor too spicy. Unlike other festival dinners, candlelighting takes place afterwards, marking the official start of Yom Kippur and the fast.

After eating and before lighting the festival candles, it is traditional to light a candle in memory of family members who have died. Special *yahrzeit* ("year's-time") candles are available in Judaica shops and some supermarkets. These candles are lit without a formal blessing, though some people say a silent prayer. It is a nice time to talk to children about the person being remembered.

After eating, the Yom Kippur candles are lit with the following blessing:

בָּרוּךְ אַתָּה יְיָ, אֱלֹהֵינוּ מֶלֶךְ הָעוֹלָם, אֲשֶׁר קִדְּשָׁנוּ בְּמִצְוֹתָיו
וְצִוָּנוּ לְהַדְלִיק נֵר שֶׁל יוֹם הַכִּפּוּרִים.

*Baruch Ata Adonai, Eloheynu Melech Ha-olam, asher kid'shanu
b'mitzvotav vitzivanu l'hadlik ner shel Yom HaKippurim.*

You Abound in Blessings, Adonai our Lord, You make us holy
with commandments and call us to kindle the lights of Yom Kippur.

Yom Kippur ends with a light meal to break the fast. This repast has no formal rituals or ceremony apart from the blessing over bread, *Hamotzi.*

Food prepared in advance is usually set out, buffet style, while family and friends discuss the relative difficulty of their fasts and the content of their rabbis' sermons. It is a *mitzvah* to invite to your table anyone who might have nowhere else to break the fast.

Many families contribute both money and canned goods to help feed the hungry. Synagogues often collect food for distribution to local pantries.

Synagogue Observance Services begin with the haunting melody of *Kol Nidre*, the opening prayer and also the name of the evening service. *Kol Nidre* is an Aramaic declaration that nullifies all the vows and promises that each person will make to God and to him/herself in the coming year, an acknowledgment of the weakness of human resolution.

One feature of the *Kol Nidre* liturgy is the communal confession, called the *Viddui*. Repeated several times the following day as well, this is an alphabetical listing of communal sins: "We abuse, we betray, we are cruel. We destroy, we embitter, we falsify." *Kol Nidre* is the only evening service at which congregants wear prayer shawls. There are other distinctive customs regarding clothing on this holiday as well. Some people dress in white, a sign of purity. Some wear a *kittel*, a white robe. Some wear sneakers or other rubber-soled shoes out of deference to the ancient practice of avoiding leather shoes, which were a symbol of luxury. Some people pray barefoot to show humility.

Yom Kippur services run throughout most of the day: *Shacharit*, the morning service, includes a Torah reading from Leviticus that describes the sacrificial rites for Yom Kippur in the Temple.[27] Some congregations choose to substitute another Torah reading, often Deuteronomy 29:9–30:20, which ends with the lines "I have put before you this day life and death, blessing and curse. Choose life." The morning *Haftarah* reading is Isaiah's passionate sermon demanding justice and decrying religious hypocrisy.

Musaf, the "additional" service that follows *Shacharit*, includes recitation of the martyrology, which begins with a list of the murders of Talmudic sages by the Romans, and describes other persecutions culminating with the Nazi Holocaust.

Sometime during the day, there is a memorial service called *Yizkor*, which recalls loved ones who have died. In general, young children do not attend this service.[28]

Mincha, the afternoon service, traditionally includes a reading from the Torah that outlines the laws of incest (Leviticus 18), though this too is often replaced with another Torah portion (Leviticus 19), referred to as "the holiness code," which includes the injunction to "love your neighbor as yourself." The *Haftarah* reading in the afternoon is the Book of Jonah.

Yom Kippur services conclude with *Ne'ilah*, from the Hebrew "to lock," referring to the symbolic closing of heaven's gates and the "book of life." Many people stand throughout this short service, which ends with a final *shofar* blast. In some congregations, *Ne'ilah* may be followed by a short evening or *Ma'ariv* service, and/or *Havdalah*, the ceremony that ends this holiday as well as the Sabbath.

An Alternative   Some families forgo synagogue observance on these holidays, and spend the day in the woods or at the beach. Surrounded by the quiet beauty of the natural world, parents and children read prayers and poems, talk about forgiveness, and discuss family goals and Jewish resolutions for the coming year: Where should our *tzedakah* money go this year? How can we make our Shabbat observance better for everyone in the family? Is this the year we join a temple or look for one that better meets our family's needs?

HIGH HOLY DAYS: AGES AND STAGES

Rosh Hashanah and Yom Kippur demand a great deal of self-reflection and self-control. While this might, at first glance, make them seem irrelevant or even oppressive to children under the age of ten or even thirteen, the gravity and universal pull of these two holidays—when American synagogues are filled beyond capacity—is felt by youngsters, too.

While the meaning and impact will be far less intellectual or spiritual for children, these holidays are impressive in their solemnity and sheer size. In addition to special meals and attention from family and friends, children will notice the crowds and expanded size of the sanctuary. The annual beginning-of-school excitement will become associated with the start of the Jewish year and for kids who attend secular schools, the fact that they miss school to observe these Jewish holidays seals their importance.

As children grow, they understand more about the themes of the liturgy and grapple with the powerful stories in the Torah readings. But even for very young children, participating in the Jewish community's biggest convocations—from infants to grandparents—lets them feel that the Jewish community is big and vital, and that "this is where we belong."

Babies and Toddlers   Bringing babies and toddlers into the sanctuary is an individual call; sleeping or cooing infants add a beautiful presence to services, but a wailing baby can be terribly disruptive and should be soothed outside.

Synagogues vary in the quality of baby-sitting and early childhood programs for children, and even if good care is available in your temple, some children will not tolerate being left if they know that Mommy or Daddy are on the premises. Often, hiring a baby-sitter at home or taking a toddler to his regular daycare is the best option available, especially if parents want to participate in the service. Besides, some children are too sensitive to the noise and crush of a big crowd to be anything but miserable in the synagogue.

If you are not sure how your baby will react and want to try bringing him to temple, be prepared to leave if he gets fussy. If you can let go of expectations of what Rosh Hashanah and Yom Kippur are "supposed" to be like, you may find your religious experience in the lobby with the nursing mothers, or watching your child run around in the temple playground.

Preschool Children   Children in the preschool years may enjoy parts of the service. If your family attends Shabbat services with any regularity, you can point out how different the music is and how the Torah is "dressed" differently—just like the people. On Rosh Hashanah, the crowd tends to be upbeat and festive—great for people-watching. Remark on all the different faces, the different ways there are to "look Jewish."

Serve any snacks outside the sanctuary. Be sure to keep food out of the synagogue on Yom Kippur; children should eat at home, or in the car, if necessary.

School-age Children   As children mature, parents can offer fuller synagogue attendance as coming-of-age rewards: "Now that you can read Hebrew so well, I think you can stay in the service a little longer." Or, "I think you're old enough to come to *Kol Nidre* with us."

If you think your child is ready, talk to him/her about the issues in the Torah readings, which present troubling scenarios of family life: a father who casts his firstborn son out in the desert, where he's likely to die. The same father will take his second-born son up a mountain with every indication that he's going to kill him.

Solicit her opinions about what Isaac must have thought when his father took him up the mountain, or why Jonah ran away when God asked him to try to help the people of Nineveh. She may well have discussed some of this in class, and may enjoy sharing what she knows in the car to and from services.

There is a fine line between exposing children to the experience of services and causing them pain. Yom Kippur can be arduous for adults, let alone children. "It's so boring," is an accurate description from a child's point of view, so do not ignore your ten-year-old's fidgets. Be judicious about insisting on a child's presence in the sanctuary, otherwise the holidays will be overshadowed by dread and a terrible war of wills. Make sure there is decent programming for your child's age group—a junior service or other activities.

Many school-age children are fascinated—and some are a little worried—by the idea of the Yom Kippur fast. No one under the age of thirteen is expected to fast, nor is anyone who might suffer because of it supposed to try. If your child is curious or wants to try fasting, talk about the reasons why it's done. The notion of self-purification may not make much sense to a child and the idea of "rehearsing one's own death" may be too frightening. But some children may want to experience real hunger in order to empathize with people who are hungry, not just once a year but every day.

You can help children learn how to fast in stages, which is a nice way to acknowledge their desire to take part while recognizing their limits. Start by suggesting s/he forgo snacks all day, or try a half-day fast with water. The following year, suggest fasting morning to evening, with water. Children might also be encouraged to try a different kind of "fast:" giving up television or a favorite food for a full twenty-four hours.

If a child decides to fast, offer support and respect for the impulse, but don't make too much of it or else s/he may feel terrible about "failing."

Adolescents Once children turn thirteen—the age of bar and bat mitzvah and religious maturity—they have the right to decide on how to observe *mitzvot*. Besides, as much as you might want your seventeen-year-old to attend Yom Kippur services with the rest of the family, he may be beyond the age of forcing.

This does not mean you can't require your young adult to make a thoughtful choice about the holiday, and you might even offer some choices: "If you don't want to sit in services, would you like to help out with a program for the younger children?" Or: "Do you want to be on duty to collect food for the temple's Yom Kippur canned-goods drive?" Or: "How about getting the youth group to run Rosh Hashanah services at the nursing home this year?"

In the days leading up to the High Holy Days, parents have an opportunity, indeed a responsibility, to raise the themes of repentance, self-examination, and resolving to be a better person—all of which are resonant for adolescents, who are struggling to figure out who they are.

Try talking to your teenager (side-by-side in the car is probably the best venue) about your own reflections and desire to be a better person. In the spirit of *teshuvah*, offer an honest apology yourself: "I'm sorry for nagging so much about your homework. I really do have a lot of faith in you. I am going to try harder to remember that you're growing up and are more responsible for yourself." If you are silent and patient, you may hear some *teshuvah* from your teenager, but even if he says nothing, you have doubtlessly initiated some reflective thought. Modeling is one of the best methods for teaching serious religiosity—at any age or stage of development.

Celebrating the High Holy Days with Your Children

- Bring apple juice, a round challah, sliced apples and honey to your child's secular preschool or public school class. Explain the meaning of the holidays and how you celebrate them.
- Bake or decorate a birthday cake in honor of the "birthday of the world"; encourage young children to make birthday cards and table decorations.
- Bake or shop for a round challah (raisins in the dough add to the sweetness). And save some crusts or crumbs from your Rosh Hashanah challah to use for *Tashlich*.
- Decorate a paper bag for *Tashlich;* older children can sew a bag and decorate it with fabric paint.

- Plan a *Tashlich* picnic with other families; meet at a duck pond and enjoy the afternoon together.
- Make a special bowl or dish out of clay for apples and honey.
- Read books about the holidays, listen to tapes that include holiday melodies and themes.
- Write "I'm sorry" notes, and put them in lunch boxes, or at a holiday table.
- Make a label for a jar and start collecting pennies for playing *draydl* at Hanukkah.

SUKKOT AND SIMCHAT TORAH

The second pair of fall holidays is as joyful as the first pair is somber. Sukkot ("huts") and Simchat Torah ("joy of the Torah") celebrate the pleasures of nature, of community, and of learning in visual, tactile, and physical ways that make them wonderful to share with children. They are linked to the first pair of fall holidays by the injunction to start building your *sukkah* immediately after breaking the Yom Kippur fast. (Hammering a symbolic nail is enough.)

Sukkot is a harvest festival of seven (or eight) days that begins on the full moon of the month called Tishri. Synagogue observance includes services on the first (and in some congregations the second) day of Sukkot, with a memorial, or *Yizkor,* service at the end of the week.

But the primary symbol, activity, and *mitzvah* of this holiday is the *sukkah,* a temporary hut reminiscent of structures the ancient Israelites built near their crops during harvest time—a reminder, too, of the exodus from Egypt. Spending time in a *sukkah* is a way to slow down, reconnect with the natural world, and offer up one of the most fundamental human prayers: "Thank You."

Home Observance Most synagogues construct a congregational *sukkah,* but since it is incumbent upon every Jew to "dwell" in a *sukkah,* it is essentially a home-based *mitzvah.* Once little known to American Jews, the pleasures of the *sukkah* have been rediscovered, with more *sukkot* (the plural of *sukkah*) going up every year. Prefabricated kits are widely available by mail order, on the Internet, and in some lumberyards.

A *sukkah* is a small, temporary structure that can be built as a lean-to against the outside wall of a house or as a freestanding hut. All kinds of materials can be used to construct the sides: pine boards, bamboo, Plexiglas, aluminum poles, canvas, cotton bedspreads, plywood paneling.

The most important part of the *sukkah* is the roof, which is made of a layer of cut branches. This material, called *s'kach,* should provide shade from the sun without totally obscuring the sky; starlight should be visible through the branches at night. Evergreen boughs make good *s'kach,* as do palm branches and corn stalks.

How much you "dwell" in a *sukkah* depends on the climate and how late in autumn Sukkot falls in a given year. But it's also a matter of your family's style: hikers and campers will jump at the chance to use sleeping bags in the backyard, while confirmed urbanites will be happy with breakfast and dinner on the patio.

Any way you use a *sukkah,* however, Sukkot is likely to turn into one of your children's favorite holidays, and for good reason. Having a *sukkah* in your backyard or porch is like having a Jewish clubhouse, an informal space that children can help erect and decorate, show off and share with friends and neighbors.

Sukkot begins with a festive meal—inside a *sukkah* if possible. In addition to the blessings for candles, wine, bread, and a *Shehechiyanu,* there is a special blessing for being inside a *sukkah:*

בָּרוּךְ אַתָּה יְיָ, אֱלֹהֵינוּ מֶלֶךְ הָעוֹלָם, אֲשֶׁר קִדְּשָׁנוּ בְּמִצְוֹתָיו וְצִוָּנוּ לֵשֵׁב בַּסֻּכָּה.

Baruch Ata Adonai, Eloheynu Melech Ha-olam, asher kid'shanu b'mitzvotav vitsivanu leyshev ba-sukkah.

You Abound in Blessings, Adonai our King, You make us holy with commandments and call us to dwell in the *sukkah.*

The other symbols of Sukkot are the *etrog* (citron, a lemon-like fruit), and the *lulav,* a green bouquet of palm frond, myrtle branch, and willow bough. The *lulav* and *etrog*—which are said to comprise "four species"[29]— are part of an ancient and mysterious ritual that involves waving them toward the four points of the compass, then up and down, a gesture indicating that God is everywhere. Judaica shops stock *etrogim* and *lulavim* and many synagogues order them in bulk for congregants. You can also make your own *lulav* by binding together stems from each species—a favorite Hebrew school and family education project.

Celebrating Sukkot with Children

- Plan a family outing in search of *s'kach*.
- Go to a farm stand for pumpkins, gourds, corn stalks, and other decorations for your *sukkah* and/or your home.
- Decorate the *sukkah* with posters, paper chains, paper flowers, dolls, toys, the Rosh Hashanah cards you received.
- Make your first pumpkin pie or honey cake of the season.
- Bob for apples with fruit from your pre–Rosh Hashanah apple-picking trip.
- Electrify the *sukkah*. Hang strings of lights, encourage children to do their homework, listen to music, and even watch TV in it.
- Encourage children to have sleep-outs and sleep-overs in the *sukkah*.
- Invite your child's teacher and classmates to visit the *sukkah* and have your son or daughter explain what it means and how your family built it.
- Track the moon's progress. Using a silver marker, have children draw pictures of the moon, which is full when Sukkot begins.
- Sukkot is associated with hospitality and festive gatherings, so have a *sukkah* decorating party, organize a *sukkah* dinner party, invite Shabbat guests to your *sukkah,* or hold an annual "open *sukkah*" on a weekend afternoon.
- According to an ancient tradition, the spirits of different *ushpizin,* or "Biblical ancestors" (i.e., Abraham and Sarah, Moses and Miriam), will visit your *sukkah* if invited. In this spirit of connecting with the past, tell stories about great-grandparents; take out old photo albums or home movies and introduce your children to their ancestors.
- Put the family *tzedakah* box in the *sukkah* and have children put

change into it daily. At the end of the week, take the money to the store, have the children select some canned goods, and bring them to a local food pantry.

- Above all, have fun in your *sukkah*. Play cards. Get a new board game. Sing silly songs. Howl at the moon.

Just because you can't build your own *sukkah* doesn't mean you can't get into the spirit of the holiday:

- Make a child-sized *sukkah* out of an empty appliance box. You can even "make" *s'kach* by drawing, coloring, and cutting out leaves for the roof.
- Make a tabletop model of a *sukkah* out of a shoebox or craft sticks and use it as a centerpiece all week.
- Decorate the house with autumn leaves, gourds, and Jewish holiday cards.
- Raise a "roof" complete with *s'kach* (made of paper or pine boughs) over the dining room table.
- Attend synagogue events in your congregation's *sukkah*.
- Build a *sukkah* with a few other families or ask if you can use your synagogue's *sukkah* for a pot-luck supper or weekend lunch.

Simchat Torah, the last of the fall holidays, arrives at the very end of Sukkot.[30] The name of this holiday means "Joy of the Torah," and it celebrates the completion of a year's Torah reading and the immediate renewal of the cycle of Torah reading. Unlike Sukkot, this holiday takes place almost entirely in the synagogue. But like Sukkot, it is observed with joy and enthusiasm and with a special role for children.

Simchat Torah is celebrated with all the energy associated with Jewish weddings, complete with singing, dancing, and special food and drink. The Torah reading often takes place under a *huppah*, a wedding canopy made of a large *tallit,* and there is even a ceremonial couple, since the person who reads the last portion of Deuteronomy and the first words from Genesis is called the bride (*kallah*) or bridegroom (*hatan*) of the Torah.

At the evening Simchat Torah synagogue service, all the Torah scrolls are removed from the ark and paraded around the sanctuary in seven circles, or processions, called *hakafot*. The honor of carrying the Torah is shared, and in some congregations everyone takes a turn. Some temples unfurl an entire Torah scroll in a huge circle, with people carefully holding the parchment, an unforgettable sight for adults and children.

Many congregations liven up the celebration after services with music, dancing with the Torahs, and champagne—just like at a wedding.

Children participate in the *hakafot*, carrying flags and miniature Torah scrolls or Torah ornaments. In some temples, children in the kindergarten or entering Hebrew school are "consecrated" or welcomed into the religious school on Simchat Torah, each child given a small *tallit* or Torah scroll of his or her own. The rabbi may call all the children up to the *bimah* for a special blessing. Little ones will either be enchanted or terrified by the commotion at Simchat Torah; take your baby's and toddler's temperament and sleep cycles into account before bringing them to this happy but noisy event.

Most preschool-age children revel in the free spirit of Simchat Torah, the chance to march around the sanctuary or social hall with flags and banners, and the opportunity to dance with their parents.

Simchat Torah is a wonderful occasion for giving school-age children new Jewish books in honor of the beginning of a new year of Jewish study. Donations to literacy programs and libraries are especially appropriate forms of *tzedakah* at this time of year. Make sure your children know why and to whom you are making contributions; let the little ones lick the stamp and put it in the mailbox. Older children might go through their own collection and donate books they have outgrown to children who can't afford to buy books at all.

BOOKS FOR CHILDREN

The Birthday of the World, by Barbara Diamond Goldin (Harcourt Brace & Jovanovich, 1990). For Rosh Hashanah.

Happy New Year, Beni, by Jane Breskin Zalben (Simon & Schuster, 1995). For Rosh Hashanah.

Jonah and the Two Great Fish, by Mordecai Gerstein (Simon and Schuster, 1997). For Yom Kippur.

Tikvah Means Hope, by Patricia Polacco (Turtleback, 1996). For Sukkot.

When Zayde Danced on Eldridge Street, by Elsa Okon Rael (Simon and Schuster, 1997). For Simchat Torah.

WINTER

HANUKKAH

Hanukkah is one of the most home-based and family-centered of the Jewish holidays. Full of gift-giving, games, and good food, it is a child's delight. Like all Jewish holidays, it is an opportunity for children to learn —not only by hearing and reading about Hanukkah or mastering a new blessing, but also by watching their parents enjoy themselves.

Hanukkah in History   The story of Hanukkah is found in the Book of the Maccabees, part of the Apocrypha, a collection of ancient writings not included in the Hebrew Bible.[31] In the second century B.C.E., Antiochus Epiphanes of Syria ruled the land of Israel and persecuted Jews who continued to practice their religion. When Antiochus ordered the desecration of the Temple in Jerusalem, he precipitated a rebellion led by Mattathias and his five sons, the Maccabees, who defeated the Syrian forces after a three-year war. The Maccabees rededicated the Temple in 165 B.C.E. and proclaimed that their victory be commemorated with an eight-day celebration. "Hanukkah" is based on the Hebrew word for "dedication."

Hanukkah was a radical innovation in the Jewish calendar because it honored the role of human beings, rather than God. The rabbis who codified Jewish law in the Talmud several hundred years later, were disturbed by the holiday that celebrated a military victory; they feared it might inspire dangerous risk-taking among Jews in their own day.

But the people were not going to give up their midwinter celebration of lights and merrymaking, which was probably borrowed from pagan solstice celebrations. The rabbis injected God into the consecration of the Temple with a story about how the Maccabees found only enough consecrated oil to last for one day but that miraculously the oil lasted for eight days. The tension between the modest miracle and the military victory is part of what keeps Hanukkah interesting.[32]

Hanukkah Lights Like many other religious traditions, Judaism brightens the darkness of the winter solstice with a holiday centered around light. The most familiar symbol of Hanukkah is the eight-branched candleholder, which goes by two names: "menorah," which could be used to refer to any candelabra, and "*hanukkiah*," the special eight-branched version used only at Hanukkah.

The *hanukkiah* is the hearth of the holiday, warming home and heart. The custom is to place the *hanukkiah* near a window, to brighten up the night for passers-by and to "proclaim" the miracle of Hanukkah and the very idea that miracles can happen. A menorah in the window is also an affirmation of Jewish pride.

You can light as many menorahs as you wish anytime after sunset. On Shabbat, Hanukkah candles are lit before the Sabbath lights.

Begin with the *shamash*, or "helper," candle—the one that's set apart either by height or distance from the rest, and then use it to light the other candles. Add one more on each night, filling the *hanukkiah* from right to left, but lighting them from left to right so the newest candle is always kindled first.

As you light the candles, two blessings are recited or sung:

בָּרוּךְ אַתָּה יְיָ, אֱלֹהֵינוּ מֶלֶךְ הָעוֹלָם, אֲשֶׁר קִדְּשָׁנוּ בְּמִצְוֹתָיו
וְצִוָּנוּ לְהַדְלִיק נֵר שֶׁל חֲנֻכָּה.

Baruch Ata Adonai Eloheynu Melech Ha-olam asher kid'shanu be-mitzvotav vitsivanu l'hadlik ner shel Hanukkah.

You abound in blessings, Adonai our Lord, You make us holy with commandments and call us to light the Hanukkah lights.

בָּרוּךְ אַתָּה יְיָ, אֱלֹהֵינוּ מֶלֶךְ הָעוֹלָם, שֶׁעָשָׂה נִסִּים לַאֲבוֹתֵינוּ,
בַּיָּמִים הָהֵם בַּזְּמַן הַזֶּה.

Baruch Ata Adonai Eloheynu Melech Ha-olam sh'asa nissim lavoteynu bayamim hahem bazman hazeh.

You abound in blessings, Adonai our Lord, You performed miracles for our ancestors in days of old, at this season.

On the first night, the *Shehechiyanu* is added:

בָּרוּךְ אַתָּה יְיָ, אֱלֹהֵינוּ מֶלֶךְ הָעוֹלָם, שֶׁהֶחֱיָנוּ וְקִיְּמָנוּ וְהִגִּיעָנוּ לַזְּמַן הַזֶּה.

Baruch Ata Adonai, Eloheynu Melech Ha-olam,
shehechiyanu v'kiamanu v'higianu lazman hazeh.

You abound in blessings, Adonai our Lord, You have kept us alive, You have sustained us, You have brought us to this moment.

According to tradition, no one is supposed to do any work while the candles are burning; the light marks a period for relaxation. Right after the blessings, it is customary to sing *"Maoz Tzur"* ("Rock of Ages"). Families who know other Hanukkah songs sing them as well; preschoolers will be glad to teach you "I Had a Little *Draydl*" and *"Sivivon"* (the Hebrew word for top). If you want to learn Hanukkah songs, ask your cantor or rabbi for song-sheets or tapes, and explore the growing selection of Hanukkah CDs and tapes.

Hanukkiot (the plural of *hanukkiah*) are available in a dizzying array of styles, shapes, sizes, and prices—everything from Mickey Mouse to Waterford crystal. You can also make a Hanukkah menorah out of materials ranging from ceramics to potatoes. Everyone in the family can have his or her own menorah, and guests can bring theirs, too. The more candles, the brighter the night.

Gift-giving   Most families exchange gifts after the lights are lit. The custom of giving Hanukkah *gelt* (Yiddish for "money")—either real coins or chocolate coins wrapped in gold foil—dates back to seventeenth-century Poland. This practice has evolved into the giving of elaborate presents, mostly because of the proximity of Hanukkah to the consumer frenzy that surrounds Christmas.

Some parents make the mistake of trying to compete with Christmas by giving gifts on every night of Hanukkah, saying something like, "Their holiday lasts one day but ours goes on for eight." That approach tends to encourage indulgence and greed.

There is nothing inherently wrong with gifts at Hanukkah. In fact, they can provide opportunities to teach children about the pleasures of giving as well as receiving. Many families institute a "designated gift-giver rule" so that each child has a night on which she chooses and gives presents but receives none. Giving is a good way to teach children why the words "Thank you" are important. It's also a chance to practice empathy, putting themselves in someone else's shoes by thinking about what Mommy might really like.

Some families designate one night for homemade gifts, or for giving and getting books. It is possible to skip gifts on one or more nights; the family can go out to a play or movie. You can dedicate one night to *tzedakah;* count and roll the change you've been using for playing *draydl* and decide where to send the money. Hanukkah's political themes suggest contributions to organizations that work for religious and political freedom for Jews and for all oppressed people.

Food   Traditional Hanukkah foods are fried, recalling the story of the miracle of the oil. Ashkenazic Jews eat potato pancakes, called *latkes,* which are traditionally served with applesauce and sour cream. In Israel, jelly donuts, *sufganiot,* are the specialty of the holiday. Sephardic Jews favor fritters with sweet syrup. Italians and Moroccans serve chicken that has been fried. Russian Jews drink "flaming tea," adding to the light of the candles by dropping flaming, brandy-soaked lumps of sugar into their cups or glasses.[33]

Parties   Hanukkah parties can be held on any or all eight nights. Most synagogues run family programs that might include a *latke* dinner or even a competitive *latke* "cook-off," song festivals, storytelling, games for children, and musical concerts. At home, it's traditional to invite family and friends over for *latkes,* singing, and *draydl.*

The most universal Hanukkah party activity is *draydl,* a gambling game of dumb luck. Each player antes up, using chocolate coins, buttons, peanuts, or pennies, and takes a turn spinning the four-sided *draydl* (or top). Each of the four sides bears a Hebrew letter. If the *draydl* falls on the letter *nun,* you get nothing; on *hay,* you take half the pot; on *shin,* add something to the kitty; and if on *Gimel,* you get the entire pot. The letters are an acrostic for the Hebrew sentence: "*Nes gadol haya sham,*" "A great miracle happened there." (In Israel, the Hebrew letter *pey* is substituted for *shin* and the letters stand for "*Nes gadol haya po,*" "A great miracle happened here.")

Little kids love the game, and older children usually enjoy helping them play. To play "human *draydl,*" children spin till they drop and the last one standing wins a prize.

Still, *draydl* has its limits, so you might also plan activities that suit your family's interests: make Hanukkah the occasion for an annual charades party or Scrabble tournament; or stage a formal debate on the relative merits of *latkes* versus *hamentaschen* (the traditional food for Purim).

Celebrating Hanukkah with Children

- Decorate the house with blue-and-white homemade paper chains, store-bought tinsel banners and centerpieces, or anything you like.
- Use Hanukkah napkins all week, and eat off Hanukkah place mats—store-bought or homemade—and Hanukkah plates made with plastic "make-a-plate" kits.
- On Sunday have an annual Make-Your-Own-Hanukkah-Sundae party.
- Get Hanukkah cookie-cutters and decorate the cookies with frosting or colored sugar.
- Post a tally sheet of *draydl* winners and losers on the refrigerator all week.
- Collect *latke* recipes and make different kinds; potato, leek, sweet potato, apple, etc.
- Start a *draydl* collection, with tops made out of every kind of material: plastic, wood, ceramics, metal.
- Give every child a different *draydl* every year and save them in a special box.
- Make menorahs out of food, recyclables, treasures from nature: potatoes, seashells, eggshells, cupcakes, spools, tin cans, pizza dough, Play-dough, stones, sea glass.
- Scatter small plastic and wooden *draydls* on window ledges and

tabletops as decorations (so long as there are no toddlers in the house, of course).

- Read a Hanukkah story every night while the candles are still burning.
- Act out the Hanukkah story with props and costumes. Put the names of all the characters (including God) into a bag and have everyone draw their parts.
- Make edible *draydls* out of marshmallows or gingerbread, or cut peanut-butter sandwiches into *draydl* shapes. See Joan Nathan's book *The Children's Jewish Holiday Kitchen* for ideas and easy recipes.
- Go outside to admire the candles in your window. Displaying the Hanukkah menorah celebrates religious freedom today, just as in the days of the Maccabees. Talk about the fact that for much of Jewish history, this would have been a dangerous thing to do.
- Talk about the meaning of the word "miracle." On which day did the Maccabees decide that the long-lasting oil wasn't just luck but a miracle? Are miracles limited to gigantic events, like the parting of the Red Sea? Can everyday things be miracles, too? Go around the dinner table and have everyone name an "everyday miracle." Keep the conversation light: "It's a miracle that the *latkes* didn't burn tonight" ("that the puppy didn't poop on the carpet all week"; "that the baby got a new tooth"; etc.).
- Look up the word "dedication" (the meaning of the word "Hanukkah") in the dictionary and thesaurus. Dedicate yourselves to doing something in the coming months: more reading aloud to your children, or having Shabbat dinner more regularly.

Christmas and Hanukkah Christmas confronts American Jews with the undeniable fact of our difference in an overwhelmingly Christian culture. Adults make their peace with this over time, but the issue is revisited every time parents see their children discover and confront their outsider status. As much as we might want to protect them from the disappointment of the season, there is no way to shield Jewish children from the onslaught of Christmas, which is not only a cornerstone of Christian and secular culture, but also of the national economy.

Learning that you are an outsider is never particularly easy. But to be a child with his/her nose pressed up against the glass at Christmas is doubly hard because the season is especially geared to seduce and delight the very young. Christmas-envy is not a religious issue for children. They want the tinsel, the flashing lights, the candy, and, most of all, the toys.

Jewish children react in different ways to Christmas and prohibitions against their full participation: jealousy, sadness, outrage. Little children may cry. School-age kids, obsessed with the idea of "fairness," sometimes express anger at all the TV commercials and holiday decorations. "Why aren't there as many Happy Hanukkah signs as Merry Christmas signs?"

Some children find it easier to hate everything about Christmas, which is a hard way to live in America from October through January. On the other hand, some kids say they feel "sorry" for their non-Jewish friends who don't have as many holidays to celebrate.

Whatever their position, it's pointless (and even harmful) to try to talk your children out of their feelings. Why try to get your child to "be reasonable" about Christmas, which itself is all about unreasonable expectations? If your child says, "I don't like Hanukkah. I want Christmas," don't tell him he doesn't mean it. If she says, "I hate Christmas lights," don't defend them as pretty. Just listen and sympathize. Explain how you handle your feelings about the holiday. It's fine to talk about why you like Hanukkah and how it fits into a whole year of Jewish celebrations, but try to keep this from becoming an argument about which is better.

Besides, your child's passionate position will change as s/he grows. By the time they start grade school, most children understand that every family has its own way of doing things, so a parent might say, "I know Jane's Christmas tree is wonderful, but that's not part of our religion. We do Hanukkah as part of a whole year's worth of Jewish holidays, including Shabbat." Children who participate in the whole cycle of Jewish holidays—not just Hanukkah but Sukkot (the big hut to decorate and play in), Purim (dress-up and sanctioned noise), Passover (the family feast)—are less likely to feel "robbed" at Christmastime. Even so, they probably won't stop wishing they could have their own celebrations *and* Christmas. Many Jewish children have friends from intermarried families who seem to get it all, lighting menorahs *and* hanging stockings. The argument for celebrating both holidays may seem very persuasive to a child if one of her parents is a non-Jew.[34]

Christmas often brings up different issues for Jews-by-choice, whose extended families include Christian in-laws and grandparents who want to share the holiday with grandchildren, nieces, nephews, and cousins. Some families try to make Thanksgiving the big extended-family get-together and avoid visits in December—especially if long-distance travel is involved. However, many liberal Jewish families feel quite confident about sharing Christmas with non-Jewish relatives and friends, as long as the celebrations take place outside their own homes.

By the age of six, most children understand that celebrating Christmas at Grandma and Grandpa's house is like going to a friend's house for a birthday party. You enjoy the cake and ice cream, you give a gift and accept a party favor, but when you go back to your own house, the celebration is over because it isn't *your* birthday. The same holds true when non-Jewish family and friends come to your house to share *latkes* and candlelighting on Hanukkah.

Synagogues and Jewish agencies run "December Dilemma" workshops, mostly for intermarried couples trying to decide how to juggle the complicated emotions and family expectations of the season. But December raises issues for Jewish families of all constellations. Do we send "Season's Greetings" or Christmas cards to Mom's parents and siblings? Do we let our ten-year-old go to Midnight Mass with his best friend since the friend came with him to the synagogue Hanukkah party? How should we respond to Christmas-tree decorations at school, or Christmas music in the school's annual Winter Concert? Are we making too big a deal out of Hanukkah and turning it into "the Jewish Christmas?"

Some Jews object to celebrating Hanukkah with the same cultural "vocabulary" as Christmas (blue-and-white gift-wrap, six-pointed tinsel stars, strings of lights in the shape of *draydls*, etc.). Critics fear the transformation of what is usually dubbed a "minor" festival (compared to Passover, for example) into a "Jewish-lite" version of Christmas.

But making Hanukkah into a bigger party than it once was does not nullify its Jewishness—especially when it is part of the whole Jewish holiday cycle. Hanukkah exemplifies innovation in the Jewish calendar; the eight-day festival of light was inserted into the biblical holiday cycle to commemorate a victory against total assimilation. What lesson could be more relevant?[35]

December can be a tough month for Jewish parents. There are so many competing demands and emotional pulls. As you fry the potatoes and try to decide what to answer when the supermarket clerk wishes you a "Merry Christmas," try to stay consistent about your family's traditions, avoid getting defensive, and, most important, celebrate with joy.

HANUKKAH: AGES AND STAGES

Infants and Toddlers   The sights, smells, nonverbal and verbal associations of Hanukkah imprint on young eyes and ears. And although children don't actually remember their first holidays, the photographs of "Jessie's first Hanukkah" and "two-year-old David lighting the menorah with a little help from Grandma" will eventually become indelible and precious memories.

Preschool and School-age Children   Hanukkah is adored by all children, and for good reason: the arts and crafts, songs and games, stories and activities are sure to find a match in every child's developing abilities and interests.

The holiday is also a natural focus for lessons and celebrations in Jewish school settings, and public schools in many communities also acknowledge and even teach about the "Festival of Lights" along with the other holidays of the seasons.

You can supplement and support your child's Jewish curriculum by borrowing or buying new Hanukkah picture books. Do some bedtime reading together and talk about the meaning and values of the holiday in age-appropriate terms.

Hanukkah presents a story of heroes and bad guys. The Maccabees—crafty underdogs who outsmart and outfight a more powerful enemy—appeal to childhood fantasies, especially common among young boys, who love to copy superheroes. While some parents may want to avoid glorifying fighting and military victories, the fight between good and evil—with good triumphant—appeals to children's growing understanding that there are bad people in the world. Pretending to be one of the good guys is a way of asserting control.

Hanukkah also raises the issue of standing up for what you believe in. Parents can ask children if they can think of ways to take a stand without resorting to violence and discuss the question of when fighting is justified.

Adolescents Teenagers will expect and want Hanukkah presents, but will probably feel that the holiday games are too babyish for them. Putting them in charge of entertaining younger children provides a way to join in without sacrificing dignity, and high school students often help run synagogue parties for little kids. Jewish schools and youth groups often run toy and book drives for needy children at this season, or bring a Hanukkah party to a nursing home.

Standing up for your beliefs is a topic of great interest to teenagers. Hanukkah is an opportunity to raise a few provocative questions with your adolescent: "What would it take for you to take a risk for your beliefs? When do you tell a friend you're uncomfortable with him using racial slurs or telling gay jokes? Would you organize a protest if your public school suddenly mandated a daily prayer? What about dances on Friday night? High school graduation on Shabbat?

Were the Maccabees right in going to war because their temple was messed up? What would you fight for? Do the ends ever justify the means?

These questions are offered as conversation-starters, which, depending on your teenager, might be more effective during the car-pool ride to school than over a family dinner.

TU B'SHVAT

Tu B'Shvat, the fifteenth day of the Hebrew month of Shvat, is described in the Talmud as the "New Year of the Trees." It probably began as a way to date trees so that farmers would know when a fruit tree was old enough to be tithed, a percentage of its crop sent to the Temple in Jerusalem. Today, Tu B'Shvat is celebrated as a kind of Jewish Earth Day, connecting traditional Jewish values with contemporary efforts to protect the planet from climate change, pollution of air and water, deforestation, and other ecological ills.

For Jews in the Northern Hemisphere, Tu B'Shvat arrives "just in time." Midway between Hanukkah and Purim, in the dreary heart of winter, a holiday that anticipates the coming of spring is most welcome. The rediscovered Tu B'Shvat seder, a once-arcane celebration invented by the sixteenth-century mystics of Safed, provides the template for celebration.

History   The dispersion of the Jews from the land of Israel (first in 586 B.C.E. and again in 70 C.E.) changed Tu B'Shvat from an agricultural festival into a way of maintaining a connection to a place where, in the month of Shvat, the winter rains end and the first signs of spring appear. For centuries, Jews in the Diaspora have kept the connection alive by eating things grown in Israel. Because it traveled well, carob (also known as bokser, and Saint John's bread) became the traditional food of the holiday among Ashkenazic Jews. Sephardic Jews celebrated Tu B'Shvat with special fruit platters, songs, and games for children. Throughout the Jewish world, the *mitzvah* of eating fruit from Israel was considered important enough that efforts were made to give *ma'ot perot* ("money for fruit") to the poor.

Schoolteachers in prestate Israel reinvented the holiday with songs and tree-plantings, and after the founding of the State of Israel in 1948, Tu B'Shvat became Jewish Arbor Day. Jewish children around the world planted seeds in paper cups and raised money for the Jewish National Fund, which continues to support forestation efforts in Israel.

Tu B'Shvat has become a great platform for connecting ecological activism to Jewish values. The Torah itself is called a tree of life, and planting trees is considered a holy activity. According to Rabbi Johanan ben Zakkai, a sage of the first century, "If you have a seedling in your hand, and someone says to you, 'Look, here comes the Messiah!' go and plant the seedling first, and then come out to meet the Messiah."[36] The Torah forbids the cutting down of an enemy's fruit trees in times of war, even if the wood is needed for the siege of a city.[37]

The Tu B'Shvat curriculum in supplementary and day schools may focus on the Israeli landscape, and introduce the concept of humankind as *shomrei adamah*, keepers of the earth who are responsible for the stewardship of God's creation. The holiday exemplifies the Jewish connections between "secular" concerns and "religious" values. Linking science to *mitzvah*, Jewish programs stress *tikkun olam*, repair of the world. Working for the environment within a Jewish setting—cleaning up a park, recycling paper, collecting money for trees or endangered pandas—gives children a sense of accomplishment as it imparts lessons in religion, ecology, and teamwork. Children also get the message that they can make a difference and that, as Jews, they are expected to try.

Celebrating Tu B'Shvat with Your Family

- Do an arts-and-crafts project: make *tzedakah* boxes in the shape of a watering can, forests made of recycled paper-towel rolls, a collage of flowers and trees, decorated paper cups for planting seeds.
- Give each child a "pet plant." Try a cactus or other low-maintenance plant for little kids, flower bulbs for older children (amaryllis is a particularly dramatic choice).
- Plant something edible. If your climate does not permit outdoor gardening at this time of year, try a window box with parsley seeds to be harvested for the Passover seder.
- Visit a greengrocer and count the fruits. Look for a fruit or vegetable you've never tasted before.
- Shop for Israeli produce, such as olives, dates, figs, almonds, persimmons, oranges. Try a sabra, a cactus fruit also called "prickly pear," spiny on the outside but sweet inside, or a giant pomelo, a cross between grapefruit and orange.
- Feed the neighborhood wildlife. String popcorn and hang it on the deck or around the bushes for the birds; scatter cracked corn for pheasants and squirrels; make a birdfeeder by smearing peanut butter on a pinecone to hang from a tree branch.
- Play tasting games. Take turns with a blindfold and guess some fruits by smell, touch, or taste.
- Go through seed catalogues and make selections for the coming spring.
- Visit a botanical garden.
- Tour your yard to see if any of the trees need attention.
- Donate money to the Jewish National Fund for the planting of trees in Israel (800-542-TREE); or to Mazon: A Jewish Response to Hunger, so others may eat (310-442-0020); or support national and international organizations dedicated to protecting the environment.
- Increase your family's environmental efforts: Weigh the garbage your family makes in a week and try to reduce the amount

through recycling. Install space-occupiers in the toilets. Get a rechargeable battery set.
• Have children decorate the table or make placecards for your Tu B'Shvat seder.

The Tu B'Shvat Seder   The word "seder" means order. As with the Passover seder, the Tu B'Shvat seder is a liturgy for the table that includes prayers, songs, eating, drinking, and discussion. Unlike the Passover seder, which is laden with historical and family expectations, this one is new to most people and thus wide open. It's a great time to invite friends and neighbors for a vegetarian potluck. And encourage your children to invite their friends, too.

Many synagogues run Tu B'Shvat seders, which are almost always geared to families. Or you can make your own at home. Either create your own *haggadah* (literally, "the telling") or buy one of the published versions listed below.

Your seder can be as simple as reciting the blessing for wine and for fruit before enjoying a meal. Or you can organize the courses to correspond with the seasons and have a conversation about the meaning of the holiday. Custom and tradition are so new and fluid regarding this seder that there really is no way to do it wrong.

The mystics who invented the Tu B'Shvat seder, organized it around four cups of wine and four types of fruit. The first cup of wine is white, the second and third are mixtures of white and red (rosé or blush), and the last is red. Or you can substitute white and red grape juice.

The same blessing is recited before each cup:

בָּרוּךְ אַתָּה יְיָ, אֱלֹהֵינוּ מֶלֶךְ הָעוֹלָם, בּוֹרֵא פְּרִי הַגָּפֶן.

Baruch Ata Adonai, Eloheynu Melech Ha-olam, boray p'ree hagafen.

You Abound in Blessings, Adonai our Lord, You create the fruit of the vine.

115

Fruit is the culinary focus of the menu, and some people try to serve fifteen varieties, to correspond with the date—the fifteenth of Shvat. The fruits are divided into four categories that are metaphors for the seasons, the elements, human characteristics, and mystical emanations of God.[38]

The same blessing is recited before eating from each category of fruits:

בָּרוּךְ אַתָּה יְיָ, אֱלֹהֵינוּ מֶלֶךְ הָעוֹלָם, בּוֹרֵא פְּרִי הָעֵץ.

Baruch Ata Adonai, Eloheynu Melech Ha-olam, boray p'ree ha'aytz.

You Abound in Blessings, Adonai our Lord, You create the fruit of the tree.

The four categories of fruit represent increasing levels of closeness to God:

Level One: Fruits that are hard outside and soft inside: nuts, citrus, melon, pineapple, pomegranate, and coconut. Winter. Earth. The body.

Level Two: Fruits with a soft outside and hard inner core: cherry, peach, plum, date, olive and avocado. Spring. Water. Emotion.

Level Three: Fruits that are totally edible or have only small seeds: strawberry, apple, fig, grape, raisin, pear. Summer. Air. Intellect.

Level Four: As the highest and purest level—beyond being consumed—these fruits are purely symbolic and inedible to human beings, such as pine cones and acorns (though maple syrup or maple sugar candy may be used as edible symbols). Autumn. Fire. Spirit.

Menus Although the food at Tu B'Shvat seders often consists of raw fruit platters, piles of apple slices and melon wedges do not live up to the promise of the word "seder," which conjures associations with a mouthwatering feast.

Inventive cooks can have a lot of fun planning the menu for a Tu B'Shvat seder. For example:

Israeli Hummos, tabouli, felafel with pita bread, chopped salads, citrus salad.

Vegetarian Gourmet Pumpkin soup, polenta vegetable lasagna, green beans with almonds, tarte Tatin.

International Guacamole, bean-and-cheese enchiladas with green salad, lemon flan. Or egg-lemon soup, eggplant moussaka, cucumber salad, peach ice cream.

BOOKS FOR CHILDREN

Hanukkah
Just Enough Is Plenty, by Barbara Diamond Goldin (Viking, 1988).
Herschel and the Hanukkah Goblins, by Eric Kimmel (Scholastic, 1989).
The Power of Light, by Isaac Bashevis Singer (Farrar, Straus, and Giroux, 1990).
The Tie Man's Miracle: A Chanukah Tale, by Steven Schnur (Morrow Junior, 1995).
On videotape: *A Rugrats Chanukah* (VHS 1997).

Tu B'Shvat:
Pearl Plants a Tree, by Jane Breskin Zalben (Simon and Schuster, 1995).

BOOKS FOR PARENTS

A Seder for Tu B'Shvat, by Harlene Winnick Appelman and Jane Sherwin Shapiro (Kar-Ben Copies, 1984). An illustrated seder for families with children, containing activities, discussion questions, and songs.
Seder Tu B'Shevat: The Festival of the Trees, by Adam Fisher (Central Conference of American Rabbis, 1989). Two seders actually, one for use with children.
The Jewish Vegetarian Year Cookbook, by Roberta Kalechofsky and Rosa Rasiel (Micah Publications, Inc., 1998). The chapter on Tu B'Shvat contains a seder as well as recipes.

SPRING

PURIM

Purim is a Jewish Halloween, a Jewish Mardi Gras, and a secular New Year's Eve all rolled into one. The fourteenth of Adar, which falls near the vernal equinox, celebrates springtime with a loud, bawdy shout to remind us that laughter is a religious act—a *mitzvah.*

Purim is the polar opposite of Yom Kippur. Where Yom Kippur is probably the most "adult" holiday of the year, Purim is the most childlike. Indeed, Purim encourages grown-ups to act like children. Children are indulged, dressed up in costumes, given noisemakers, and told to make a racket in the temple.

Purim is a holiday free from normalcy and rules. On Purim, Jews are encouraged not only to gamble, cross-dress, and drink to excess,[39] but even to make fun of our most sacred texts. And yet, Purim is not considered a trivial or minor holiday. According to the Talmud, only Purim will be celebrated even after the Messiah comes; evidently, even in a perfect world, we will still need to laugh at ourselves.

There is no requirement to refrain from work or study on Purim. The only *mitzvah* (religious commandment) is to hear a public reading of the Book of Esther. The holiday begins with the reading of the story at the evening service. But the reading or chanting of *Megillat Esther,* the scroll of Esther[40] is unlike any other biblical reading. For one thing, it is sometimes acted out by costumed players using funny voices. And listeners are encouraged to participate by drowning out the name of the villain, Haman, using any means at hand: yelling, whistling, banging on pots, blowing horns, or special Purim noisemakers called *graggers.*

Purim Torah is the name for the sacred nonsense of the holiday. Rabbis deliver sermons about the Jewish significance of Cookie Monster's relationship to all things round and sweet; synagogue newsletters will announce congregational rodeos and advertisements for kosher lobsters; traditional prayers may be sung to Broadway show-tune melodies. Theatrical offerings called *Purimshpiels* make fun of national, international, and congregational politics and personalities.

Some synagogues and Jewish organizations raise funds with costume parties and Las Vegas nights, since gambling, generally forbidden by Jewish law, is permitted on Purim.

The story of Purim takes its name from the Hebrew word *pur,* which means "lot" (as in lottery), because in the Book of Esther Haman cast lots to pick a date for the slaughter of the Jews. There is no evidence that the events described in this book have any basis in history. Indeed, there's evidence that the *ganze megillah* (the whole story) is based on a Persian legend since the protagonists' names belong to local deities—fertile Ishtar (Esther) and warlike Marduk (Mordechai)—and the holiday's masks and drunkenness recall ancient Persian springtime revels.

The Book of Esther is one of the oddest tales codified in the Hebrew bible. The name of God does not appear anywhere, and its sexual shenanigans, philandering king, and violence are the stuff of burlesque. It is a story not appropriate for children, and it is always cleaned up for them. Still, the dark undertones and giddy triumph over mortal danger make it a favorite among a people with a long history of persecution and unhappy endings.

The Book of Esther

Once upon a time, a large and prosperous Jewish community flourished in Persia. Mordechai, a Jew, was a member of the court of King Ahasuerus. One day, the king banished his queen, Vashti, for refusing to appear naked before his guests, as he had commanded her. To replace her, Ahasuerus held a beauty contest which was won by Esther, a relative of Mordechai's.

Meanwhile, Haman, a dreadful anti-Semite, was named Grand Vizier. When Mordechai refused to bow down before him (because Jews are allowed to bow only to God) Haman plotted revenge with plans to kill him and massacre all the Jews in the kingdom.

Esther ultimately foils the plot, the Jews take revenge, and the king commands that Haman be hanged on the scaffold built for Mordechai, who was then appointed Grand Vizier.

And then Esther, Mordechai, and the Jews of Persia lived happily ever after.

Food Traditional Purim foods are sweet. Ashkenazic Jews make a three-cornered pastry called *hamentaschen* ("Haman's pockets"), a filled pastry that has been part of Purim celebrations in Eastern European communities since at least the twelfth century. Legend has it that poppy seeds (a favorite filling for *hamentaschen*) were used in memory of Queen Esther's three-day fast before she approached the king, during which time she ate nothing but seeds while praying to God to repeal the decree against her people.

Sephardic cooks make confections called *orejas de Aman* ("Haman's ears"). These are deep-fried or baked and served with syrup.

It is traditional to share sweets with others through the custom of *shalach mones*—a Yiddish term meaning "sending portions," which refers to a passage in the Book of Esther that commands Jews to give two portions to the poor. As at every Jewish holiday, giving to the poor is considered both a responsibility and a privilege. In some congregations, *tzedakah* money is collected before reading from the *megillah*.

Additionally, there is a custom of bringing food to neighbors and friends, a kind of reverse trick-or-treat. Some families deliver plates or goodie bags of homemade cookies, Israeli candies, and dried fruit.

Celebrating Purim with Children   Kids rule at Purim. Synagogue and Jewish community centers sponsor carnivals, costume contests, and parades. Jewish day schools and preschools hold parades and puppet shows.

There are, however, serious lessons hidden within the silliness. The story of Purim teaches that the world is a changeable and sometimes dangerous place for Jews, and that in order to survive, Jews have had to take risks and stick together. The book of Esther presents children with the model of a Jewish heroine who is not only a beauty queen but a real human being, a person who, despite her fears, acts to help her people.

Older children know that, despite the happy ending of the Purim story, the victory did not last; many "Hamans" far more terrible have risen up against the Jews. And yet, the message is still relevant: we are still here telling the story. The ultimate triumph belongs to the living.

But these lessons are mostly implicit. Purim is, first and foremost, a party for children who are young enough to enjoy dressing up and making noise. Teenagers—far too old for face paint—often participate by running the synagogue Purim carnival as a way to help the temple and raise money for the youth group or for charity. This gives them the chance to be silly (some are even willing to wear funny hats or dress up as clowns) in the service of the little kids' fun.

With dress-up and masks, Purim looks like the Jewish Halloween, but the "content" of the holidays couldn't be more different. Purim costumes are always for fun rather than to scare people. And Purim is all about giving (*shalach mones* and *tzedakah*) rather than getting (trick-or-treat).

Purim Fun

- Make masks and crowns using glitter, feathers, metallic paper, plastic "gems," etc.
- Create a cast of stick puppets to act out the Purim story.
- Deliver *shalach mones* goodies early in the morning—in pajamas.
- Make *hamentaschen* and have a bake-off with friends or at the temple. Or buy *hamentaschen* from several different bakeries and have a tasting.
- Make a three-cornered Purim plate for *hamentaschen*.
- Bring boxes of brownie mix to a local food pantry to share the sweetness.
- Give each child a new *gragger* every year and keep them in a special Purim box.
- Take an annual snapshot portrait of the whole family wearing masks or costumes. Or have a family portrait taken at a photo studio that provides fancy dress costumes.
- Make it a backwards day; serve pizza for breakfast and pancakes for supper. Wear funny hats to the dinner table.
- Have a family joke-fest at dinner.
- Introduce your kids to the Marx Brothers or Mel Brooks on video.
- Invite another family over for charades, paper-bag dramatics, skits, and a potluck supper.

PASSOVER

Passover is the most treasured of all Jewish holidays, the richest, the sweetest. Celebrated as springtime and sunlight make their return, Passover expresses Judaism's profound optimism, resolving the great dualities of existence in favor of light over darkness, birth over death, freedom over slavery. Passover begins with the retelling of the Exodus from Egypt and is given form for a week by eating slave food, *matzah*.[41]

The word "Pesach," the Hebrew word for Passover, refers to the last of the plagues that God unleashed upon the Egyptians to force Pharaoh to free the enslaved Israelites.[42] Moses tells the Hebrews to paint their doorposts with the blood of a lamb so that the angel of death will "pass over" those houses during the killing of the firstborn.

The biblical saga that begins in the Book of Genesis continues in Exodus, telling how the Jews came to Egypt and how they left: there is the story of Joseph's rise to power, the tale of Moses' birth and religious calling, the resistance of the midwives who refused to kill Hebrew baby boys, the entry of God into human history.

This is the story told at the seder (literally, "order"), the feast held on the first and second nights of the seven- (or eight-) day festival. (See page 82 for an explanation of one-day versus two-day observances.) But the mandate of the Passover seder is not merely to tell the tale, but to reenact it so that everyone—especially children—will feel that they were there.

The seder is a unique proceeding: pageant, living tableau, master class. The table is an altar and a stage set. The ritual objects are props, the *haggadah*, the book that contains the liturgy of the seder, is both a script and a lesson plan. The goal is to talk, think, eat, and argue our way back in time and bring the experience into our daily lives, to savor the freedoms we enjoy.

Jews have always pulled out all the stops for Passover. The best china emerges from the cupboards; special recipes make an annual appearance; the house is turned upside down in a frenzy of cleaning, cooking, and preparation. Family members travel to be together for the seder.

The only holiday that compares to Passover is Christmas. Just as many secular and unchurched Americans anticipate, celebrate, and love Christmas, so do unaffiliated and secular Jews who celebrate no other Jewish holiday make a point of being at a seder.

Like Christmas, Passover takes over the whole house—especially the kitchen. As with Christmas, the attachment to Passover is rooted deep in evocative, formative childhood experiences, which include beautiful religious observances and in-gathering of relatives with children at center stage. The Torah is explicit about the importance of passing this crucial story on to the next generation, with the phrase, "You shall tell your child on that day."[43] At the seder table, children play a vital role in the drama; their participation and their questions are precious and crucial.

There are two major *mitzvot* to fulfill during Passover: the first is to attend a seder, hearing and telling the story. The second is to avoid all leavened foods for a week, which is a way of reenacting the Exodus and the transformation from slavery to freedom. Every part of Passover—from the planning to the preparing and celebrating—provides opportunities for your children to participate, learn, enjoy, and grow.

The anticipation begins as soon as you put away the Purim *graggers* and masks. Involve your children in every step of your plans. Explain what you're doing and why.

Getting Ready for Passover with Children

- Starting on Purim, begin the process of "eating up" the leavened foods in your cupboards. Explain why you're not buying new boxes of macaroni and crackers.
- Get a new recording of Passover songs and start playing them a few weeks before the seder.
- Go to the library, bookstore, and video store and get new Passover books and tapes. Let children watch Passover videotapes as often as they like.
- Make a poster with photographs from family seders of years past.
- Attend a workshop on how to make a seder. Offered at many synagogues, these can provide basic information about the holiday, show you how to keep your children entertained, and inspire your own creativity.
- Sign up to host a Jewish traveler, college student, or serviceman/woman at your seder.
- Find out if your synagogue matches families with widowed or single members in your own congregation who might otherwise not have a seder to attend.
- Bake your own *matzah!* In order to prevent even the possibility of fermentation, the *matzah* must be baked precisely 18 minutes after water is added to flour.[44] Some synagogues run a *matzah*-baking session around Passover. Be aware that since it is nearly impossible to purchase the special kosher-for-Passover flour used by commercial bakeries, this will not be kosher-for-Passover

matzah. However, the process will give you a new appreciation for the "bread of affliction."
- Tell your children how the family is helping with a Passover food drive so every member of the Jewish community can afford *matzah* and wine for the holiday.
- Bring your child with you to donate foods containing leavening (*hametz*) at local food pantries.

Planning the Seder   The seder is full of teachable moments and the makings of joyful Jewish memories—but only if you take the time to think it through and plan. Start by asking yourself: How long can our kids sit at the table? What kind of seder will keep our children engaged? What messages do we really want them to get from the evening?

Seder hosts often feel pressure to serve a delicious meal, set a beautiful table, and meet various family members' expectations of what a seder "should" be. But do not lose sight of your child's learning experience.

The primary purpose of the seder is to pass the story on to the next generation. Indeed, some of the "traditional" Passover rituals—such as lifting the *matzah* plate high and hiding the *afikomen*—were probably invented as playful ploys to keep children involved and to get them to ask "Why?" The Four Questions were once read at the end of the meal (where they logically belong) but were moved up earlier in the seder, to a point where it was more likely children would still be awake.

Customizing your seder to suit your children's needs and abilities is a venerable idea. Although many people are distressed by the categories in the parable of the Four Children, the story reflects a basic appreciation of the fact that children learn differently and thus require different methods of instruction. We teach "the one who can't ask"—babies, toddlers, and preschool children—the words *haroset* and *maror* and leave it to teenagers to debate the meaning of "redemption."

Try to avoid having your kid be the only child at the table. If there won't be any cousins or other children near your child's age, have him/her invite a friend. Since most Jewish kids will be with their families, this usually means there will be non-Jewish children at the table. This is usually a boon, since non-Jews tend to treat the invitation as an honor, take the seder seriously, and provide your child a fresh perspective and new respect for his/her own traditions. Make it clear to your guest that he or she is welcome to participate and that at a seder every question is a good question.

You may not wish to turn your whole seder into a puppet show geared toward preschoolers, however. That approach may alienate older children and even send the message that Passover is not for adults. There are ways to achieve a balance. If, for example, most of the children at the table are very young, you might consider having two totally different seders, the first night given over to teaching children, and the second geared to adult consideration of the meaning of the holiday—which might even entail hiring a baby-sitter.

Another strategy is to excuse children during abstract discussions or longer readings from the *haggadah*. You can summon the kids back for all the high points—the cups of wine, the Four Questions, the plagues, the Hillel sandwich, etc.—by banging a drum, sounding a gong, or blowing a whistle.

Of course, if you are attending a seder at someone else's home, you have less control over the proceedings. Some people have fixed expectations about what should happen at a seder and how children ought to behave; in the past, children were expected to sit still and be quiet while the adults read every word in the *haggadah*. But do not assume your hosts' resistance to change; many a seder has been transformed for the sake of young guests—especially grandchildren. If you are going to be a guest at a seder, ask whether you can add some special elements for your children, such as puppets, song-sheets, or other props.

Selecting and Using a Haggadah A *haggadah* (literally, "a telling") is a book that contains the seder liturgy.[45] Many *haggadot* (the plural) also include a great deal of information about everything from the history of Passover to the details of setting the seder table. Choosing a *haggadah* that's right for your family is one of the most crucial decisions in seder planning.

There are dozens of *haggadot* from which to choose. Some are mostly Hebrew, others are mostly English, with just a few transliterated Hebrew blessings. There are lavish, museum-quality *haggadot*, with long scholarly footnotes, and cartoon versions with pages to color and puzzles to do. Several *haggadot* are geared to families with young children and some provide helpful "menus" to help you construct the right seder for your family.

In addition to bookstores and libraries, you can often find a good selection of *haggadot* in a temple or Jewish community center book fair held just prior to Passover. Your rabbi, cantor, or temple educator can also make suggestions.

Once you've made a choice, get enough copies for the table. Concentration and participation is much easier when every person has a book, but at least try to make sure that no more than two people have to share.

Whichever *haggadah* you use, take time to edit or customize the service. Decide which readings to include this year and which to leave out until the children are older. Think of your *haggadah* as a series of stage directions or prompts, and the seder itself as an improvisation.

Are there sections you want to do in unison or responsively? Participation always makes for a livelier seder, but "participation" does not necessarily mean going around the table taking turns reading from the *haggadah*. Pick some readings you hope will act as springboards for discussion, and think of open-ended questions to ask.

The leader(s) should annotate their copy of the *haggadah*, with notes for where to pause for the puppet show, when to serve the next course, when to ask what you hope will be a provocative question. The leader's copy can help you plan next year's seder: Do we need to serve the soup earlier? Can we learn a new melody for this song?

One way to increase participation is to share leadership of the seder by assigning sections of the *haggadah* to guests in advance. Photocopy the pages each person will lead in his or her own style: with music, or props, or alternate translations, or a debate proposition.

It is also possible to create your own *haggadah* by copying readings, poems, artwork, and songs from various sources. Though time-consuming, this process is perfect for customizing the seder to children's developmental stages and can be updated as they grow. Young children can contribute artwork; older kids can help put the service together, write poems, and take part in leading the seder. A collection of family *haggadot* (with snapshots from each year) can become a priceless record.

The Meal and the Menu   The Passover seder is the culinary high point of the Jewish calendar. There is no feast to match it. Main courses vary from household to household, of course, but among Ashkenazic Jews, roast chicken or turkey, or beef brisket is traditional. Sephardic Jews often serve roast lamb.[46] Spring foods, such as asparagus and strawberries, recall the seasonal aspect of the holiday. There are many Passover cookbooks, and all Jewish cookbooks have Passover chapters with special recipes and menus.

There is a danger, however, in too much focus on the food. Cooks should not feel too overwhelmed or resentful to enjoy the seder, which is why potluck seders are now common. With large crowds, some hosts even hire caterers to cook or just to help serve and clean up.

A long-standing issue around the meal comes from the custom of eating only after the readings and table rituals are complete. When people are hungry, reading and talking through the progress of the *haggadah* becomes an ordeal—especially for children. One way to avoid rushing to dinner is to serve food during the first part of the seder. After the blessing for *karpas* (green vegetables), it is "kosher" to eat; punctuate the ensuing rituals, blessings, and conversations with appetizers, hors d'oeuvres, and light finger foods.

Setting the Holiday Table The seder table is not just a place where you eat, it is an altar. Your dining room is not just a dining room anymore—it is a stage set for the telling of a great story.

In many homes, the best linens and fanciest china appear to create the most beautiful meal of the entire year. Nevertheless, since the point of the seder is to engage children, this should not be an overly formal event. And indeed, the *haggadah* instructs us to recline at the seder, a posture reserved for free men in the ancient world and a custom preserved by placing cushions or pillows on the chairs. A young child who walks into the dining room and sees pillows and fancy dishes is sure to be struck by the change and ask what it's all about—which is the goal of Passover.

Another way to reenact the Exodus is to postpone sitting down at the table and hold the premeal rituals in a den or family room. Sitting on couches or reclining on floor pillows changes the atmosphere from one of waiting for dinner to one of relaxed conversation. Set out some mats or tablecloths over the carpet, and munch on vegetables, olives, and other hors d'oeuvres during the early part of the seder. You can even hang sheets or bedspreads to create a "tent."

On the Table In addition to the candlesticks and kiddush cup used at other Jewish festival tables, the seder table calls for several more ritual items, including:

The Seder Plate   This plate, the centerpiece of the Passover table, holds six traditional items:

- A roasted shank bone from a lamb, to symbolize the ritual sacrifices brought to the Passover feast in Temple times. You can substitute a roasted chicken or turkey bone; vegetarians use a roasted root vegetable, such as a beet or turnip.
- A roasted egg—another reminder of sacrificial Temple practices, and a harbinger of springtime and rebirth.
- Bitter herbs, usually horseradish, to recall the harshness of slavery.
- Salt water—the tears shed by Hebrew slaves.
- *Karpas*—a green vegetable, often parsley or lettuce, to symbolize springtime. (Ashkenazic Jews sometimes use potatoes.)
- *Haroset*—a sweet paste of fruit, wine, and nuts, symbolizing the mortar the Israelites made.

Many liberal Jews now place an orange on the seder plate. This unusual addition begs the question (always a good thing) "Why an orange?" The answer is based on an apocryphal story from the 1970s, when a man is said to have opined, "Women belong in the rabbinate like an orange belongs on a seder plate." The story spread and with it oranges, which affirm the importance of women's roles in all areas of Jewish life.

Matzah Plate and Cover   Three *matzot* (plural of *matzah*) used during the seder are covered by a napkin or special *matzah* cloth with "pockets." The middle piece of *matzah*, which is called the *afikomen* (probably from a Greek word for "dessert") is eaten at the end of the meal.

Elijah's Cup   A goblet is filled with wine for the prophet, the legendary visitor who brings the promise of hope for the future. A brimming cup is an invitation to Elijah, in hopes that he will arrive and announce the redemption of the world at your seder. Alternately, Elijah's cup may be left empty and at an appropriate moment after the meal, passed around for everyone to fill with wine from their own glasses, to show that everyone must help to bring peace to the world.

Miriam's Cup   A goblet is filled with water—like the orange, this is a new ritual object that celebrates the role of Jewish women. Moses' sister,

Miriam, is associated with a mythic well whose water quenched the thirst of the desert wanderers. Miriam, it is written, led the Hebrew people in song when they escaped their Egyptian pursuers.

Wineglasses   The blessing and drinking of four cups of wine is an integral part of every seder.

Hand-washing Stations   Bowls of water, with a cup and hand-towel, at either end of the table.

Invite your children to help set the seder table and prepare the seder plate. Depending on their ages, they can make place cards for your guests, create a *matzah* cover, help grate horseradish root, mix *haroset* and form it into a pyramid, harvest parsley planted at Tu B'Shvat, watch the egg brown in the oven, pick out the best Jaffa orange at the grocery store, select three "perfect" sheets of *matzah* for the table, fill the cups for Elijah and Miriam.

The Structure of the Seder in Four Parts

Haggadot may vary, but the following elements are part of virtually all seders. The asterisks denote the most child-friendly moments. If you're letting the little ones come and go from the table, these are times to call them back to watch, listen, and participate. Remember: the seder is an outline. It's up to you to fill it in with meaning through storytelling, lively conversation, and laughter.

Part I: Introduction
*Candlelighting.
*Blessing over the first cup of wine (kiddush).
Shehechiyanu (the prayer for having reached this moment).
*Ceremonial hand-washing (no blessing).
Karpas—a blessing is recited over the green vegetable, which is then dipped into salt water and tasted by everyone.
(Suggestion: Serve finger foods/hors d'oeuvres and keep them on the table.)
Afikomen—the middle of the three *matzot* on the covered

plate is broken and the larger piece hidden so it may be searched out and "ransomed" later by the children.

Part II: Telling the Story

The *maggid* (story) begins with the line, "This is the bread of slavery which our ancestors ate in Egypt when they were slaves. Let all who are hungry come and eat."

Traditional *haggadot* don't actually contain the story of the Exodus; it was assumed that the leader(s) knew it and would tell it in their own words in ways their children could understand. Telling the story with dramatic flourishes, costumes, puppets, and flair makes it a high point for kids and adults.

*The Four Questions. Children's participation in the seder is crucial. Indeed, Maimonides instructed parents to do anything and everything—even remove the table—to get children to ask questions. At some point in history, the child's role was ritualized into these four questions, which the youngest son was expected to recite or chant.

The questions are: Why do we eat matzah? Why do we eat bitter herbs? Why do we dip our vegetables twice? Why do we recline? (In other words: What are we doing here?)

Applaud any and all questions from the children at your seder table.

(Suggestion: Serve the soup.)

*The Four Children. This is a parable about how parents should answer children's questions in a fashion appropriate to each one's abilities. The traditional version mentions sons only and describes four types of sons as wise, wicked (or stubborn), simple, and one who is too young to ask. Contemporary *haggadot* often change the four to include daughters as well as sons.

*The Ten Plagues. The list of calamities that befell the Egyptians as punishment for Pharaoh's unwillingness to let the Hebrews go is a dramatic moment in the seder. As each plague is named, every participant takes a drop of wine from his or her glass and drops it on a plate, symbolic of the sufferings visited upon the Egyptians, and of our sympathetic self-denial.

*"*Dayenu*"—a song that lists the miracles God performed to free the Jewish people from slavery.

Part III: Blessings and Meal
*Blessing over the second cup of wine.
*Ceremonial hand-washing, with the blessing.
**Motzi* and the blessing over *matzah*.
*Blessing over the bitter herbs.
*Hillel sandwich—a mixture of *maror* (bitter horseradish) and *haroset* (sweet nut paste) is prepared and eaten on *matzah*, to simultaneously recall the sorrow of slavery while savoring the sweetness of freedom.
*The rest of the meal is served.

Part IV: Finale
*The *afikomen* is "bought back" from children, and a piece is eaten by everyone.
*Blessings after the meal—*Birkat Hamazon*.
*Blessing for the third cup of wine.
*The door is opened for the prophet Elijah.
*Singing.
*Blessing for the fourth cup of wine.
**"L'shanah ha-ba'a b'Yerushalayim"*—the phrase, set to music, means "Next year in Jerusalem" and expresses the hope that next year all will be free and none will be enslaved.

Seder Fun with Children   There are so many ways to help your children feel that the seder is theirs.

Arts and Crafts   Kids can make a welcome sign for the front door, or drape the door with a wide red ribbon to symbolize the lamb's blood that saved the Jews that first night of "passing over."

Using a large white handkerchief and fabric paint, make *matzah* covers as "seder favors" for every family taking part in your seder, or decorate pillowcases for reclining during the seder.

A seder plate can be made out of clay, or from a paper plate decorated and covered with clear plastic wrap. Kids can create a whole set of miniature Passover ritual objects out of clay or recycled objects, so stuffed animals and dolls can have their own seder. These and other projects can be made in advance of the seder, or, if the grown-up talk gets to be too much, during the meal at a separate table.

Set Up a Tent   During parts of the seder that don't hold their interest, create a special space under a table or sheet to give children a place to pretend they are Israelites. Set out crafts or games inside. Let little ones fall asleep inside.

Bring the Story to Life   Encourage children to do skits, puppet shows, or pantomimes to tell the story of Moses and the Exodus from Egypt. There are lots of ways to do this; the story can be scripted, with parts drawn from a hat (Miriam, Moses, frogs, God, Pharaoh, narrator, and so on). Supply a costume box or let children make masks for each role. Parents can either participate or be the appreciative audience.

Jazz Up the Plagues   Collect origami frogs, plastic bugs, red food coloring dropped into a clear bowl of water (for blood), a burned-out lightbulb or dark glasses (for darkness), rice (for lice) Ping-Pong balls (hail), bubble wrap (boils), toy barnyard animals (cattle disease). With older kids and teenagers at the table, go around the table and name current plagues: AIDS, homelessness, poverty, cancer, racism, anti-Semitism, pollution, etc.

Get Up and Move   Too much sitting is hard for children—and grown-ups, too. At the point in the story when the Israelites leave Egypt, Sephardic Jews get up and walk around the table; in some households, they also "lash" one another with the greens of leeks or scallions, in imitation of the taskmaster's whip. When the Hebrews rejoice at having reached the other side of the Sea of Reeds, put on some music and dance.

Fun with Afikomen   The seder ends when everyone eats a bite of *afikomen*. There is a long-standing tradition that children steal this otherwise ordinary piece of *matzah*, and then sell it back to the grown-ups. There are several ways to "ransom" the *afikomen*. You can hide pieces of *matzah* all over the house—one for every child under the age of thirteen—and make it a game of "You're getting warmer." Or you can have a treasure hunt with clues. When the children find the *afikomen*, you can buy it back with a gift rather than the traditional silver dollars.

Do not make *afikomen* presents too elaborate: stick to simple things, like kaleidoscopes, puzzles, puppets, or extra-soft stuffed animals named Pesach, Miriam, or Nisan (the name of the Hebrew month).

Laughter   Give a silly prize to the first person who spills their wine. Ask everyone to bring a Passover-related joke. Have a contest to see who can be the fastest in reciting all the verses to "Dayenu" or "Who Knows One?" ("Echad Mi Yodeah").

Celebrate freedom by eating dessert first! Start with a chocolate *matzah*.

Singing   All *haggadot* contain lyrics, and some even have music. While there's nothing like singing to make a meal festive, this fizzles if only one or two people know the songs. Play tapes or CDs in the weeks before Passover, so everyone in your family becomes familiar with a few tunes. Encourage people to sing "ya-da-da" if they don't know the words. Hand out song-sheets and include English tunes that most people are likely to know, like "If I Had a Hammer." If you have a piano or guitar on hand, encourage accompaniment.

In the spirit of keeping your seder light, include a song parody, such as "There's No Seder Like Our Seder" (to the tune of "There's No Business Like Show Business").[47]

Elijah   Opening the door for Elijah is one of the most dramatic moments of any seder for children. Send one or all the kids to open the door and peer into the night. When they return to the table, ask if anyone saw a miracle. Look at the wine in his cup and see if some is missing.

Refraining from Leavened Food   After the seders, Pesach continues with a personal and family "fast" from all leavened foods. This relatively modest form of self-denial recalls the poverty of slavery in Egypt and the privations faced by the Hebrews as they wandered in the desert after leaving. Another interpretation of the fast from *hametz* sees yeast as a metaphor for the "evil inclination" (*yetzer harah*) or an inflated sense of self-importance. Passover becomes an opportunity to rededicate ourselves to living a good and balanced life.

The Jewish dietary laws, called *kashrut,* change during Passover to include a new category of foods, *hametz,* which describes all foods to be avoided during the holiday. *Hametz* (literally "fermentation") includes wheat, oats, rye, barley, spelt and millet and food made with yeast or any leavening agent, and foods that can easily ferment. According to Ashkenazic (Eastern European) custom, *hametz* also includes beans, peas, lentils, rice, corn, and legumes. Sephardic Jews, however, eat all of these during Passover.

Some families get ready for Passover with a thorough spring cleaning to make sure every square inch of their home is free of *hametz.* This process is especially intense in the kitchen; some Jews discard all food that contains *hametz,* donating unopened boxes and cans to charity. Others store their *hametz* (which includes beer and other liquors, and prepared foods, such as ketchup, vinegars, and confectionery sugar, which contains cornstarch) in a box or cupboard that is marked and taped shut all week.[48]

Over the centuries, Passover traditions came to include a complete changeover in the kitchen, so that only special kosher-for-Passover plates, silverware, linens, pots and pans could be used. The dramatic transformation of the home at Pesach is an enduring memory for children, who look forward to the annual appearance of the Passover dishes. (Glass dishware is favored because it can be used for either meat or milk meals.)

Some liberal Jews observe the fast from leavened foods by changing their diets without changing dishes; they simply buy and eat nothing that contains *hametz.*

In supermarkets that serve Jewish communities, special Passover shelves are stocked with packaged foods designated "Kosher for Passover," which means they were prepared under rabbinical supervision. This display may not include everything you need during the week, which means you'll have to read labels extra carefully.

Ask your children to act as "detectives," checking labels for leavening agents. As you walk up and down the aisles, make a game out of your shopping list: Will granulated sugar be okay for Passover or not? What about mustard? Let them pick out some special treats for school lunches in the Passover section.

The spring cleaning rituals for Passover can be a lot of work for adults and even for children who are enlisted to clean their rooms and help with the changeover to Passover dishes. Reward yourselves, and your kids, by adding some fun to the project:

- Put fresh spring flowers in as many rooms as possible.
- Move the furniture around, or change the placement of artwork on the walls.
- Buy new toothbrushes for everyone in their favorite colors.
- When you've finished all the work of making your house "kosher for Pesach," do something fun to celebrate. Visit your children's favorite playground for an hour; toast yourselves with milk shakes served in wine glasses.

Starting The ancient ritual called *Bidekat Hametz* seems as though it was invented with children in mind. This symbolic search for the last leavened food in the house is a game of hide-and-seek, hunting for strategically hidden crusts or wayward Cheerios. (Some people save a piece of last year's *afikomen* for this purpose.) Turn the lights off and, using a candle or flashlight, brush the crumbs onto a paper plate, using a feather if possible. The night before or the morning of the first seder, the crumbs are taken outside and burned. Alternately, you might consider feeding them to the birds.

The blessings for this ritual are found in most *haggadot* and include a wonderful disclaimer that demonstrates how cleaning for Passover is really a symbolic act:

> All *hametz* in my possession, whether I have seen it or not, and whether I have removed it or not, shall be nullified and ownerless as the dust of the earth.

After the *hametz* is ritually removed, it is traditional to avoid eating bread or *matzah* until the seder.

Feeding Children During Passover Generally, children follow their parents' example in keeping kosher for Passover without much fuss, especially if they are presented with it matter-of-factly: "During *Pesach* the whole family eats differently." For the most part, kids do accommodate to change, although some have an easier time accepting it than others. Some parents worry that a kosher-for-Passover kitchen will be an impossible hardship on children who subsist entirely on breakfast cereal and spaghetti, but most survive without a problem, even if they wind up eating a diet heavy on kosher-for-Passover brownies and potato chips for the week.

Sticking to this kind of rule is harder in families where children generally have a great deal of choice in what they eat the rest of the year, or where parents are beginners to Passover rules. In some households parents permit children to eat a regular diet even if the adults are avoiding *hametz*. If this is the case in your home, be sure to point out and explain why you are not eating bread or cereal. And you might explain that while fasting of any kind is really for grown-ups, when they are old enough to choose, they may want to join you.

School-age children who attend secular schools are faced with a particular challenge at lunchtime. Non-Jewish friends may be curious and want a taste of *matzah;* some will like it enough to want to trade for their regular sandwich. Other non-Jewish kids may think the whole thing "weird" and tease. This is one of many good reasons to offer to visit your child's classroom to explain the holiday and to hand out samples of *matzah* and other holiday foods.

Lunch menus can be a real challenge for kids who don't love peanut-butter-and-*matzah* sandwiches or yogurt. Offer hard-boiled eggs, or *matzah* crackers with favorite cheese or nut spreads, or dips such as hummus or cream cheese. Ask the principal if your child can reheat a precooked, stuffed baked potato, or a portion of last night's dinner in the microwave. And be sure to pack fruit and dessert.

Passover Eating for Kids

- Have them make a poster of things the family won't be eating during Passover with a collage of advertisements for bread, pizza, etc., and draw a universal "No" sign over it.
- Pack marshmallows and chocolate-covered *matzah* in their school lunches.
- If your child enjoys only certain Passover foods, indulge her in *matzah-brei* (the *matzah* equivalent of French toast, served with maple syrup or brown sugar) at breakfast; *matzah* lasagna (layers

of tomato sauce, vegetables and cheeses between water-softened matzah) for supper; *matzah* with cream cheese at lunch.

- Encourage all forms of fruit to prevent constipation. Serve fruit salads, smoothies, sorbets, strawberry sundaes, etc.
- Encourage children to participate in Passover cooking and baking; this makes it more likely they will eat the muffins that taste "different."
- To counter any sense of deprivation, serve special desserts as the week progresses.
- Rediscover the joys of potatoes; homemade French fries might become an annual Passover treat.
- Plan a potluck Passover meal in the middle of the week with other families who have children around the same age as yours; it's not only fun for the kids, it makes a nice break for the cooks.

Ending the Fast   Passover starts with a bang, but in most families it tends to peter out with a whimper. Any Passover "break-fast" meal can become a special memory for children regardless of the menu simply by doing the same thing every year. Just as you build anticipation for the first taste of *matzah,* remind your children about how delicious it will be to bite into your special "Passover's Over Macaroni and Cheese." Likewise, if your family's custom is to go out to the Lotus Blossom Chinese Restaurant at the end of Pesach, that will become "traditional" and children will be surprised to learn that other people eat pizza at the end of the fast.

If the cupboard is bare of forbidden foods, go for a celebratory trip to the market to stock up on breads, cereal, pasta, and cookies. Take a ride to a local bakery and buy loaves in different varieties for a bread tasting.

A Moroccan Jewish custom called *maimuna*[49] offers another model for concluding Passover. Served on tables decorated with flowers and wheat stalks, traditional *maimuna* feasts feature a special pancake, or crêpe, called *muflita.* But whether your *maimuna* meal consists of homemade pancakes or take-out pizza, it's a wonderful meal to share with friends, family, and members of your congregation. Say or sing the *Hamotzi* (at the top of your lungs, for fun) and then take time to savor the taste of leavened bread.

Synagogue Observance   The first one or two days and the last one or two days of Passover are festival days. Some Jews refrain from working or going to school and attend holiday services, including a memorial *Yizkor* service on the last day, when loved ones who have died are recalled.

Some congregations hold a community seder, which ensures that everyone has a place to celebrate. Interfaith seders and intercommunity seders such as Black-Jewish and Jewish-Irish seders, are teaching-and-fellowship events; these are usually held before the holiday or on one of the intermediate days of the week.

PASSOVER: AGES AND STAGES

Infants and Toddlers   No matter how early you start, the seder always goes long past babies' bedtimes. On any other night, you might leave tiny ones at home with a sitter, but most parents want their babies with them for seder, even if they won't understand what's going on.

Toddlers will respond to the excitement, but the seder will be beyond their ability to understand. Parents with children under the age of three should expect to spend a good part of the seder away from the table. If you're going to feel deprived by this reality, consider hiring a sitter to supervise when children need to get up and play.

Preschool Children   This is a prime age for learning about Passover. From age three to six, children will feel the anticipation and notice how the seder table is different from a regular dinner table—or even a Shabbat table.

In a way, the seder really is geared to the preschool mind. The Four Questions in the *haggadah* are, developmentally speaking, questions that might be asked by a preschool child who is still learning the basics. (By the time a child is seven, he or she will know the answer to the question, "Why do we eat *matzah* tonight?") Preschoolers who delight in imaginative play and pretend can enter the story of the Exodus wholeheartedly through dramatics, puppets, and the like, which are great ways to keep them engaged and at the table.

Try to get young children to nap in the afternoon with the promise they can stay up as late as they wish; and if they conk out in the living room while the adults finish the seder, that's fine, too. It makes a great picture and a sweet memory.

School-age Children   By this age, children enrolled in any kind of formal Jewish schooling will be learning about Passover in class. Many teachers help their students prepare for the formal recitation of the Four Questions in Hebrew, which is a coming-of-age moment acknowledging that a child is mature and accomplished enough to take part in the ritual. The custom in many homes has been for the youngest child who was able, to stand and perform alone. For kids who enjoy being the center of attention, this is a great opportunity to bask in adult adulation; it is, however, an ordeal for shy children. Alternately, the questions can be shared by all the pre–bar and bat mitzvah kids, either taking turns or in unison.

Although the questions themselves have become formulaic, this is a prime moment to stop for a conversation about questions. Are the questions in the *haggadah* good questions? Can you come up with better ones? If a Martian were seated at the table, what question would he or she ask?

Children should be included as serious participants wherever possible. Do not condescend. Everyone deserves a respectful hearing, regardless of age. And while no one should be forced to participate, make sure it feels safe to offer an opinion.

School-age children run the gamut in their ability to sit and participate. Some kids will want to be at the table throughout, but others may find it boring beyond endurance. Some families permit all children to take breaks; you can set up a Passover video in another room, or put out arts-and-crafts materials. Kids can be summoned back with a gong or a whistle at key moments in the seder.

Consider bringing Passover to your child's public-school classroom. Not only is it a more important holiday than Hanukkah, it is more fun to present and explain. Bring in a real horseradish root and let everyone taste the bitterness of slavery. Explain why *haroset,* which symbolizes the mortar used by the Hebrew slaves, was turned into something sweet. If your child is willing and knows the Four Questions in Hebrew, have her chant or recite it—and make sure you provide a translation.

Since questions are the core of the seder, invite your child's classmates to come up with questions and hand out pieces of chocolate-covered *matzah* as reward for the funniest, the hardest, the most thoughtful question.

Adolescents   Teenagers have a wide variety of reactions to the seder. They may want to sit with the adults and assume a grown-up role as full participants. Others may prefer to come and go, to help supervise the little kids. Although you can't force it, there are several ways to encourage your teenager's participation. Invite local college students to your seder, and suggest your son or daughter invite a friend to your table. Ask if s/he would like to lead part of the seder.

Teenagers who attend secular schools will be making their own decisions about observing the fast from *hametz*, at least insofar as what they eat outside your home. Although you can't enforce your choices, you can certainly raise questions—and thus awareness—about theirs just by asking, "What's it like in the cafeteria over Passover? Do they put out *matzah* for the kids?" Or, "Do kids who bring *matzah* from home get teased about it?"

BOOKS FOR CHILDREN

The Carp in the Bathtub, by Barbara Cohen (Lothrop, 1972). Leah and Harry make friends with the fish that Mamma is going to cook for Passover.

Matza Ball Fairy, by Carla Heymsfeld (UAHC Press, 1996). Lighter-than-air dumplings for the seder.

Miriam's Cup: A Passover Story, by Fran Manushkin (Scholastic Press, 1998). Retelling the story from the perspective of Miriam, Moses' sister, with an explanation of the new seder tradition of the *kos Miryam* (Miriam's cup).

Only Nine Chairs, by Deborah Uchill Miller (Kar-Ben Copies, 1982). A "tall tale" about what happens if there aren't enough chairs for the seder. Preschool and up.

VIDEOS FOR CHILDREN

The Animated Haggadah (Scopus Films, 1985, 1987).
A Rugrats Passover (VHS, 1995).
Prince of Egypt (Dreamworks, 1998).

BOOKS FOR PARENTS

Keeping Passover: Everything You Need to Know to Bring the Ancient Tradition to Life and to Create Your Own Passover Celebration, by Ira Steingroot (HarperCollins, 1995).

The New York Times Passover Cookbook, by Linda Anister and Joan Nathan (William Morrow, 1999).

The Passover Gourmet, by Nira Rousso (Adama Books, 1987).

Family-friendly Haggadot

A Children's Haggadah, by Howard I. Bogot and Robert J. Orkand (Central Conference of American Rabbis, 1994). Stunning illustrations by Devis Grebu in a very simple seder.

A Family Haggadah, by Shoshana Silberman (Kar-Ben Copies, 1987). Contains two versions: one for use with little kids, another for school-age children and young teens.

We Tell It to Our Children: A Haggadah for Seders with Young Children, by Mary Ann Barrows Wark (Mt. Zion Hebrew Congregation Rabbis' Publication Fund and Mensch Makers Press, 1984). To order: 1588 Northrop, St. Paul, MN 55108. Funny song parodies are a highlight, and the leader's guide contains stick-puppet cutouts.

A Different Night: The Family Participation Seder, Noam Zion and David Dishon (The Shalom Hartman Institute, 1997). To order: Haggadahs-R-Us, 1888 South Compton, Cleveland Heights, OH 44118, or www.thumpers@apk.net). A remarkable resource if you take time to edit and select. A "Leader's Guide" is available, as is a "Seder Planner" that gives you a form to make an itinerary for your seder.

A Night of Questions: A Passover Haggadah, edited by Rabbi Joy Levitt and Rabbi Michael Strassfeld. (Reconstructionist Press, 2000). To order: call 877-573-7827 (toll-free).

YOM HASHOAH, YOM HAATZMA'UT, AND LAG B'OMER

Yom HaShoah (Holocaust Remembrance Day) and Yom HaAtzma'ut (Israel Independence Day) are relatively new and public commemorations. Although there are really no home-based traditions to them, they provide children with a living connection to the two crucial events in twentieth-century Jewish history that changed the world and shape Jewish consciousness. Together, they echo the theme of Passover, they move from darkness to light, from slavery to freedom.

Holocaust Remembrance Day is observed on the twenty-seventh of Nisan, twelve days after the start of Passover. Israel Independence Day is celebrated eight days later, on the fifth of Iyar—the Hebrew date corresponding to May 14, 1948, the date Israel became a sovereign nation.[50]

Yom HaShoah   Holocaust Remembrance Day may be the most difficult of all Jewish observances for parents. But keeping alive the memory of those who died in the Holocaust—and the resolve to never let it happen again—is a sacred obligation that Jewish parents must pass on to their children.

Like other difficult subjects, some parents try to protect their children from knowledge of the horror and postpone discussing it. But the Holocaust echoes through the Jewish universe in many subtle and unconscious ways that children learn even before they know the facts. The toll of the Nazi's "final solution" is recalled at Passover seders and at Yom Kippur services, in references at religious school and the dinner table. In families directly touched by the Shoah (the Hebrew word for "Holocaust"), children may have heard stories or seen photographs of relatives who were killed in concentration camps or while fighting in World War II. By grade school, most children recognize "Holocaust" as a Jewish term and identify the Nazi swastika as an emblem of evil that relates to them personally.

Children who ask about the Holocaust at any age should be given an appropriate answer. To say, "You're too young to hear," can make children very anxious. Not knowing what the nightmare is about does not make the nightmare go away. While very young children need to be protected from the gruesome details, they will be better reassured by a simple explanation than silence: "The Holocaust was a time when it was very dangerous to be Jewish because of some very bad people. These people, called Nazis, hated Jews so much, they wanted to get rid of us all. But they didn't. A war was fought to stop the Nazis, and the Jewish people are still here today."

There are many excellent books about the Holocaust for children as young as six. Children in grades five and up—in secular school as well as in Jewish schools—are often assigned to read works of fiction based on historical accounts of the Holocaust.

Yom HaShoah is observed in a variety of public commemorations. Synagogue liturgies are varied, but often use testimony from Holocaust victims, survivors, and witnesses in addition to prayers and poems and psalms. Services may upset some children as they witness adults crying or talking with great sadness. However, they will ultimately be comforted to see the adults recover and smile after the service. Older children may be consoled to find adults confirming their own feelings after being moved by Holocaust reading or classroom conversation. However, never force a child or teenager to attend Yom HaShoah services.

In addition to religious services, many cities and towns hold secular, civic ceremonies in memory of victims of the Holocaust. These solemn events usually include testimony from survivors and are attended by public officials and clergy of all faiths. If you are planning to go, tell your children about it and (if appropriate to their age and maturity) offer them the opportunity to accompany you.

In Israel, all public entertainments are closed on what is there called Holocaust and Resistance Remembrance Day. At noon, a three-minute siren blast is heard throughout the country. People stop whatever they are doing—even getting out of cars and buses—and everyone stands in silence.

Yom HaShoah with Children

- Light six memorial candles, one for each of the six million Jews who were killed.
- Light a seventh candle in memory of non-Jews who were killed in the Holocaust, or to honor the righteous non-Jews who risked their lives to help Jews.
- Plant six yellow tulips in your garden, or put six yellow tulips in a vase.
- Lay six flowers in memory of Jewish victims at a local Holocaust memorial.
- Read a book about the Holocaust with your children. If your son or daughter has been assigned a Holocaust novel in school, read it and talk about the characters and why they did what they did.
- Give *tzedakah*.

BOOKS FOR CHILDREN

Parents should preview these titles before giving them to a child. Read them together with younger children.

Grades 3 and Up

The Number on My Grandfather's Arm, by David A. Adler (Union of American Hebrew Congregations, 1987). A clear, first-person narrative that avoids explicit photos or graphic descriptions.

Promise of a New Spring, by Gerda Klein (Rossell Books, 1981). An introduction to the subject of the Holocaust for young readers.

Grades 5 and Up

Number the Stars, by Lois Lowry (Houghton Mifflin 1989). Fictionalized account of the Danish rescue of the Jews.

Island on Bird Street, by Uri Orlev (Houghton Mifflin, 1983). A twelve-year-old boy hides for five months in an unnamed ghetto.

Diary of a Young Girl, by Anne Frank (Doubleday, 1967). The classic, tragic memoir by the Dutch Jewish teen.

Junior High and Up

The Sunflower, by Simon Wiesenthal (Schocken Books, 1998). A dying German officer confesses to killing Jews in the Holocaust and begs a Jewish survivor for forgiveness.

The Devil's Arithmetic, by Jane Yolen (Viking Penguin, 1988). A novel about an American girl who time-travels to a Polish shtetl in the 1940s.

Yom HaAtzma'ut   After nearly two thousand years in exile, the establishment of a Jewish state in the land of Israel transformed the Jewish world and connected Jews around the world in support of its existence. While Israel Independence Day is celebrated without religious ceremony as a secular festival, the connection to the land is rooted in the Torah, where God promises Abraham, "I give all the land that you see to you and your offspring forever."[51] This theme is reiterated annually at the Passover seder, which concludes with the words, "Next year in Jerusalem" ("*L'shanah ha-ba'a b'Yerushalayim*").

In Israel, Yom HaAtzma'ut is celebrated with flags, band concerts, fireworks, picnics, and street parties. Israel also observes Yom HaZikaron (Remembrance Day), the day before Yom HaAtzma'ut, to honor the memory of those who died defending the State of Israel. Yom Yerushalayim (Jerusalem Day), three weeks after Israel Independence Day, celebrates the reunification of Jerusalem by Israeli forces in 1967.

In America, Israel Independence Day is celebrated in synagogues and Jewish community centers with Israeli dancing, film festivals, Israeli foods, and lectures. In some cities there are also parades, street fairs, and rallies.

Jewish supplementary schools and day schools often focus some part of their curricula on Israel and conclude the day with a party.

Participating as a family in congregational and/or communal observance is a great way to reinforce the idea of *klal Yisrael*, the community of Israel, the common bonds among Jews around the world, and the unique connection to the land of Israel.

Celebrating Israel Independence Day with Your Children

- Attend celebratory events in your community and/or synagogue. If your temple is not running a special program, check listings and see what other congregations are doing.
- Make an Israeli flag out of blue and white construction paper.
- Call or e-mail family or friends in Israel.
- Arrange for an Israeli e-mail pal for your son or daughter.
- Eat at an Israeli restaurant; cook an Israeli meal; buy Israeli fruit or candy.
- Look at pictures from your last trip to Israel, or if you haven't been there yet, plan an itinerary with a map and guide book.
- Read a picture book set in or about Israel with younger children. Give older children a book about or set in Israel.
- Give *tzedakah* to an Israeli charity.
- Rent an Israeli video, or the Hollywood classic, *Exodus*.
- Learn to say some new words in Hebrew.

BOOKS FOR CHILDREN

Kids Love Israel, Israel Loves Kids, by Barbara Sofer (Kar-Ben Copies, 1996). For updates and changes, go to www.karben.com.

A Kids' Catalog of Israel, by Chaya M. Burstein (Jewish Publication Society, 1988).

Lag B'Omer Lag B'Omer is the thirty-third (*lag* in Hebrew) day in the counting of the *omer,* an ancient measure of grain. In ancient Israel, the

Jewish people would send one *omer* of barley per day to the Temple in Jerusalem for a period of forty-nine days, beginning on the second day of Passover and ending with the holiday of Shavuot.

Over the course of Jewish history, the *omer* represented a period of semimourning during which people would not cut their hair, and weddings were not celebrated. The thirty-third day of the *omer*-counting was a time-out from these restrictions and thus became a favorite date for weddings.

In Israel the holiday is celebrated with bonfires and barbecues. In America, Lag B'Omer is the Jewish "field day." Synagogues hold congregation-wide family picnics, with softball or volleyball games, three-legged races and other outdoor fun.

Books for children
Jewish Sports Legends: The International Jewish Sports Hall of Fame, by Joseph M. Siegman (Brassey's Inc., 1997).

SUMMER

SHAVUOT AND TISHA B'AV

These two summer holidays are unfamiliar to many American Jews. Since they tend to fall near or after the end of the school year, Shavuot and Tisha B'Av are often not given much attention in Jewish curricula. And because they lack a tradition of family gatherings and home-based customs (at least in Ashkenazic culture), they lack the emotional connections attached to other holidays in the Jewish calendar.

The summer can, however, be a time for creative Jewish family celebrations. Shavuot observances can be meaningful and lovely. And Shabbat is especially sweet when the days are longer and the weekly schedule is more relaxed. You can make a date to watch the sun set on Friday nights at a nearby park, or from your own window.

Shabbat on vacation—in a distant country, in a seashore cottage, or in a tent—can be a focal point for Jewish memories. Bring along a set of traveling candlesticks or create your own out of a pair of beautiful seashells;

make kiddush in a hotel room; see if you can find a challah in the local stores, and if there is no challah, buy the best loaf of bread you can find and make a blessing over that. Shabbat on the road can be a welcome time-out from too much sightseeing, a way to gather everyone in the family at the table for a real meal, and a lesson in the portability of Jewish tradition and ritual.

Shavuot The name of this holiday, which celebrates the giving of the Torah, is the Hebrew word for "weeks." Seven weeks after the Hebrew slaves left Egypt—seven weeks after Passover—they were given the Torah, ("teaching" or "guidance") which transformed them into the Jewish people. Just as Passover encourages every Jew to feel as though he or she is a freed slave, Shavuot encourages us to imagine ourselves as receiving the Torah at Sinai.[52]

Shavuot takes place in late May or early June. It begins with a festival meal and starts with the blessings for candles, kiddush, *Shehechiyanu,* and *Hamotzi.* Shavuot meals are traditionally dairy, a custom that may date back to our days as shepherds, when the holiday coincided with a spring-time abundance of milk.

Ashkenazic Jews cook blintzes, crêpes filled with a sweet cheese mix-ture. Fruit soups are another favorite for this seasonal holiday table, and cheesecake is the traditional dessert in many families.

It is customary to have two loaves of challah on the table. Sometimes these are baked side-by-side so they will look something like the two "tablets" Moses brought down from Mount Sinai; the Torah portion for the Shavuot morning service includes the reading of the Ten Utterances ("Commandments" is really a misleading translation).

For many congregations, Shavuot (or the Shabbat closest to it) has be-come linked to congregational life-cycle milestones. Some synagogues hold a confirmation or graduation from the temple religious school. And be-cause it is traditional to read the Book of Ruth on Shavuot, some temples have a special service then that acknowledges or welcomes new converts to Judaism.

Ruth, who became part of the Jewish people not by birth but by choice, embodies the Jewish notion of revelation as a covenant—a contract that requires the consent and participation of each individual Jew. The story of Ruth has probably never been more relevant than it is today, when religious affiliation and practice are increasingly a matter of individual self-expression, and converts to Judaism are such a visible and vital part of the community.

Shavuot celebrations can provide powerful lessons for children. Watching high school kids at a confirmation ceremony is a demonstration that Jewish learning continues after bar or bat mitzvah, and makes the high school program something to look forward to. Seeing converts welcomed to the community—not only formally, during the service, but also during the festivities at the Oneg Shabbat or kiddush afterwards—is a vivid demonstration that Judaism is an open community and a worthy choice.

In many synagogues, Shavuot evening services are followed by a study session called a *tikkun*. This custom dates back to the sixteenth century, when the mystics who lived in the city of Safed in Israel (then Palestine) stayed up all night long to study the Bible and the *Zohar*, a mystical text. The goal of the session is to be spiritually prepared to hear and accept the Ten Utterances at services in the morning.

Obviously, late-night study is a grown-up activity. But when possible, bringing children to a *tikkun* (with sleeping bags, snacks, and toys) gives them the chance to see adults enjoying Jewish study in an informal setting, and gives them a new way to "own" their own synagogues.

Celebrating Shavuot with Children

- Put fresh roses in your children's rooms.
- Bake your own challahs in the shape of the two "tablets."
- Make yogurt cheese.
- Check the *mezuzot* on your doorways; open them up and show your children the scroll (the *klaf*) inside, which contains a passage from Deuteronomy (see above, pages 19–20).
- Make a Shavuot *tikkun* at home by inviting other families to read stories or watch Bible movies on video. And let children stay up extra late.
- Arrange for a family visit to see your temple's Torah. Point out the "clothes" and "jewelry" that the Torah wears and unroll it to the Ten Utterances.

- Use a calligraphy pen to copy the first words (in Hebrew, if you can) of Genesis.
- Read over the Ten Utterances (Commandments). Talk about which is the hardest one to follow, and which is the easiest.

Tisha B'Av   The ninth day of the summer month of Av (in Hebrew: Tisha B'Av) usually falls in late July or early August. This is a day of mourning for the destruction of the Temple in Jerusalem, first in the year 586 B.C.E. and again six centuries later in 70 C.E. Over the course of Jewish history, other losses and dispersions were commemorated on this day, which is why weddings are not held on or just prior to the ninth of Av.

Some congregations hold somber, candlelit observances for Tisha B'Av that include chanting from the biblical Book of Lamentations and sitting on the floor—a visible symbol of being laid low by grief. This is the only holiday, apart from Yom Kippur, that is observed with a full day of fasting. Children who attend Jewish summer camps are often more familiar with Tisha B'Av than their parents, since many camps plan programs to commemorate this, the only Jewish holiday of the summer season.

Chapter 5

Conflict

- I hate Hebrew school!
- You never go to temple with me.
- You're *not* wearing ripped jeans to services.
- Why can't you get home for Shabbat dinner on Fridays?
- Please don't wear your *kippah* to the baseball game.
- I don't want to go to Grandpa's seder this year.

Happy couples argue. Healthy families bicker. Much as we wish our homes could be peaceful all the time, conflict is normal. Happy, healthy Jewish families clash about sharing housework and finishing homework, and also about going to Shabbat services and choosing a synagogue to join.

Tensions arise about how to be Jewish—and how Jewish to be—in virtually all Jewish households. For the most part, Jewish conflicts are grounded in the same underlying issues as other kinds of family conflicts: communication, differing expectations, power. Peeling back the Jewish pretext for the conflict usually reveals one of these.

The following pages "unpack" some of the emotional baggage that lurks inside religious flash points, such as when spouses differ on how they want to celebrate a holiday, or when a teenager announces that she's becoming a Buddhist.

First, parents must be in agreement on the basics. If one of you is ambivalent, hostile, or opposed to the goal of raising Jewish children, conflict can become chronic and corrosive. But when both of you are committed to the same goal, most disagreements can be resolved, or at least defused, if you:

- are honest and clear about your feelings and goals;
- are able to tolerate and respect differences of opinion;
- are flexible enough to find solutions that accommodate differences.

> "I don't want to go."
> "I hate Hebrew school."
> "Grandpa's seder is too boring."
> "I'm too exhausted to go to Friday night services."

It hurts to be on the receiving end of comments like these, especially if you hear them as: "I don't want to be Jewish," or "I don't want to be like you," or even "I don't love you anymore."

It is difficult to respond thoughtfully when you're feeling hurt and defensive, which is why people often lash out with statements such as, "I don't care what you want. You're going." But the last thing you want to do is turn your family's Jewish choices into a tug-of-war, because the harder you pull, the more resistance you create.

It is impossible to encourage positive Jewish memories or teachable moments in an atmosphere of anger and resentment. So the next time you hear, "I don't want to go," stop and ask, "Why not?" and listen to the answer without interruption or argument. Try to put aside hurt feelings and assess the substance of what is being said:

Maybe the child who doesn't want to go to Hebrew school is telling you that his teacher is boring, or the books outdated, or the other kids in class loud and disruptive.

Maybe it's true that Grandpa's seder really does put your children through too many incomprehensible, hungry hours.

Perhaps the spouse who doesn't want to go to temple feels intimidated or alienated by the Hebrew in the service.

If there are genuine issues behind the "I don't want to," acknowledge them and strategize ways to improve the situation:

Tell your child you are concerned about what's going on in his classroom. Explain that you want Hebrew school to be a good experience and that you will talk to his teacher or principal about the curriculum (or the materials or classroom dynamics). Then follow through by meeting with the educators and getting involved in the school as a volunteer or board member.

Talk to the grandparents about adding some new, child-friendly elements to the family seder.

Request and/or organize a learner's service at your synagogue so your spouse can become familiar and comfortable with the prayers.

Of course, an easy "fix" is not always possible. Many ten-year-old boys would simply rather play soccer after school than sit in a classroom. But if Jewish education is a priority, you have to be clear and consistent about the family rules. "Because I say so," is not enough of an explanation, however; "Hebrew school is just as important as regular school. I will work to make it a better experience, but you are going to go. In our family, kids go to Hebrew school through the twelfth grade. This is not negotiable." Then, be prepared to live with the whining or resentment that will continue until your child finishes testing your resolve.

Invite grandparents to a workshop on reworking the *haggadah* for toddlers, or propose doing a little puppet show in the middle of the seder. Or you may have to explain to your children that doing it Grandpa's way is an act of respect for their elders and a way to connect with the extended family, and then make the second night seder into a totally kid-centered event.

Empathize with the spouse who feels alienated by worship services. Does his or her choice feel like a threat to the relationship or to the family? Are you willing to consider other alternatives, such as finding another synagogue that uses less Hebrew, taking a Hebrew class together, or agreeing to attend services on your own?

When Parents Disagree Few couples are ever precisely in synch regarding their religious or spiritual lives—nor is that a healthy goal. Better to try and evolve a Jewish family culture that tolerates your differences.

When you do disagree, stay on guard against ultimatums ("I will only join a Reform temple"; "We have to do the whole seder the way my father did it"; or "My kids will never attend a Jewish day school"). If you find yourself taking a hard line, step back and ask what's going on. Is your only positive Jewish memory bound up with a Reform Jewish youth program? Would changing the seder seem like an act of disrespect? Does the term "day school" sound too much like the unhappy "parochial school" of your own childhood?

Try to sort out what is bubbling up from your childhood, or whether your spouse genuinely needs more information before making a decision or a change. These kinds of conversations often make people fearful to say what they really feel. If you get stuck or are unable to talk these issues through on your own, consider getting help (see page 156).

Remember that not all Jewish choices have to be "unanimous." Some decisions require both parents' full support (We will observe Shabbat as a family. We will send our child to a Jewish day school). But there is no reason that both parents have to be equally involved in congregational life, or Jewish communal activities, or Torah study, or regular synagogue worship.

Parents who agree to disagree about how they express their Jewishness should explain their choices to their children. Don't worry about talking "over their heads"; you can explain what you mean again when they are old enough to grasp the finer points. Couples who respect, tolerate, and support each other's Jewish choices without hidden animosities or agendas teach their children that there are different ways to be Jewish. Always be careful to speak respectfully of the other parent's choices and always be honest: "I can't really explain what Mommy thinks. Ask her and she will tell you."

Consistency and Flexibility Children need and thrive on consistency, but they suffocate without flexibility. Balancing these twin needs is one of the challenges of good parenting. While parents are far better off being unanimous about the specifics of bedtimes and homework rules, Jewish commitment can be taught and modeled as a serious commitment that takes different forms and changes over time.

Shabbat is a good example of how to balance consistency and flexibility. Children who live in a home with a weekly commitment to Shabbat observance acquire a built-in Jewish clock (see Chapter 4). But that clock is not destroyed or undermined by doing Shabbat on paper plates, or at the beach, or as guests in a home that does the rituals very differently.

The tension of balancing consistency and flexibility sometimes gets played out between parents over issues of continuity (doing things the way my parents did them) and change (doing things differently than my parents did them):

• "Why can't we go to Jewish family camp this summer?" versus "Why should we mess with our standard trip to the beach?"

- "I want to join the Reform temple, which has a stronger youth group" versus "I grew up Conservative and could never be comfortable with Reform services."
- "I want to stop doing food shopping on Shabbat" versus "Saturdays are for chores and Sundays are for play."

If you find yourself digging in your heels, ask yourself (and each other): What am I really afraid of? Do I think it's not a "real" seder if we don't read the whole *haggadah*, exactly like my grandmother did? Do I really think we're on a "slippery slope" if there is more English in the service?

Balancing the needs for consistency and flexibility requires compromise; it means there will be times when you honor the traditions of your childhood and times when you try something entirely different, times to insist that your teenager attend Rosh Hashanah services and times to let her meditate in the garden instead.

Boundaries The essential ties of affection and need that bind families together sometimes make it hard for us to see one another clearly. It's a fact of family life that parents and children are routinely "mortified" by one another's behavior. Thus, mothers squirm when their children don't say "please" or "thank you"; teenage daughters cringe at their fathers' attempts at humor.

We tend to see our children and spouses as extensions of ourselves: sometimes we bask in their reflected glory; sometimes we are afraid we'll be judged by what they say or do. This confusion about the boundaries between "me" and "you" is part of Jewish family conflict as well. The parent whose teenager wears ripped jeans to temple may feel that his kid is being disrespectful. When the flight attendant asks who ordered the kosher meals, teens may hide their faces and moan, "Why do we have to be different?" The parent whose son decides to wear his *kippah* to the ball game may be embarrassed by the public announcement of Jewishness in a secular place. A spouse who sees his newly kosher-keeping wife refuse to eat the elaborate shrimp dish prepared and served by a neighbor may be furious at her "rudeness."

When a child or spouse is "not Jewish enough," or gets "too Jewish," it can feel like a challenge or even a repudiation of you or of the family's Jewish choices. Stop and ask yourself why certain behaviors drive you crazy: Are you fighting about your kid going to temple in jeans (even though all the other teenagers wear them) because you know how that would have horrified your father?

Of course, parents have every right to insist that their children behave in accordance with certain family norms. But don't sweat the small stuff. If you pick at every word and choice, your child will eventually tune out everything you say. Think about what really matters to you. Are you really more concerned about the pants your son is wearing than about having him hate going to temple with you?

Getting clear about the boundaries between ourselves and our loved ones is an on-going challenge but a crucial task. Parents raising children to make their own authentic Jewish choices have to face the fact that those choices may differ from their own—especially as children become young adults.

One of the primary developmental tasks of adolescence is to define new boundaries between parent and child. As teenagers build a distinct and separate identity, they practice making decisions about how to look, whom to emulate, and what to believe. In the process, many teens turn away from family beliefs and customs, though most return in adulthood.

This time of experimentation and individuation can be confusing for teens; it is often painful for parents, who experience the process as a repudiation. Adolescence certainly reveals to you the limits of your influence.

Nevertheless, despite what they say or how loud they say it, teenagers value their parents' opinions and support. It is crucial to maintain open lines of communication with adolescents, to listen to them, and to affirm the indelible and unconditional connections between parents and kids. (See Chapter 9, "Ages 15 to 18.")

"Why Can't I Go to Church with Daddy?" If you are reading a book entitled *How to Be a Jewish Parent,* you and your partner have probably already chosen a Jewish path for your children. However, if one of you is also practicing another religion, some confusion or conflict is likely. At the very least, children are bound to have questions about their non-Jewish parent's beliefs and practices.

These questions, which sometimes make the Jewish parent panic, can be opportunities for important conversations. If your child asks why Daddy isn't Jewish, or why you decided on Judaism instead of Christianity for the family religion, or whether she can attend church with Mom sometime, take advantage of the opening to explain the family's Jewish commitment, to affirm respect for each another, and to reassure children of their place in the family.

Children's questions sometimes stem from worries about divided loyalties, or about hurting the non-Jewish parent. Sometimes, church-versus-synagogue conflicts have nothing to do with church or synagogue. If a child declares, "I don't want to go to Sunday school, I want to go to church with Daddy," find out what she is saying. At various ages and stages, children identify with one parent more than the other. It may be that what she means is, "I want to spend more time with Daddy."

If you know what your child needs, you can answer appropriately: "Sunday school is important. But when you come home, you and Daddy will have a special afternoon together."

If your two faiths become an area of persistent tension and conflict, consider talking to other families, to clergy, or to a professional with experience in the field of interfaith relationships.[1]

Getting Help   You are not the first or the only family that fights about how to be Jewish or how Jewish to be. If you feel isolated, stuck, or overwhelmed, talk to someone outside your immediate family. Parents of your child's religious school classmates can provide a great reality check and suggest some strategies, too.

Make an appointment to speak to the Jewish professional in your congregation or day school with whom you are most comfortable. Some rabbis, cantors, and educators are skilled counselors. For help with a specific topic, you can ask for—or perhaps organize—a workshop for parents on topics such as: "Strategies for Raising a Jewish Teenager"; "Feeding Your All-Pasta Kid During Passover"; "The Bar/Bat Mitzvah Blues."

If you decide that counseling or therapy would be appropriate, select a clinician who will be supportive of your choices as a religious person. Your rabbi may be able to recommend someone. At your first meeting, tell her or him that religious belief and identity are important and listen for a supportive response.

BOOKS FOR PARENTS

The Intermarriage Handbook: A Guide for Jews and Christians, by Judy Petsonk and Jim Remsen (William Morrow, 1988).

Mixed Blessings: Overcoming the Stumbling Blocks in an Interfaith Marriage, by Paul Cowan with Rachel Cowan (Penguin, 1989).

PART II

Ages
and Stages

Every phase of childhood brings new blessings and new challenges. Judaism gives you a voice for expressing your joy and gratitude with rituals and celebrations, prayers and parties. Every phase of childhood also means new choices and demands. The Jewish community provides support, both formal and informal, for everything from choosing a summer camp to finding a family therapist.

Part II of *How to Be a Jewish Parent* follows the stages of childhood from infancy through adolescence. Each of the next four chapters is divided into three sections, beginning with a description of the Jewish developmental task of each phase (early childhood, primary school years, early adolescence, and late adolescence). Next, you will find information about the Jewish life-cycle rituals and celebrations associated with the age. Finally, there is a discussion of key choices in Jewish education, informal learning, and leisure activities.

Much of Part II is concerned with Jewish education. The task of teaching children is considered so central a *mitzvah* that it is recited at every worship service as part of the *Shema:* "These words that I command you this day shall be upon your heart . . . and you shall teach them to your children."

This is a command that Jewish parents continue to take very seriously. Approximately 80 percent of all Jewish children are given some kind of formal Jewish education. All dire pronouncements to the contrary, the American community today is probably the most Jewishly literate in history. With boards of Jewish education in over sixty communities in North America, there are more varied and more comprehensive options in Jewish education than ever before. It is thus easier to do this *mitzvah* than ever before. If you understand this responsibility as a *mitzvah*—a good and holy action—rather than as a chore, it can be a great gift not only to your children, but also to you and your family as well. Schools are centers for community-building: as your child learns and grows, so will you.

Please Read Ahead   Inevitably, parents turn to the section that is most pressing. If you have a toddler, reading about "choosing a college" may seem absurdly remote. Nevertheless, many choices made during the early years have long-term implications. Read ahead and also look back. If you are researching educational choices for teens, much in the section on school-age children will also apply to your situation.

Chapter 6

Birth to Age Four:
The Foundation
of a Jewish Self

For any parent who wants to establish and nourish a child's Jewish self, the years between birth and kindergarten are all about creating an indelible association between Jewishness and sweetness, between Jewishness and home, between Jewishness and the unconditional love of parents for their children.

From helpless infancy through rambunctious toddlerhood, young children learn with every waking breath. Infants begin to associate the sounds and smells of family and home with warmth and safety even before they realize that they are separate from the people who hold them close. As they start to discover their fingers and toes, babies grow attached to the adults around them and learn the most important thing of all—how to love.

Healthy, beloved babies absorb the basics of the civilization into which they are born. During their brief Edenic residence in the world before "No," their growing brains integrate the fundamentals of grammar, receive a million subtle cues about gender, and learn the unconscious etiquette of their own family's culture—things like how loud one speaks, how close one stands, how much one touches. By the age of four, most children have acquired their parents' taste for chili peppers and/or blintzes, Mozart and/or klezmer. If they have been exposed to books and reading, they will be eager for literacy and school. And if they have tasted challah and grape juice on a weekly basis, they will expect Shabbat the way they expect night to follow day.

Parents today are keenly aware of the developmental importance of the first years of life. We are vigilant about our babies' nutrition, we play classical music and hang stimulating mobiles in the nursery, we avoid using baby talk. For Jewish parents, it is never too early to include Jewish elements and to pay attention to the ways we nourish the Jewish self—or soul—in our care.

Every family shapes its weeks and its seasons, with events like Sunday visits to museums, September back-to-school shopping trips, family camping expeditions. Jewish families can shape the week with Sabbath rituals, the arc of the seasons with holidays and family visits. For little ones, early exposure to the rhythms of Jewish life becomes deeply embedded, not as memories so much as expressions of themselves.

Parents can help create a solid foundation for a child's Jewish self in a myriad of ways, many of which are discussed in earlier chapters about home and holidays. For parents who are new to Jewish practice or to Judaism itself, infancy and toddlerhood give you a wonderful chance to discover the Jewish world along with your baby, to try out new customs (feeding the ducks for *Tashlich* on Rosh Hashanah afternoon) and to find ways to use new words (*kiddush, b'racha*).

But for the most part, education at this stage has less to do with language than with the senses. Introduce your baby to the sensual universe of Judaism, a place filled with the smell of challah on Shabbat, cuddly Jewish bedtime routines (singing the *Shema* and reading Jewish books), soft stuffed animals with Hebrew names (*Dov* is Hebrew for "bear"), trips to the orchard for apples at Rosh Hashanah, face-painting at Purim at the synagogue or Jewish community center.

LIFE CYCLE

Baruch habah.
B'rucha haba'ah.
Blessed is your coming.[1]

These are the words that begin the Jewish ceremonies that celebrate the birth of a baby. Anyone who has ever been in a delivery room or held an adopted child for the first time knows the meaning of the word "blessed." The arrival of a child is one of the most exciting, terrifying, and holy moments in life. Jewish tradition gives parents a way to name this unspeakable wonder, to share the joy with family and friends, to make promises to our baby and to ourselves, which is why the arrival of a child can be a Jewish turning point, a time to connect to community and tradition.

Brit, the Hebrew word for "covenant," is the way Jews describe and define their relationship to God. Jewish babies enter into this covenant through a ceremony also called a *brit*. A covenant is a contract, a mutual understanding. The Torah itself (the first five books of the Bible) is a covenant between God and the Jewish people. God's covenant with the Jewish people was personalized for male Jews through the covenant of circumcision (*brit milah*), which was commanded of Abraham and all his descendents.[2] Since the late 1960s, Jewish parents have extended the ritual imagery of the covenant to include daughters with the *brit bat* (a covenant ceremony for a daughter).

Brit milah and *brit bat* share the wonder and joy of new life, the need to express these within the Jewish community, and the idea that each and every Jew is part of the *brit*, the covenant, and the people of Israel.

BRIT MILAH (THE COVENANT OF CIRCUMCISION)

Brit milah is Judaism's oldest continuous ritual, practiced by Jews throughout the ages and across cultures. Throughout Jewish history, Jews of all backgrounds and beliefs have fulfilled what may be the most difficult of all biblical commandments.[3] Even when it was illegal and dangerous—as in the days of Antiochus (the villain of the Hanukkah story) and in the time of Hitler—Jews have circumcised their sons.

The reasons why Jews circumcise are complex: *brit milah* is a sign of faith in God, a way of connecting with our most ancient roots, an affirmation of Jewish life for another generation. The most compelling answer to the question of why we do this to our sons is that if we stop doing *brit milah* we stop being Jews. Deciding to circumcise a son in a traditional manner announces your identification with Judaism in a powerful, unequivocal way.

Today, circumcision faces opposition not from anti-Semitic despots but from an anticircumcision movement that brands the procedure "sexual mutilation." The medical community remains neutral on the health benefits of the surgical removal of the foreskin, the sheath that covers the glans of the penis. The American Academy of Pediatrics policy statement on circumcision (March 1999) noted findings of modest health benefits and extremely low complication rates, but found "no overwhelming reason to recommend routine neonatal circumcision."[4] However, Jews have never circumcised sons for medical reasons.[5]

Indeed, the medical procedure of circumcision performed by a physician in a hospital is not, in itself, a *brit milah*. A *bris* (the more familiar Ashkenazic Hebrew pronunciation of *brit*) is a ritual circumcision, defined by prayers and the intention of entering a son into the covenant of the Jewish people.

The difference between a ritual and a strictly medical circumcision is not limited to prayers. Hospital circumcisions are performed in chilly operating rooms where the newborn may be immobilized for as long as ten minutes, while a more-or-less experienced doctor (or intern) performs the procedure. The baby is not permitted to eat for a few hours before the circumcision, and it may take some time before a nurse returns him to his mother.

At home, the room will be warm, the surroundings familiar, the practitioner experienced and skilled. Rarely will the child have an empty stomach, and he is usually given a taste of wine before the procedure begins. Loving hands hold him, and if a safety restraint is used, it is only for the few moments of the circumcision itself. Afterward, the baby is swaddled and immediately returned to his mother.

There is an important difference in timing, too. Medical circumcisions may take place any time between the second and sixth day after birth, but *brit milah* is never performed before the eighth day, when the baby is larger and better able to heal.[6] *Brit milah* is not simply a circumcision, but a powerful, dramatic gesture that requires us to stop and wonder over the miracle of a new baby, a new generation, the future of the Jewish people.

Planning a Bris According to Jewish law, *brit milah* is scheduled eight days after birth—which is when Abraham circumcised his son, Isaac.[7] Unless there is a medical reason, the eighth day is sacrosanct, which means that *bris*es are done on Shabbat and holidays, including Yom Kippur.[8] (*Brit milah* will be postponed, however, if the baby is ill or weak.)

According to the Jewish calendar, days begin at sundown, which means that a son born on a Monday evening will be circumcised the following Tuesday before sundown. Most *bris*es take place at home and are performed by a *mohel*, a person trained in both the procedure of *milah* and the prayers of the *brit*.

Traditionally, *mohelim* (the Hebrew plural of *mohel*) learned the history, lore, prayers, and procedures of *brit milah* through apprenticeship to an established practitioner. Today, the Reform and Conservative movements train licensed Jewish physicians (male and female) in the law and liturgy of *brit milah* and certify them as *mohelim* for the liberal communities.[9] If you live in a community where there is no *mohel*, a rabbi or cantor may be able to refer you to a Jewish physician who will perform the ritual.

Unless you are certain that your baby will be a girl, contact at least one *mohel* a few months before your due date. Rabbis and cantors are the best sources for recommendations, but you can also consult Jewish newspapers for advertisements. Find out whether the *mohel* will be in town, and ask about fees, though most will reduce the price in case of need.

You should feel comfortable asking your *mohel* as many questions as you need to ask; if you don't like the way the *mohel* speaks to you over the phone, try to find another. One of the first phone calls after the birth of a son should be to the *mohel* to set the time for the *bris*.

A day or two before the *bris*, your *mohel* should call to see how the baby is doing and to give you instructions about supplies and setting up the room. On the day of the ceremony, he or she will arrive early to examine the baby. By then, the *mohel* will need to know the baby's Hebrew name (see below, page 171) for the ceremony.

Liturgy and Ritual As with most Jewish life-cycle rituals, the core liturgy of *brit milah* is very brief—no more than five minutes long—consisting of blessings before and after the circumcision and a long kiddush, which includes the baby-naming. If you are a member of a congregation, your rabbi or cantor may share the liturgical responsibilities, but the *mohel* usually acts as the master of ceremonies at a *bris*, which generally includes an element of informal teaching about the history and religious significance of *brit milah*.

To begin, the baby is carried into the room, usually by a grandparent or other family member. The *mohel* or rabbi greets the baby with the phrase: *Baruch habah*, "Blessed is he who comes." The baby is then set down for a moment in the *kisei shel Eliyahu* ("the chair of Elijah"), the ancient prophet who is said to be a harbinger of the Messiah and an honored "guest" at every *bris*.[10]

The *mohel* says a few words of introduction and explanation before reciting the following blessing and removing the foreskin:

> Blessed are You, Adonai our God, Ruler of the Universe, Who sanctifies us with commandments and commands us regarding circumcision.

Since the *mohel* is really only acting on behalf of the father, the baby's father (or both parents) will repeat the following blessing after the *mohel:*

> Blessed are You, Adonai our God, Ruler of the Universe, Who sanctifies us with Your commandments and commands us to bring our son into the covenant of Abraham, our father.

Everyone says amen, and the guests follow the *mohel* in reciting the traditional wish:

> Just as he entered the covenant, so may he enter into the study of Torah, the wedding canopy, and the accomplishment of good deeds.

As soon as the baby is dressed, the *mohel* (or the rabbi or cantor) recites the prayer over wine (*kiddush*), drinks some wine, and gives a few drops to the baby. This is followed by a longer, chanted prayer that includes the baby-naming.[11] The baby is then returned to his mother.

Most parents personalize the ritual by including a brief speech about the baby's namesake. Since most American Jews name their children in memory of a loved one who has died, this is usually a very moving and beautiful moment in the service. Some families also include a reading by grandparents, siblings, or other close family members.

The ceremony usually ends with *Shehechiyanu*, the prayer of thanksgiving for new blessings and the singing of "Siman Tov U-mazal Tov" ("good fortune and good luck"), a rousing song of rejoicing.

The meal after the *bris*, is a required part of the ritual. Called a *s'eudat mitzvah* ("meal of the commandment"), it tends to be an informal breakfast or lunch for family and friends.

The only people who absolutely must be present at a *bris* are the baby, the *mohel*, and the *sandek* (an honored family member, often a grandfather[12]), who assists by holding the baby. However, because a *bris* celebrates the addition of a new Jew to the community, it is preferable to have at least a *minyan*—a quorum of ten adult Jews—in attendance. Non-Jewish grandparents and other family members can participate by carrying the baby into the room or reading a poem or blessing, depending on their comfort level (see box below).

Before leaving your home, the *mohel* will examine the baby and provide instructions about taking care of the circumcision, which should be completely healed within a month. Complications are extremely rare, but do not hesitate to call the *mohel* and/or your pediatrician with concerns or questions.

Non-Jewish Family Members and Brit

Even a joyful Jewish ritual can be a point of contention or pain if some of the baby's grandparents are not Jewish. Deciding on a Jewish celebration may be the first concrete demonstration that you are serious about raising children as Jews. This can feel like rejection to non-Jewish family members, who sometimes have genuine concerns about the immortal soul of an unbaptized grandchild.

Parents in such situations should be patient and sensitive; explain the meaning of the ceremony and stress the continuities between your two traditions.[13] If appropriate and possible, invite non-Jewish grandparents to participate in the festivities by, for example, offering a toast at the celebratory meal. Usually, the joy at the birth of a grandchild is enough to overcome awkwardness and fears—especially if the family is able to ask and answer questions.[14]

⊠

BRIT BAT (COVENANT FOR A DAUGHTER)

Brit bat emerged during the late 1960s when Jewish parents became aware of the disparity between the ritual celebration surrounding the birth of a boy and the relative absence of Jewish ceremony for the arrival of a girl. The need to give Jewish expression to the joy that attends the birth of a daughter gave rise to all kinds of liturgical experiments.

In less than a generation, covenant ceremonies for daughters have moved from the experimental fringe to the mainstream center. Although there is no single normative liturgy, *brit bat* is now an established part of the American Jewish life cycle.[15]

Actually, contemporary *brit bat* ceremonies are not entirely new; Sephardic Jews have greeted the birth of daughters with lovely traditions for centuries. The Jews of Spain, for example, performed a ceremony in which the baby was brought into a room on a pillow and passed around so that each guest could give her a blessing. The rabbi recited a blessing for her health and happiness, and a lavish meal was served.[16]

Planning a Brit Bat   There is no normative liturgy for a *brit bat* and no rules about where or when to hold it. *Brit bat* takes place either at home or in a synagogue. Generally, parents pick a day when the mother feels well enough to enjoy the festivities, a date that is likewise convenient for out-of-town family and friends. While there is no mandated time frame for the ceremony, many families select one with historical and religious resonance.

Scheduling a ceremony on the eighth day recalls the ancient rite of *brit milah* and ensures that the wonder of birth is still fresh in the parents' mind. Thirty days is a popular choice because it allows for recovery and planning; it also has a basis in tradition, since according to the Talmud, that is when babies were considered to be viable. Some parents schedule the ceremony on the first day of the next new moon, *Rosh Hodesh*, a day for new beginnings.

A *brit bat* on Shabbat can take place during synagogue services either on Friday night or Saturday morning. In some congregations, it is customary for parents and sometimes grandparents to take the baby up to the *bimah* (the raised platform in the synagogue), where the rabbi conducts a brief ceremony. This may include several blessings, announcement of the baby's name, and a parental talk about her namesake(s). Afterward, the *Oneg Shabbat* or Shabbat kiddush may be sponsored by the new parents or in the family's honor.

Another Shabbat option is to hold the *brit bat* immediately following the morning service but preceding the kiddush, or the celebration can coincide with the midday meal, either in the synagogue or at home. Finally, *brit bat* is sometimes included at *Havdalah,* the ceremony that marks the end of Shabbat and celebrates distinctions.

Blessings, poems, readings, or prayers can be offered by as many guests as you choose. People can be honored with such tasks as reciting the *Hamotzi* (the blessing over bread, traditionally a braided challah) before the meal, or holding a prayer shawl over the parents and baby during the ceremony. Grandparents are usually given the most important honors at these ceremonies.[17] Non-Jewish grandparents and family members can participate in many ways, depending on their comfort level (see box, above).

Because *brit bat* ceremonies are still relatively new, and because many guests—Jews and non-Jews alike—are unfamiliar with the prayers and symbols, many parents prepare a printed guide to the proceedings.

Liturgy and Ritual For all the variations among *brit bat* ceremonies, there is a basic four-part structure to most: introduction, covenantal ritual, naming, and celebratory meal (*s'eudat mitzvah*).

Part I: Introductory Blessings and Prayers. Most *brit bat* ceremonies begin with the greeting, *B'rucha haba'ah* ("blessed is she who comes"), followed by prayers or readings by the parents and/or rabbi. Some families adapt the custom of bringing the baby to the *kisei shel Eliyahu* (Elijah's chair); the prophet Elijah, harbinger of the days of the Messiah, is said to "attend" all *brit* ceremonies.[18]

Candlelighting (with or without a blessing) can make another beautiful beginning; parents have made use of a braided *Havdalah* candle, a pair of white Shabbat candles, heirloom candlesticks, or a new set that is a gift to the baby.

Kiddush, the blessing over wine, is invariably a part of a *brit bat*. After the blessing, the cup is shared and the baby given a drop. Often the cup itself will have some special meaning—perhaps the goblet used at the parents' wedding, a gift to the baby, etc.

Part II: Covenant. Using blessings and symbolic actions, a baby daughter is entered into the covenant of the people of Israel. Daughters are most commonly entered into the covenant with a *b'racha,* a blessing, such as this one:

> You have sanctified Your beloved from the womb, establishing Your holy covenant throughout the generations. May devotion to the covenant continue to sustain us as a people. Praised are You, Eternal God, Who has established the covenant. Blessed by the Presence Whose sanctity fills our lives, we give thanks for the covenant.[19]

Many parents feel that the *brit bat* requires a symbolic action as well as words. Some of the gestures that have served this purpose include candle-lighting, touching the baby's hand to a Torah scroll, wrapping or covering the baby with a prayer shawl, or some form of washing or immersion.

Water is probably the most popular covenantal symbol for daughters.[20] The well-known Hebrew (and Jewish summer camp) song, "Mayyim" ("Water") is a wonderful accompaniment.

Before the washing, the rabbi or leader says:

> Blessed are You, Adonai our God, Ruler of the Universe, Who is mindful of the covenant.

After the washing, the parents say:

> Blessed are You, Adonai our God, Ruler of the Universe, Who is mindful of the covenant through the washing of the feet.[21]

The three-fold wish for Torah, marriage, and good deeds, often follows the covenant ritual:

> As she has entered the covenant, so may she enter a life devoted to Torah, *huppah,* and the accomplishment of good deeds.

The following reading, which expounds on the three-fold wish, is popular in *brit bat* ceremonies of all kinds:

> We dedicate our child to Torah—to a never-ending fascination with study and learning. With a book, she will never be alone.
>
> We dedicate our child to *huppah*—to never-ending growth as a human being, capable of giving and receiving love. With loving family and friends, she will never be alone.
>
> We dedicate our child to *ma'asim tovim*—to a never-ending concern for family and community, justice and charity. While she cares for others, she will never be alone.

Part III: Naming and Conclusion. The baby's name is given in both Hebrew and English. Because most American Jews name children to honor the memory of a family member who has died, stories about the loved one create a powerful and beautiful connection between loss and hope, past and future. You can also talk about the story associated with a biblical name—such as Judith—or explain your choice of a Hebrew name—such as Aviva, which means "spring."

Prayers, poems, wishes, and readings may be added here. Siblings old enough to participate sometimes read to their new sister, and whatever grandparents say is sure to be moving. Parents might also read a letter recording their wishes and prayers, addressed to their baby daughter—a treasure to be saved and read again, perhaps at her *bat mitzvah.*

Ceremonies end with one, some, or all the following three prayers:

- *Shehechiyanu:* The prayer of thanksgiving for new blessings.
- Traditional blessing for a daughter: On Friday night, after the Shabbat table blessings are made, many families add a blessing for their children. Reciting these words for the first time at a *brit bat* can be the start of a family Shabbat practice (see pages 63–64.) You can also add the names of grandmothers and great-grandmothers to the biblical matriarchs mentioned in the traditional blessing.[22]
- The priestly or three-fold benediction, which some parents also include in Friday-evening blessings (see page 64).

Part IV: S'eudat Mitzvah. According to Jewish law, major life-cycle events are celebrated with a *s'eudat mitzvah,* or "meal of the commandment," which begins with the blessing over bread (*Hamotzi*) and ends with *Birkat Hamazon*.

Several sample ceremonies appear in *The New Jewish Baby Book*, noted at the end of this chapter.

✡

ADOPTION

The arrival of an adopted child in a Jewish family is celebrated much like the arrival of a biological child, with the same joyful rituals and celebrations. Yet adoption does add extra choices to the first rituals of childhood, since most adoptive children are not born to Jewish mothers. Because Jewishness is a legal status under Jewish law, or *halachah*, parents must decide on the question of formal conversion.

The *halachic* requirements for the conversion of children include *mikvah* (ritual immersion) for both males and females, and *brit milah* for males. Both are traditionally done in the presence of a *bet din*, a court of three adult Jews, usually three rabbis. Although conversion rituals may seem daunting at first blush, they are not difficult, and *mikvah* can add a very moving and uniquely Jewish dimension to the adoption process.

Mikvah   Since the days of the ancient Temple, *mikvah* has been used to signify changes of personal status—within the community, within relationships, and within one's own heart. The rituals of immersion, called *tevilah*, have nothing to do with "washing away sin" and everything to do with new beginnings.[23] For converts to Judaism, *mikvah* is the ritual threshold leading into the house of Israel.[24]

The Hebrew word *mikvah*, which means a pool or gathering of water, is used to refer to natural bodies of *mayyim chayyim* ("living water") such as rivers, lakes, oceans, as well as to indoor pools created specifically for ritual immersion. The building that houses a ritual bath is also called a *mikvah*.

Some *mikva'ot* (the plural) are located in modern facilities built for this purpose; others are built into synagogues, schools, or even apartment buildings. The pools themselves look like miniature swimming pools. A *mikvah* must hold a minimum of twenty-four cubic feet of water (about 200 gallons), be deep enough for the water to rise above the waist of an average-height adult, and contain a certain proportion of natural water—usually rainwater—that has been transported to the pool via natural flow. This is then diluted with tap water and the mixture treated for hygiene, as with any pool.

The water in a *mikvah* is not considered holy. It is simply water. What sanctifies the *mikvah* is the intention—expressed in words and actions—of the person who enters the water.

Planning a Child's Mikvah   Generally held as soon as possible after adoption (though some pediatricians recommend putting the *mikvah* off until children are at least six months old[25]), the ritual is nearly always conducted by a rabbi. If your rabbi is amenable and if the weather permits, it is perfectly "kosher" to do *mikvah* in a pond, lake, river, or at the ocean. If the ceremony is to take place indoors, the rabbi usually makes the appointment and will describe what you need to bring, including any fee for use of the facility. The ceremony takes place on weekdays, not on Shabbat or holidays, and during daylight hours.

Your rabbi is responsible for convening a *bet din,* a court of three rabbis (or three knowledgeable adult Jews), to witness the baby's total immersion in the water. Ask if you can bring grandparents or other family and friends to the *mikvah;* having a group waiting in the foyer makes it more festive.

One or both parents take the baby into the water for the ritual. While the adults wear bathing suits, the baby has to be completely nude. But first, everyone who enters the *mikvah* must prepare with a thorough cleansing. Adjoining the ritual bath, you will find a fully equipped bathroom with tub, shower, sink, and towels.

After you are in the water and the baby is accustomed to the temperature, which is usually warm and comfortable, the rabbi will tell you to dunk the baby completely underwater. Ducking an infant's head underwater makes most parents very anxious, but in fact, few babies object. The secret is to blow directly into the child's face just before dunking; she will reflexively close her eyes and hold her breath. Rabbis and cantors with years of experience swear this trick never fails, and parents who follow their advice are amazed at how well it works.

When the child is raised from the water, the following blessing is recited by one of the rabbis or by a family member:

> Praised are You, Adonai, God of all creation Who sanctifies us with Your commandments and commands us concerning immersion.

After one or two more equally brief immersions (depending on the rabbi and local custom), the rabbi will lead the *bet din,* parents, and anyone else present in reciting the *Shehechiyanu.*

For girls, *mikvah* is the only ritual requirement. Traditionally, girls are named after immersion. The rabbi may say a blessing and pronounce her Hebrew name right at the water's edge, or give the name during a *brit bat* ceremony at the synagogue or at home.

Brit milah for an adopted infant is very much like the *brit milah* for any baby boy. Indeed, the only differences in the ritual is the addition of a prayer before the circumcision:

> Praised are You, Adonai, God of all creation, You make us holy with Your commandments, calling us to circumcise the convert.

An uncircumcised adopted male newborn is given a *brit milah* on the eighth day after birth, or as soon as possible thereafter. For a child adopted at three months of age or older, the procedure is always done in a hospital, under a physician's care and under general anesthesia. According to Jewish law, three adult Jews (one being the *mohel*) should be present, to serve as witnesses. *Mikvah* usually follows *brit milah,* plenty of time being first allowed for a full healing.

If an adopted child was already circumcised by a physician without Jewish ritual, Jewish tradition calls for a ritual called *hatafat dam brit,* "the covenant of the drop of blood."[26] This involves drawing a tiny amount of blood from the site of the circumcision by a *mohel. Hatafat dam brit* is performed as soon as it can be arranged. It involves little pain and virtually no wound. It may be done in a *mohel*'s or a physician's office, at the synagogue, or even at a *mikvah.*

Adoption Rituals For many parents, it is enough to acknowledge the miracle of their new child within *brit milah* or *brit bat.* This usually takes the form of an additional prayer and the story of how this particular child came to your family.

Some parents choose to hold another ceremony to sanctify the act of adoption itself. Since there is little precedent for such a ritual, there are virtually no limits to it. Several of the books listed at the end of this chapter contain sample ceremonies.[27] (For more about adoptive family life, see Chapter 11.)

CHOICES

NAMES AND ANNOUNCEMENTS

Choosing a name is the first Jewish decision many parents make. It is an awesome decision, a kind of second conception, as you wonder whether your baby should be a Deborah or a Miriam, a Benjamin or a Joshua.

A Jewish name bestows not only personal identity but also connects a child to family and Jewish traditions. Since most American Jews tend to follow the Ashkenazic custom and name children after close relatives who have died, a baby named Daniel or Rebecca (Rivka in Hebrew) is often a living testament to a beloved grandparent. Your Danny or Becca is also a link to every Jewish Daniel and Rebecca all the way back to the Bible. Sephardic Jews, who name children after living relatives, have the lovely opportunity to honor grandparents who are present at the ceremony. Jewish names also link parents to children, since every full Hebrew name also includes the parents' Hebrew names as well: Daniel ben Rafael v'Malkah (Daniel, the son of Raphael and Malkah). Jewish tradition is very attentive to names and naming. The Jews enslaved in Egypt were said to have been saved from complete assimilation by two identifying signs that set them apart: the custom of circumcision and their Hebrew names. But what makes a name Jewish has always been a subject of debate.

There are 2,800 personal names in the Bible, and though fewer than 5 percent of those are in common use today, biblical names are extremely fashionable, with preschool rolls filled with Samuels and Rachels. But Jews have never limited themselves to the Bible. Throughout history, we have borrowed from other sources for naming children; for example, Alexander, which is a Greek name, has been popular among Jews since the fourth century B.C.E. The custom of naming children after deceased relatives dates back to the Egyptian Jews of the sixth century B.C.E., who probably borrowed the idea from their non-Jewish neighbors.

Since the founding of the State of Israel in 1948, the lexicon of Jewish names has expanded to include formerly abandoned biblical names such as Yoram and Tamar, and new names inspired by nature: Barak (lightning) and Ilana (tree).

The practice of giving a secular name for everyday use and a religious name for prayer and Jewish legal documents developed during the Middle Ages in Eastern Europe. This custom is still common in America, where the connection between the secular and Hebrew names may be as tenuous as the initial consonant: Sarah for Suzanne. However, a Hebrew name can also be chosen to reflect personal qualities: Shalom, for one who loved peace.

Many parents now choose identifiably Jewish names, from Abigail to Zachariah, that work well in three settings where American Jews are likely to find themselves: in secular life, in synagogue, and in Israel.

However you choose, your child's Hebrew name will be the one she or he will answer to when called to the Torah for bar or bat mitzvah. It will appear on his or her *ketubah* (Jewish marriage certificate). It is the name he or she will pass on to your grandchildren.

Names for the Adopted Child   When American Jews adopt, they tend to follow the custom of naming children to honor family members. Thus, a child's full Hebrew name will include his or her parents' names as well, as in David ben Moshe v'Rivka (David, the son of Moses and Rebecca), or Gila bat Raphael v'Leah (Gila, the daughter of Raphael and Leah). It is rare to follow the custom for adult converts, which names Abraham and Sarah as parents: David ben Avraham Avinu v'Sara Imenu (David, the son of Abraham our father and Sarah our mother).[28]

Jewish Baby Announcements   What makes a Jewish announcement distinctive is the inclusion of Hebrew letters, Jewish words, biblical phrases, or Jewish design elements. You can "make it Jewish" simply by adding the baby's Hebrew name—in English and/or with Hebrew letters, either with the help of a calligrapher or a Hebrew-language computer program. Or you can add other Jewish elements, such as giving the birth date according to the secular and Jewish calendars and/or noting if your baby was born on Shabbat or a holiday.

Since most Jewish parents name babies in honor of loved ones, you can also mention the namesake on the announcement: "Rebecca is named for her great-grandmother Rivka Felker."

Or you might consider using a phrase from the Bible, in English and/or Hebrew. If your baby has a biblical name, for instance, you might use a concordance to search out a poetic verse: "He was called Solomon, and the Lord loved him," or "Awake, Devorah, and sing."[29] Another source for a quotation is the weekly Torah portion for the week your child was born.

A few common Jewish quotations that commonly appear on birth announcements include: "For this child we have prayed" (Samuel 1:27); "With each child, the world begins anew" (Midrash).

Adoption announcements can make use of the same Jewish elements. Some adoptive parents note both the date of the child's birth and the date of his or her arrival home. International adoptions are sometimes noted by place of birth:

LISA AND JOSEPH MILLER
JOYFULLY ANNOUNCE THE ARRIVAL OF THEIR DAUGHTER
ORA RUTH
BORN: NOVEMBER 4, 1999, HUNAN, CHINA
ARRIVED HOME: JULY 15, 2000

PRESCHOOL

High-quality early childhood education is not only fun, it's also good for children's development. Which is why most toddlers attend some kind of preschool program before entering kindergarten—whether or not both parents work outside the home.

Preschool is where children pat bunnies, practice social skills such as sharing and taking turns, play in the sandbox, and learn the rules to duck-duck-goose. Preschool can also be where a child first sees a Torah scroll up close and gets to sit on the floor right next to the rabbi during story-hour.

Early childhood experts agree that preschool should not be an "academic" experience. Although there may be games that improve a child's intellectual readiness, classroom instruction, as a goal, is better left for kindergarten. The preschool years are best filled with the kind of learning described in earlier chapters—learning through the senses and by example.

An explicitly Jewish preschool will foster literacy and numeracy like any other preschool. It will also nurture a sense of Jewish identity and belonging to a larger community. It reinforces and recapitulates the rhythms of Jewish life, week by week, season by season. A Jewish preschool also provides a variety of Jewish role models—not only teachers, but other children and their parents, too. In the process of doing Jewish art projects, eating Jewish holiday foods, and celebrating Shabbat, preschool children acquire an impressive vocabulary of Hebrew and Yiddish words and concepts.

Enrolling a toddler in a Jewish preschool located in a community center or synagogue also helps mitigate or postpone some of the inevitable tensions of being a Jewish child in America: you probably won't have to explain to your three-year-old why you don't dye Easter eggs or visit Santa at the mall like the other kids in his class.

One of the less-obvious benefits of a Jewish preschool is that it provides a community of peers not only for children but also for parents. Any preschool will introduce you to a group of parents with many of the same interests: toilet training, nap management, picky eating, etc. Choosing a Jewish preschool can connect your parenting career with your family's Jewish development, integrating parts of multifaceted, often hectic lives into a more meaningful whole.

There are cases where local Jewish preschools do not work for your family in terms of coverage or special needs. Many Jewish children have had wonderful preschool experiences in community-based and even church-based preschools. People of different backgrounds share and can teach many of your basic values: respect for all people, nonviolent conflict resolution, love of learning. You can easily add age-appropriate communal Jewish elements to preschoolers' lives by bringing them to the temple Purim party, the Jewish community center's Hanukkah concert, etc.

For children enrolled at nonsectarian preschools, however, Jewish parents do need to be clear that teachers and curricula avoid espousing other religious traditions, even subtly. This may require a conversation with the preschool director about Christmas—for instance, does she understand that you do *not* consider Christmas a secular celebration, regardless of the pagan origins of the tree? It might also mean sharing your traditions with the school community. Jewish parents can volunteer to bring apples and honey in at Rosh Hashanah, and *matzah* at Passover, as well as the Hanukkah menorah. This kind of participation is usually a source of pride for the child, who watches as Mommy or Daddy explains "our family traditions."

Criteria for Choosing a Preschool   Sending your "baby" to preschool requires a huge leap of faith and trust in the people and institution you select, which is why it's crucial that you feel confident in your choice. As you gather information, always trust your instincts; you are the expert about your own child. Even if a preschool has the "best" reputation, it still might not be the right fit for your son or daughter. Visit any program you are considering more than once; after your meeting with the preschool director, schedule a second meeting to observe a class in action.

You will want to make sure the facility is licensed by the state. Also check to see if it has accreditation from the National Association for the Education of Young Children (NAEYC), the "gold standard" in the field.

Since staff is the single most important part of any school, you'll want to satisfy yourself that teachers are well prepared, that student-teacher ratios are low, and that teacher training is on-going.

Preschool teachers and staff can be a wonderful resource for guidance and strategies, so find out if regular parent-teacher meetings are scheduled, or if there is a mechanism for informal sharing. Does the staff ever offer parenting programs on subjects such as sibling rivalry, handling anger, sleep problems? Are there opportunities for parent-child learning about Jewish holidays? Some of the more common topics include: "How to Make Shabbat with Young Children," "Passover 101;" and "December Dilemmas for Intermarried Families."

Ask about the Jewish curriculum: holidays, Shabbat, blessings before meals, arts and crafts, songs, etc. Are secular and Judaic elements presented separately or intertwined?

If the school is in a synagogue setting, find out if the preschoolers are exposed to other facets of the community. Do older Hebrew school students have any interaction with the little kids? Does the rabbi visit the classroom?

BOOKS FOR PARENTS
The New Jewish Baby Book: Names, Ceremonies, and Customs for Today's Families, by Anita Diamant (Jewish Lights Publishing, 1994).

Choosing a Jewish Life: A Handbook for People Converting to Judaism and for Their Family and Friends, by Anita Diamant (Schocken Books, 1997).

The New Name Dictionary: Modern English and Hebrew Names, by Alfred J. Kolatch (Jonathan David Publishers, 1989).

Circumcision: Its Place in Judaism, Past and Present, by Samuel A. Kunin, M.D. (Isaac Nathan Publishing, 1998).

Creating Ceremonies: Innovative Ways to Meet Adoption Needs, by Cheryl A. Lieberman, Ph.D., and Rhea K. Bufferd, LICSW (Zeig, Tucker & Co., Inc, 1999).

To locate a physician-*mohel* trained under Reform-movement auspices, go to www.rj.org/beritmila/

For referrals to Conservative-movement *mohelim,* contact the Rabbinical Assembly, which is located at the Jewish Theological Seminary in New York, at 212-280-6000.

For up-to-date information about preschools and early childhood education, contact the National Association for the Education of Young Children at www.naeyc.org.

Chapter 7

Ages Five to Ten: Teaching Values, Getting to *Mensch*

Preschoolers do not understand abstract ideas. Adolescents may argue with what you have to say. But during the years from five to ten, children pay attention to the words of your mouth: the subjects you discuss at the dinner table, how you talk to your own parents, and the way you discuss friends, neighbors, and the rabbi.

Actions still speak louder than words, but school-age children do listen carefully. These are prime years for introducing Jewish terms and concepts that embody the values you want your child to cherish and embody so s/he will grow up to be a *mensch*.

A Yiddish term, *mensch* means "person," but not merely a member of the species *Homo sapiens*. A *mensch* is a person of the highest order, worthy of trust and respect. A *mensch* is someone who treats other people with respect, who honors the elderly and gives to the poor, who fights for justice and cherishes peace, who is proud to be a Jew.

Mensch is only one of many evocative words that parents can use to link basic human values—such as personal responsibility and honesty—to a child's developing sense of what it means to be a Jew. Here are a few other core Jewish values and stories that teach *menschlichkeit*, the quality of being a *mensch*:

Fairness *(Tzedek)* and Kindness *(Gemilut Hassadim)* We all want our children to behave respectfully toward others, especially those who need and deserve special consideration: "We don't make fun of people in wheelchairs. We don't tease people who aren't so great on the soccer field. Not only is acting that way mean, but the Torah tells us, 'Do not place a stumbling block in front of the blind.' That means we shouldn't trip people who can't see, and it also means we should never make fun of any person's weakness."

Fairness is a big issue for school-age children, among whom, "That's not fair!" is a common complaint. Ask what your child means by "fair." Connect their response with the Jewish idea that everyone deserves to be treated with equal respect by telling this story about Hillel:

"A wise rabbi named Hillel once said that the whole of the Torah—all of Judaism—could be summed up in one sentence. What do you think that sentence would be?"

After your children have come up with their own answers, tell them Rabbi Hillel's answer: "What is hateful to you, do not do to your fellow man. That is the entire Torah—all of it. The rest is commentary. Go and study."

Forgiveness (Teshuvah)   During the High Holy Days, it is customary to apologize to the people you have hurt through word or action. There is no better way to model *menschlichkeit* than to say to your child, "I'm sorry for the times I lose my patience and yell at you. Will you please forgive me?" Similarly, children who see their parents apologize to one another learn that reconciliation can follow conflict.

Gossip (Lashon Harah)   Talking about people behind their backs is considered a serious wrong among Jews—the term *lashon harah* means "evil tongue," or "evil speech." Confronted with tales told out of school, a parent can take the opportunity to quote one of Judaism's greatest teachers: "There was once a great rabbi named Maimonides who said that three people are harmed by gossip, but one is hurt the most. The three people are: the one who is the subject of the gossip, the one who tells the gossip, and the one who hears it. Which one do you think is hurt most by *lashon harah?*"[1]

Let your child come up with his/her own answer and then reveal that Maimonides thought the most damage is caused to the person who hears the gossip, because it cannot be forgotten.

Respect (**Kevod**)   Self-esteem can be fostered and grounded in the religious value of showing respect, *kevod,* for other people. According to Jewish teaching, every person has unique and special gifts because we are all "made in the image of God," a value nicely demonstrated by a story attributed to a Hasidic rabbi named Zusia:

"A rabbi named Zusia, who lived a long time ago, was old and ill. Knowing he would die soon, Zusia was crying. His students asked 'Master, master, are you weeping because you are afraid that God will ask you why you were not like Moses, the great prophet?' 'No,' said the rabbi. 'Perhaps you are weeping because you are afraid that God will ask you why you were not a great warrior like Joshua?' 'No,' said the rabbi. 'Perhaps you are weeping because you are afraid that God will ask you why you were not a great judge like Solomon?'

" 'No,' said the rabbi, 'I cry because I am afraid that God will ask me why I was not Zusia.' "[2]

Generosity (Tzedakah)   Philanthropy begins at home and parents foster the spirit of *tzedakah* (see pages 45–48) by setting an example of generous giving. Doing good deeds together—volunteering to deliver meals to the elderly on Christmas Day, participating in a fund-raising walk, and the like—turns *tzedakah* into a family activity.

Parents can also let children know they are expected to be generous as individuals, too. As soon as a child starts getting an allowance, make it clear that some part of it belongs in the family *tzedakah* box, a responsibility that also gives him/her the right to help decide where to send the money. Similarly, *tikkun olam,* repair of the world, is modeled by connecting Jewish values and words to aspects of daily life, such as recycling and discussing events in the daily newspaper and Jewish periodicals.

God Talk   Keep God in the conversation in ways that feel comfortable and authentic to you. One way to do this is by reading aloud from Jewish children's books. Even after they can read to themselves, school-age children enjoy the intimacy of bedtime stories. Choose books of increasing sophistication and invite your child's speculations and questions. If your child asks, "Mommy, do you believe in God?" answer by asking him what he believes. Never lie about questions of faith. "I'm still trying to figure it out," is an honest and indeed "religious" answer.

Jewishness (Yiddishkeit)   Children pick up all kinds of cues from their parents about what it means to be Jewish. There is no "faking" respect for one's rabbi or teachers or local federation leaders, nor is there any way to hide genuine excitement when Israelis or American Jews win Olympic medals.

When parents express pride in Jewish accomplishments and identify with Jewish problems, children learn that they belong to a larger world of Jewishness—*Yiddishkeit*—that transcends nationalities and distance, and ultimately even time.

Parents instill pride in belonging to the Jewish community when they express pride in their synagogue and respect for their clergy, when they insist on equal respect for teachers in religious school and public school, and when they speak well of their other Jewish affiliations. This isn't to say that parents should never criticize a fellow Jew, or sugarcoat problems. Be aware that your overall attitude—pride or ambivalence, identification or distance—sets a crucial example.

Keep the Lines Open   From ages five to ten, parents lay the groundwork for conversations in the years to come. If you take advantage of their openness and talk to your children about sex and drugs, about God and doubt, about making mistakes and making amends, your children will learn that no subject is out of bounds between them and you. And this is a lesson remembered long after the specific content of these conversations is forgotten.

Make sure to listen at least as much as you speak. Children who feel their parents do not listen will eventually stop talking to them.

Listening is not a passive activity, but it does require that you do not rush to judge or fix or comfort. Parents who are dismissive or get angry may instill fear and silence. Parents who want to take charge and make everything immediately better risk inspiring passivity, secretiveness, or rebelliousness. Parents who cannot tolerate their children's growing pains may encourage them to hide problems.

Whatever you do say, your children will compare your words with what you do. If you say "Jewish learning is important" but permit your child to miss Hebrew school in order to go shopping, she will learn the meaning of "lip service." If you say "Jewish ways are beautiful" but make no effort to beautify them in your life, your child will learn cynicism. If you say "Ours is a meaningful way of life" but make no mention of Jewish values when you talk politics or pass a beggar on the street, children will learn that Judaism is an empty label.

If, however, your Jewish words and your Jewish actions are consistent, your children will learn how to be a *mensch* from a *mensch*.

LIFE CYCLE

JEWISH EDUCATION

There are no major rituals associated with these years. However, in line with customs dating back to rabbinic times, synagogues, schools, and families usually make a lovely fuss over the beginning of a child's formal Jewish education. In the Middle Ages, little boys would be given honey cakes on their first day of *cheder* (religious school) so that they would always associate learning their Hebrew letters with sweetness. Today, families are invited to celebrate the start of Jewish learning in synagogue schools and day schools.

Consecration is a synagogue custom usually held during Simchat Torah or on Shavuot, two holidays that celebrate the relationship between Jews and the Torah. Children in the kindergarten or starting first grade may be called up to the *bimah* or gathered under a *huppah*, a canopy made of a large prayer shawl. Some synagogues give each child a toy Torah or a small prayer shawl on this occasion, to mark the official beginning of a child's religious education.

Day schools sometimes mark the end of kindergarten with a celebration called *siyyum ha-sefer* ("completion of the book"), in which each child is given a *siddur* (prayer book) in honor of having learned all their Hebrew letters.

These are wonderful times to convene grandparents, other family members, and close friends. Make sure to have film in the camera.

CHOICES

As nearly every page in this book stresses, Jewish identity is forged at home. Jewishness, that ineffable sense of belonging, is grounded in melodies and aromas, in family jokes and recipes, in preverbal and nonverbal memories and associations. Jewish schooling cannot be a substitute for the kinds of teaching and modeling from parents and family life, or for the multilayered communal experience of synagogue life.

And yet, Jewish tradition values the life of the mind. Indeed, Jewish study is considered one of life's great pleasures, as well as a primary obligation. Jewish culture—which begins with a vast library of sacred texts and also includes literature, music, art, humor—is the birthright of every Jewish child. Providing children with access to this treasure is every Jewish parent's sacred obligation.

For Jewish parents in America, the basic choice for formal education is between Jewish day school and secular school plus supplementary religious school. The vast majority of children enrolled in institutions of liberal Jewish learning go to supplementary schools, most of which are run by synagogues. Jewish day schools account for approximately one-fifth of all Jewish children in America; three-quarters of that number are in Orthodox schools, but enrollment is booming in Conservative, Reform, and interdenominational schools.

Both day school and supplementary school have strengths and weaknesses, but either can help parents achieve core Jewish goals: exposure to Jewish texts, liturgy, languages and values, a sense of Jewish community, and a Jewish peer group.

Enrollment in any Jewish school represents also a major lifestyle decision because of the likelihood that it will become a gateway into a whole community for everyone in your family. As you make this important choice, remember to: clarify your own goals; visit the school; become a full partner in your child's education.

Clarify Your Goals   What do you hope and expect your child to learn? Is it important that s/he learns modern Hebrew? Do you feel community service should be part of Jewish education? How do you want theology or God-talk handled in a classroom? How involved are you willing to be in your child's Jewish schooling?

You don't have to know the answers to these questions as you search for a school; indeed, the search itself may help clarify your thinking. Look for a setting that offers you and your child a welcoming, compatible environment for exploring Judaism.

Remember that no school can satisfy a parent's goals on all counts. Every educational setting is a compromise of some kind, so it is crucial to be clear about which goals you are giving up (modern Hebrew) in exchange for others (a vibrant Jewish high school).

Nevertheless, as parents, it is your responsibility to maintain the highest expectations. Look for quality in terms of challenging curricula, passionate teaching, respect for different learning styles, and a commitment to critical thinking.

Visit the School   Plan to visit at least a year before enrolling your child. Attend classes at different levels; after all, your first-grader may be attending junior high school in this place. While visiting, check out the "culture" of the institution; look at art on the walls, the faces of the children in the classrooms and playground. Listen to how the teachers talk to and about their students. Consider the "climate" of the day school or synagogue school. Is it welcoming and attractive? Do the other parents seem enthusiastic about their children's education; are they people you can imagine becoming your friends?

Schedule a meeting with the principal, headmaster, or director—the individual whose talents and leadership tend to set school's standards and tone. During your meeting ask him/her to address:

A Vision of the School's Mission: Every school should be able to articulate its goals, both in terms of its larger mission ("We want to produce literate, committed Jews") and on a grade-by-grade level ("By the end of fourth grade, children should be reading prayers in Hebrew"). The school's vision should be apparent in its published materials, such as newsletters and brochures.

Curriculum: Evidence of careful decision-making is a good sign. Regardless of the choices, listen for a thoughtful approach to decisions and dilemmas. For example, "We had to make a decision about whether to teach spoken Hebrew or prayer-book Hebrew. This is what we chose and why."

Class trips, retreats, and other out-of-building experiences signal a program committed to community-building.

Are children taught the whys as well as the hows of Jewish life—not only how to say the prayers for lighting Sabbath candles, but also what the words mean and why Jews say them?

Do children ever use primary sources—such as the Torah and *siddur* (prayer book)—as textbooks?

Is prayer a part of the school experience? How do teachers talk about God?

How are social justice and *tzedakah* included in the curriculum?

Are subject areas developed from year to year? Are the arts integrated into the curriculum?

Teaching Staff: How long do teachers tend to stay with the school? Are they offered in-service training? Do they participate in curriculum development? How much class time is devoted to "frontal" learning, with the teacher standing in front of the room and the children seated at desks? Is dialogue and discussion stressed?

Check Out the Budget: Financial allocations speak volumes about a school's values, especially line items devoted to teacher salaries and training, special education, and family education.

Become a Full Partner in Your Child's Education Good Jewish schools welcome and enlist parent participation in a variety of ways: as classroom volunteers, school board members, parent-teacher organization leaders, etc. When you actively support school programs (showing up for assemblies, bringing in snacks, visiting the classroom when invited, signing up for family retreats), you reinforce your child's commitment, too.

Find out if the school provides opportunities for the whole family to learn and celebrate together. Schools often run family education workshops and study sessions that involve parents and children together (baking challah, learning Hebrew songs and dances) and separately (parents studying the text of the *haggadah* while second-graders are creating *matzah* covers).

Whenever possible, connect your family life with what a child is learning at school—for example, by referring to a public school canned-good drive as "*tzedakah*," using the challah cover made in art class on the Shabbat table, pulling out a map of the Middle East when the dinner conversation turns to Israeli politics.

⬦

SUPPLEMENTARY SCHOOL

They go by many names: Hebrew school, synagogue school, religious school, Sunday school. All refer to part-time Jewish schooling held in the late afternoon and/or on weekends. Most are run by synagogues for their member families. (If you are thinking about joining a congregation in order to send a child to its religious school, be sure to read Chapter 3, "Joining a Synagogue.") There are some non–synagogue-based programs run by community-based organizations[3] and by such nondenominational groups as the Yiddish-oriented Workmen's Circle and the Society for Humanistic Judaism.[4]

Supplementary Jewish education runs a wide gamut in terms of curriculum, commitment, and quality. Time requirements range from two to ten hours per week. The director might be a rabbi, cantor, or professional Jewish educator, and the school will be staffed with volunteer and/or paid teachers. In some smaller congregations, parents run the school.

Supplementary Jewish education is only beginning to recover from years of bad press, much of it from adults who remember it as oppressive or just dull. However, Jewish parents continue to endorse the effort by enrolling their children, and many have joined in initiatives to raise the quality to the levels achieved in model programs around the country.[5]

One of the inherent strengths of synagogue-based supplementary schools is that they give students a sense of belonging to a larger, multigenerational Jewish community. For children who study in the same building—and sometimes even with the same teachers—as their parents, there is no need to preach about the importance of life-long learning. The combination of supplementary school with Jewish summer camps, youth groups, Jewish community center participation, and family observance creates a powerful synergy.

Good supplementary schools can provide children with a core of basic Jewish knowledge and the skills to be life-long Jewish learners. The particulars of curriculum will vary from school to school, though virtually all devote time to the study of Bible, ethics, Hebrew, Israel, life-cycle observances, liturgy, *mitzvot,* Shabbat and the holidays, *tikkun olam,* and *tzedakah.*

In supplementary schools, children can learn how Jewish teachings and traditions are both timeless and timely, applicable to everyday decisions (how to talk to siblings, how to spend your allowance) as well as to abstract debates (the death penalty, civil liberties). Supplementary schools are a great place for children to wrestle with big theological questions: Why am I here? Is there a God? What kind of God do I believe in?

Clarify Your Goals   For many parents, one clear goal for supplementary education is preparation for bar/bat mitzvah. However, if this is your only aim, the results may be dismaying. Bar and bat mitzvah are meant to be a beginning, not an end to Jewish education.

Try to articulate why the ritual is important to you and what you hope your child will get out of the experience. But you must think past bar or bat mitzvah. Would you prefer that your son or daughter date other Jews? Do you want him/her to be part of a high school youth group? As you consider and tour synagogue schools, ask yourself whether its program can help you achieve these goals.

Visit the School   When looking at synagogue-based schools, find out how they fit into the temple community. Does the rabbi support the school and its director by teaching the children or their teachers? A good indicator of supplementary school success is the percentage of students who continue their Jewish education through high school.

Become a Full Partner in Your Child's Education   Take a positive stance toward the whole experience—starting with car-pool duties. When it's your turn to drive, be patient, positive, and bring special snacks. Serve your child's favorite meal on religious school nights. Take the whole car pool out for ice cream on the last day of Hebrew school.

Problems and Solutions   Time is a big problem. The typical supplementary school student attends for five years in grades three through seven, for an average of four to five hours per week for twenty-six weeks per year. That comes out to about a year's worth of public school instruction. Clearly, this is not much time in which to teach a 4,000-year-old tradition, and unfortunately, most kids stop going after bar/bat mitzvah, just when they have mastered the basics.

Afternoon programs put tired, restless kids into classrooms. Weekend programs mean less time to sleep late. And supplementary school is invariably in competition with sports, dance class, music lessons, and dentist appointments, creating stress if not resentment.

The time problem becomes less pressing if and when supplementary school is understood for what it is—a *supplement* to a complete and balanced Jewish life of holiday observance, parental modeling, and community ties that include youth group, summer camp, Jewish community centers, etc.

Compounding the time problem, however, is the issue of low parental expectations. Many people despair of finding quality in part-time programs and view them as merely "better than nothing." This attitude translates to disrespect for the teachers and unwillingness to participate or support the school. Children will eventually come to share their parents' disdain, thus undermining the whole enterprise. If you want your child to like his/her Jewish schooling, talk about the teachers, principal, and rabbi with respect, and show interest in what your child learned in Sunday school.

Your attitude toward attendance at Hebrew school is also crucial. Occasional absences (to study for a big math test or attend a dress rehearsal) are not the same as skipping to go shopping or for a routine soccer practice.

Soccer and all-city chorus often conflict with supplementary programs. Yet many parents expect total cooperation and flexibility on the part of the Jewish school staff but never insist that a coach or conductor permit a long string of missed games or practices in order to accommodate a child's Jewish education. Check your priorities: Which is ultimately more important—that your child become a master soccer player or a committed Jew?

DAY SCHOOL

Liberal Jewish day schools are the fastest-growing segment of Jewish learning in North America.[6] Although still the choice of a minority in the non-Orthodox community, the growth reflects the dramatic transformation of American Jewry from a community of immigrants who made public education the doorway to American society, into a fully integrated community that seeks a meaningful connection to Judaism.

Most day school parents went to public school, and for many, the choice of a Jewish school for their children is not a rejection of secular education; most non-Orthodox day school students spend some years in public school and nearly all attend secular universities. Rather, choosing a day school is an affirmation of Jewishness. Confident of their ability to provide their children a comfortable place in American society, day school parents decide that a full-time Jewish education is a way to ground children in their own heritage as preparation not only for living full Jewish lives but also for participation in the larger society. This development reflects changes in American culture itself, where the image of the melting pot has given way to the rainbow, where each color retains its individual hue while adding to the beauty of the whole.

Parents cite many reasons for choosing a Jewish day school education:

School Environment   With a few exceptions, day schools tend to be relatively small and students are known to the entire faculty. As in other private schools, class size is also small, so each child receives individualized attention. Liberal day schools are well equipped and technologically up-to-date. Curricular integration, with team teaching across disciplines, is common. Critical thinking skills are taught and prized.

General Academics   Students at day schools get a full complement of mathematics, English and language arts, history and social studies, science, physical education, and the arts. Day school graduates test well, and when they enroll in public or independent schools at middle school or high school, they excel. Graduates are routinely accepted by the universities and colleges of their choice.

Jewish Literacy   Jewish studies and general studies are given equal time at day schools, many of which stress an integrated approach (for example, Jewish history within American history). Jewish day schools provide a superb Jewish education. Although curricula vary from school to school, generally they include:

- Hebrew language as an access language (for reading and study) and/or as a second spoken language. Schools that stress verbal competence use Hebrew as a language of instruction.
- Jewish texts. Day schools provide in-depth exposure to the core texts of the Jewish people: Torah in particular, but also Prophets and rabbinic

texts, which ground and locate sources of Jewish values and ethics. The traditional form of Jewish text study—stressing the ability to ask good questions and fostering an appreciation for a multiplicity of "right" answers—teaches critical thinking.

- Jewish calendar. Through their studies, the arts, religious services, and celebrations, students live out the Jewish holidays in school. Jewish life-cycle ceremonies are also covered.
- Jewish history. Students graduate with a grasp of Jewish history, from biblical times to the modern era, including an understanding of Zionism and contemporary Israel.
- Jewish values. Day schools explicitly teach values, such as *kevod* (respect), *tzedakah* (the imperative to share with others), and *tikkun olam* (repair of the world). Already grounded in Jewish texts, these values are usually linked to hands-on projects: visiting nursing homes, canned food drives, writing letters to elected representatives, etc.
- Jewish religious skills and spirituality. The school day usually includes a prayer service. God, prayer, and faith, off-limits in public schools, are part of daily life and classroom discussion at day schools.

Social Benefits Day schools offer an integrated Jewish immersion experience otherwise unavailable to liberal Jews outside the land of Israel. At day schools, a child's peer group is Jewish and most of her/his teachers will be knowledgeable, committed Jews as well. Children are insulated from certain kinds of conflicts: if none of your child's schoolmates celebrates Christmas at home, she won't feel the absence of the holiday hoopla in the same way that a Jewish child attending public school will.

At day schools, the food in the building will not violate the basic rules of *kashrut,* and the school calendar is arranged around the Jewish calendar: no Saint Patrick's Day, no Easter, no soccer on Shabbat. While children in supplementary Jewish schools often have conflicts with sports and lessons, day school students have afternoons free for such activities.

The social dimension of day school includes the whole family. Parents meet and become friends. Commitments and communities intersect, creating a more unified and unambiguously Jewish world for adults as well as children.

Concerns and Problems The most intractable problem associated with day school education is cost: from $7,000 to $10,000 per child per year.

Sometimes grandparents help with tuition, scholarships are available, and there are growing philanthropic efforts to ease the financial burden.

There are also some social costs to day school attendance. Generally, there is little sense of neighborhood for students who often commute from various suburbs. Day school children may not know other kids on their own block which may necessitate more driving for after-school and weekend play dates with friends from school.

Some parents worry about the lack of racial and religious diversity in a Jewish school. But day school students can meet children of different backgrounds in city-sponsored sports leagues, after-school activities, and summer programs. And since most day school students ultimately attend secular high schools, and virtually all go on to mainstream colleges and universities, many parents feel that a solid grounding in Jewish learning and identity is worth postponing the experience of religious diversity.

In fact, Jewish day school populations may be no less homogeneous than most suburban public schools. Children from a wide religious spectrum (Modern Orthodox to secular Jews) attend some community-based schools. And the cultural/racial mix has been enriched through enrollment by recent immigrants from the former Soviet Union, enrollment by Israelis, and international adoptions.

Another concern is that day school children may feel marginal in the family synagogue. Since they are not part of the congregation's supplementary school community and spend the week immersed in Jewish learning and prayer, going to temple for Shabbat or even holidays may become a sore point. Parents can help mitigate this situation by making sure that day school students are on the appropriate mailing lists so they know about junior congregations, youth group events, holiday parties, retreats, and the like. Membership in a synagogue-based *havurah* (a small group that meets for holidays, study, and celebration) with other families who have children around the same age is another way to help your children feel that they belong to the synagogue and that the synagogue belongs to them.

Clarify Your Goals Be clear about why you are choosing a day school education and how it might affect your entire family. Try to be honest about your child's interests and abilities.

Day school education is not a "magic bullet" that can guarantee the creation of a committed Jewish adult or prevent intermarriage. Nor is day school a good Jewish choice if it is made solely on the basis of general academic excellence or small class size. The dual track in general and Jewish studies means more subjects, more classroom hours, and more homework. While this is a wonderful challenge for many students, it can be overwhelming for others. Know your own child's limits and respect them.

Become a Full Partner in Your Child's Education In a sense, day school is also "supplementary" in that it is just one part of the larger project of Jewish living. If school is the only Jewish experience in a child's life, she will learn that Jewishness is something to be compartmentalized and set apart from what goes on at home or in the community.

As in any school setting, parents who are involved in the life and the mission of the institution set a powerful example that their children tend to emulate. Although children can have a positive experience in a school that does not exactly mirror their family's beliefs and practices, all Jewish day schools include some level of religious practice and have some expectations about family practice. Programs are closed for all the Jewish holidays, which begs the question: "What did your family do on Sukkot?"

Special-Needs Education For the most part, Jewish day schools and supplemental programs try to accommodate children with special needs; however, the resources and commitment varies from school to school, teacher to teacher. Although there are many individual examples of schools and classrooms accommodating the needs of a deaf, blind, or learning-disabled or delayed child, by and large, Jewish institutions struggle with the costs associated with special-needs students and tend to act on a case-by-case basis. While the Americans with Disabilities Act has prompted Jewish institutions to become more accessible, few schools are equipped to take care of children with profound disabilities (see Chapter 10).

Home-schooling The home-schooling movement in North America is growing. Parents may choose this route as a way of giving their children a Jewish education if they are isolated from a Jewish community, to suit a child's special learning needs, or simply because they are not satisfied with available options. There are loads of published resources—not just books but curricula, computer programs, and a host of Web sites—that can assist home-schoolers.

Parents can compensate for the absence of Jewish classmates and peer groups with play groups, synagogue involvement, Jewish community center activities, youth groups, summer camps, and the like. However, the fact remains that Jewish study is a fundamentally communal enterprise that thrives on the heat and light generated in groups of students and teachers. Although parents and children can certainly take those roles, family dynamics tend to get tangled up in the process. Even the most comprehensive, rigorous, creative home-schooling cannot substitute for the quintessential Jewish pedagogic experience: the text-based argument.

SUMMER CAMP

Summer camp is a place where children learn new skills and discover that they can thrive away from home, where they create deep friendships, some that will last a lifetime. If camp is also a place where being Jewish is easy and fun, all of these powerful experiences become part of a child's Jewish memory bank.[7] Parents who went to Jewish summer camp themselves almost always want to give their children the experience, too.

Camps are run by a variety of organizations. Nonprofit camps run by Jewish communal agencies specialize in summers that teach Jewish skills and values, foster Jewish community, create strong Jewish memories, and encourage religious growth (along with the full complement of sports, arts and crafts, hiking, etc.). These include Jewish community centers and Zionist groups such as Young Judaea and Habonim Dror, which stress Israeli culture and Hebrew language. There are also a few secular Jewish camps that stress social-justice values, environmental issues, and Jewish culture.

The Reform and Conservative movements both sponsor large camping programs. Although different in many ways, Conservative-movement camps and Reform-movement camps incorporate Jewish learning into daily life, orient the weekly calendar around Shabbat observance, and foster a joyful sense of Jewish community.[8]

Although a handful of private, for-profit camps offer meaningful Jewish programming, most private camps run by Jews for a largely Jewish clientele do not provide any Jewish content apart from a chicken dinner on Friday night.

Facilities at Jewish camps range from rustic to very comfortable. And while every camp is different, Jewish programming generally includes a focus on Israel (with lots of singing and dancing) and connections between the environment and Judaism. Hebrew words and names are woven into daily life, and Shabbat is a weekly highlight. In addition to Jewish content, camps provide a general summer experience with water sports, team sports, arts and crafts, singing and dancing, hiking, dramatics, and games. There are only a few Jewish camps that specialize in a single skill or interest, such as tennis or drama.

The size of these summer programs is limited, which means that camps fill very quickly. It's best to start planning a year ahead and make a commitment early.[9]

Choosing a Camp   Take your time and choose carefully, because after one happy summer, most children won't even consider switching. Most families select a camp on the basis of word-of-mouth recommendations. Generally, children want to go where their friends go, or where their parents went. For other camp recommendations, consult your rabbi, cantor, and educators, who will usually, though not exclusively, suggest camps sponsored by their own movements. Staff at local Bureaus of Jewish Education may also have suggestions.

There is no one-size-fits-all camp, so it's important to find a good match for your child. Don't depend on camp marketing tools such as brochures and videos. The best way to decide is to take your child to visit some camps while they are in session.

If you can't manage a visit, try to arrange a meeting with the camp director, and bring your son or daughter. Continuity and leadership are crucial indicators of a camp, and directors are generally year-round staff, and set the tone for the program. Ask about the length of his or her tenure, and also about staff continuity. It's a good sign if many of the counselors "grew up" at the camp.

Other questions to ask a camp director:

- How old are the counselors? (Older is generally better. Do you want sixteen-year-olds in charge of your eight-year-old?)
- What is the staff-camper ratio? (A healthy ratio is four to six kids per counselor.)
- How many campers return from one summer to the next?
- What is the policy on visits and phone calls?

- What kind of training/orientation does the staff receive?
- Is there a social worker on staff?
- How is homesickness handled?

Finally, there is the question of cost. Summer camp is expensive; however, scholarships are available. Local federations provide financial aid, and some synagogues will find support for kids going to camps run by their own movement.

Readiness   Generally, children who enjoy sleepovers at other children's homes are ready for camp, but even this rule of thumb is not foolproof. You can help set the stage for camp by talking about it as something to consider "in a few years" and by introducing your child to older children, cousins, or neighbors who love going to Jewish camps. Some residential camps run a short "mini-camp" to introduce young children to camping.

Homesickness   Homesickness is a normal reaction to separation from the rhythms and comforts of home and family life, and most children experience it during their first year at camp at least. Counselors should be trained to help children handle these feelings, but parents can also do a lot to minimize homesickness and set the stage for a great summer.

It's hard to predict which kids will struggle with homesickness. While most children do fine at sleep-away camp, some cannot adjust to the change and the separation.

You can mitigate homesickness by helping your child feel competent about taking care of him- or herself. In the months before camp begins, younger children may need practice putting themselves to bed, managing laundry, and toothbrushing.

Face up to your own separation issues. Do not project your anxieties on your child or set him up by dwelling on how much you're going to miss him when he's away. Emphasize how much fun camp will be and do not make deals like, "Just try it for a few days and if you don't like it you can come home . . ." Reassure your child that most kids get homesick, that it's normal and that it stops.

Start writing letters before your child leaves so that a letter will be there on the first day of camp. And keep writing—every day if possible.

Day Camp   Most Jewish community centers offer day camps at urban campuses and/or at facilities in the country, with programs for children from preschool through elementary school. Some have programs for junior high and even high school–age kids, which tend to be heavy on day trips and short overnight adventures. Bring your child for a visit while the camp is in session so that you can check out the activities, counselors, and facilities together.

In addition to swimming lessons, arts and crafts, sports, and games, Jewish day camps provide a multifaceted Jewish experience, highlighting Shabbat observance, Hebrew songs, and Israeli dancing. Day camps can also introduce and/or reinforce the use of Hebrew words and prayers before and after meals, while fostering connections between Jewishness and the environment.

When considering a day camp, ask the director some of the same questions as those listed above. Also consider the duration of the bus ride. (Is an hour commute each way a good idea?)

Day camps usually offer an overnight program each session, which is a good way to introduce your child to the idea of being away from home, and to see how s/he handles the separation.

While less expensive than residential camp, day camp fees can be quite high; again, scholarships are available.

BOOKS FOR CHILDREN AND PARENTS TO READ TOGETHER

Does God Have a Big Toe? Stories about Stories in the Bible, by Marc Gellman (HarperCollins, 1989).

The Book of Miracles: A Young Person's Guide to Jewish Spirituality, by Lawrence Kushner (Jewish Lights, 1997).

A Coat for the Moon, and Other Jewish Tales, selected and retold by Howard Schwartz and Barbara Rush (Jewish Publication Society, 1999)—plus many of Howard Schwartz's retellings.

SCHOOL RESOURCES

The Congress of Secular Jewish Organizations runs programs that study Jewish tradition, history, literature, music, art, languages (Yiddish as well as Hebrew), and creative, nonreligious approaches to holiday celebrations. Contact Rifke Feinstein, Executive Director, 19657 Villa Drive, Southfield, MI 48076, www.csjo.org.

The Jewish Community Day School Network (JCDSN) is an association of Jewish community day schools not affiliated with any one movement but committed to pluralistic Jewish learning environments.

You can write them at 255 College Cross, Unit 61, Norfolk, VA 23510, www.jesna.org/jdcsn/index.htm.

The Jewish Educational Service of North America, a national research and development organization, is located at 111 Eighth Avenue, New York, NY 10011, www.jesna.org.

The Progressive Alliance for Reform Day Schools (PARDeS), an affiliate of the Union of American Hebrew Congregations, is located at 633 Third Avenue, New York, NY 10017, www.rj.org/pardes.

The Solomon Schechter Day School Association, associated with the Conservative movement, is located at 155 Fifth Avenue, New York, NY 10010, www.uscj.org (click on "day school").

The Workmen's Circle (*Arbeiter Ring*) runs secular Jewish schools and summer camps that stress Yiddish language and culture and social-justice values. They are located at 43 East Thirty-third Street, New York, NY 10016, www.circle.org.

For more information about supplementary schools associated with Conservative, Reconstructionist, and Reform synagogues, see movement listings in Chapter 3.

CAMP RESOURCES

The American Camping Association, the primary industry-wide organization, provides an interactive database on its Web site (www.acacamps.org) with links to many Jewish camp Web sites.[10]

The Association of Jewish Sponsored Camps, a membership organization of over forty camps, provides referrals free of charge to both sleepaway and day camps. You can reach them at 130 East Fifty-ninth Street, NY, NY 10022; 212-751-0477; or www.jewishcamps.org.

The Foundation for Jewish Camping, which supports camp construction, recruitment, and program development, can provide a directory of all Jewish camps in North America. For information, contact them at 6 East 39th Street, 10th Floor, New York, NY 10016, 212-792-6222: or www.jewish-camping.org.

Chapter 8

Ages Eleven
to Fourteen: Fitting In,
Coming of Age

E arly adolescence is a time of radical change and rapid growth on many fronts: physical, emotional, intellectual, social, and moral. Children who were mostly unaware of their bodies, become hyperaware of their appearance ("I hate my hair"; "Why aren't I taller?"), compare their looks to those of friends and media role models, and become self-conscious sexually. Early adolescence is also an age of unacknowledged losses. The blissful sense that "My parents are the smartest and most attractive people in the world" gives way to the shock and embarrassment of seeing that your father's jokes are stupid and your mother's clothes are frumpy. Young teens face up to a liberating but terrifying insight: I want to be separate from my parents.

Somewhere between the ages of eleven and fourteen, the center of the universe shifts from family life to peer-group life. Friends, classmates, and teammates become a primary source of identity and validation, and the primary attraction of school is what happens *between* classes—in the hallways and the lunchroom, on the bus and on the playing field.

Early adolescence is a challenging time for parents. Your once-pliant and loving child may push you away, insist on more independence, and challenge your authority on every front. But despite the fact that your child *seems* to care more about what her friends think and say than what you think and say, parental modeling remains primary. Even when teens temporarily (sometimes vehemently) reject their family's ways, the overwhelming evidence shows that most people eventually reproduce their parents' basic values and life choices as adults. Nevertheless, being an accepted part of a group is crucial to teens at this stage, which means that Jewish parents should focus, in large measure, on fostering Jewish peer groups. There are several ways parents can provide one or, even better, several Jewish teen communities; these include living in a city or town with other Jewish families (see the discussion "Your Jewish Neighborhood," in Chapter 3), supporting youth group activities, sending young teens to Jewish summer camp, and encouraging their continued attendance in Jewish schools.

The Jewish life cycle helps by providing a Jewish peer group at this point in children's development, since these are the years when the vast majority of Jewish children are preparing for bar and bat mitzvah. In addition to classroom interaction, bar and bat mitzvah often becomes a focus of a child's social life for nearly two years, as he or she attends the ceremonies and *simchas* (joyous celebrations) of friends and acquaintances. For students enrolled in both supplementary and day schools, the grade-grouping becomes even closer-knit as a whole seventh grade cycles through this rite of passage.

LIFE CYCLE

BAR AND BAT MITZVAH

Bar and bat mitzvah are an organizing principle of American Jewish life. A large percentage of American Jews join synagogues in order to prepare their children for the coming-of-age ceremony. Even people who have been disaffected from the Jewish community for years will reconnect for this purpose; for some families, bar/bat mitzvah prompts the first contact with the Jewish world since a wedding or a parent's own bar/bat mitzvah.

Bar and bat mitzvah are public statements of Jewish identity, ways to please grandparents (a perfectly honorable goal), and a pledge to the Jewish future. They can become emotional benchmarks for families, peak experiences for children and parents alike.

For the child, bar or bat mitzvah is a moment of triumph. The otherwise painfully self-conscious thirteen-year-old boy or girl faces a sanctuary filled with family, friends, and congregants who are rooting for them, overwhelming normal adolescent self-doubt with love, respect, pride, and honor.

More important than a performance or a recital, more personal than a report card, it is an affirmation of a child's whole self, with every aspect of development on display, from a new physique to the emerging spiritual-moral-Jewish voice explaining the week's Torah portion.

For parents, bar/bat mitzvah is a crowning moment. To watch a son or daughter stand, Torah in arms, before family, friends, and congregation is a moment of great pride and joy—but one tinged with sadness as well. This young woman or man is not a baby, nor are you "young parents" anymore.

With bar/bat mitzvah, mothers and fathers mark a kind of midpoint in their parenting careers. You pull out the baby pictures and marvel at the transformation of the chubby infant into a long-limbed person with preferences and passions of his or her own. And when you get the bar/bat mitzvah portraits back from the photographer, you catch a glimpse of what she or he will look like as a grown man or woman.

Like all other life-cycle events, bar/bat mitzvah embodies profound changes in your family life. Parents need to recognize the child's developing maturity: this is a budding adult who needs practice in making his or her own choices. The bar/bat mitzvah itself marks the start of this new stage.

For the extended family, gathered from around the country, or even around the world, a bar/bat mitzvah can have effects beyond all expectations. Family feuds may be reconciled, long-lost cousins rediscovered. Divorced parents remember the dreams they once shared, now realized in the young person standing on the *bimah*.[1]

Although there are many stresses associated with planning the Big Event, the forces of normal adolescence, which ordinarily tend toward chaos, are contained and held together. Even though your child thinks you are weird and your child is driving you crazy, a bar/bat mitzvah requires everyone to sit down and talk—with the rabbi and cantor, with the caterer, and most of all, with one another. The talking sometimes leads to a big fight about skirt lengths or haircuts, but even the arguments are part of the whole holy package.

History   Although according to Jewish law, all Jewish thirteen-year-olds acquire the status of ritual adulthood whether or not they participate in a bar or bat mitzvah ceremony, it has become a major life-cycle event for families and for the whole Jewish community. In fact, bar mitzvah is a relatively "new" ritual in the grand sweep of Jewish history. Unmentioned in the Bible or Talmud, it became customary only in fourteenth-century Germany and Poland.[2] The central act of the ritual was—and remains—the honor of getting an *aliyah*, a call to the *bimah* to bless and/or read from the Torah at a regular congregational service. The ritual expanded to include a discourse (*d'rash*) on the Torah portion by the bar mitzvah; in some synagogues it also became customary for accomplished students to lead part of the service. The bar mitzvah boy thus demonstrated his erudition and intellectual maturity by taking his place among the other men of the community, who regularly read from the Torah.

Bat mitzvah has a much shorter history. Since women were not, historically, given public religious honors such as reading from the Torah or being counted for a *minyan* (a prayer quorum of ten), girls' coming-of-age was accorded no communal recognition until the twentieth century. The first recorded bat mitzvah was celebrated in the United States in 1922 by Judith Kaplan (Eisenstein), the eldest daughter of Mordecai Kaplan, the founder of the Reconstructionist movement. Bat mitzvah finally became fully normative for liberal Jews in the 1970s, and it is now virtually indistinguishable from bar mitzvah in most liberal congregations.[3] At the age of thirteen, Jews automatically become bar mitzvah "son of the commandment" or bat mitzvah "daughter of the commandment." Although thirteen-year-olds are not treated as adults, the rite of passage acknowledges the beginnings of maturity, starting with the fact that parents are no longer fully responsible for their children's religious obligations. For example, on Yom Kippur, a person who has attained the age of bar/bat mitzvah is expected to fulfill the adult obligation of fasting. Thirteen-year-olds may fulfill adult responsibilities, such as being counted in the *minyan* or serving as a legal witness at a Jewish wedding.

Current Practice   A bar or bat mitzvah ceremony can occur during any congregational service where the Torah is taken out and read: at morning services (*Shacharit*) on Monday, Thursday, and Shabbat, at the afternoon service (*Mincha*) on Shabbat, and on holidays. The majority are scheduled on Shabbat morning. Unlike a wedding or a baby-naming, bar and bat mitzvah are not meant to be invitation-only, private celebrations since each one honors the addition of a new Jewish adult to *klal Yisrael*, the people of Israel.

The specific customs for bar/bat mitzvah ceremonies vary from one congregation to the next: in some synagogues, the young man or woman leads part of the service, reading prayers in Hebrew and English, leading songs and responsive readings; in others, participation is limited to reading a Torah portion and making a speech, or *d'rash;* some congregations mandate the same liturgical participation for all *b'nai mitzvah* (plural of bar/bat mitzvah), but elsewhere more adept students are encouraged to lead more of the service. Special-needs children who wish to become bar or bat mitzvah are almost always accommodated with sensitivity and respect (see Chapter 10).

Despite the variety of customs, there are three universal elements in virtually all bar and bat mitzvahs: the *aliyah,* the speech, and the celebration.

The Aliyah Receiving an *aliyah* means being called up to the *bimah,* the raised platform in the synagogue, to recite the blessings for the Torah reading and then to chant or read from the scroll. The bar or bat mitzvah may read or chant as little as three verses or as much as the entire weekly Torah portion; then he or she will read a *Haftarah,* a selection from the prophetic writings, along with its blessings, before and after.

Family and friends of the bar/bat mitzvah are usually given *aliyot* (the plural of *aliyah*). Parents, grandparents, siblings, uncles, aunts, and cousins may be called up to recite the Torah blessings or chant from the Torah. Other honors include opening the ark where the Torah is stored, lifting and dressing the Torah in its decorative cover before it is returned to the ark. In some congregations, the Torah scroll is passed from grandparents to parents to the bar/bat mitzvah, in a gesture that symbolizes the passing of the tradition from one generation to the next.

***The Speech, or* D'rash** With this address, the bar or bat mitzvah student demonstrates his or her understanding of the Hebrew text s/he has just read. Although the speech often includes a list of "thank you's" to parents, teachers, and siblings, the main point is to showcase the young person's approach to Jewish belief and learning in front of family, friends, and community. Focusing on the content of the weekly Torah portion or *Haftarah* reading, the bar/bat mitzvah often extrapolates a moral teaching that applies to his/her real life.

The rabbi generally also delivers a *d'rash* or sermon, and/or a "charge," which is a kind of personal sermon addressed to the bar or bat mitzvah and his or her family. In many synagogues, parents also make a short speech or give a blessing to their child.

The Celebration As with every Jewish life-cycle event, bar/bat mitzvah comes with the obligation of a *s'eudat mitzvah,* a festive meal. Often, the family will sponsor a kiddush buffet or luncheon immediately following services, where the Shabbat kiddush blessing and the blessing for bread start the meal. While this lunch may comprise the entire celebration, many families also hold afternoon or evening parties at home, at the synagogue, or in a hotel ballroom or hall.

Nearly all bar/bat mitzvah ceremonies are held in synagogues where families are members. Unaffiliated families borrow a Torah scroll and hold their bar/bat mitzvah in function halls, living rooms, even outdoors. Since Jewish worship services do not require the presence of a rabbi, the proceedings may be led by a family member or friend, or by the bar/bat mitzvah. This kind of do-it-yourself ceremony celebration tends to be intimate and modest.

Israel Some parents plan an additional religious celebration of bar/bat mitzvah in Israel as an affirmation of the family's connection to the land and as a special gift. In Israel, the ceremony can be arranged at a number of sites, the most popular being the Western Wall in Jerusalem (for boys only, since Orthodox rulings restrict public and communal observances and services for women at the Wall) and at the historical ruins of Masada (for both boys and girls). It is also possible to arrange for a bar/bat mitzvah at a Reform or Conservative congregation in Israel. Remember, though, that the entire service there will be in the vernacular, which is Hebrew.

A bar/bat mitzvah trip of this kind can become a turning point in Jewish identity and commitment, especially if it is your family's first time in Israel. Tour companies that specialize in bar/bat mitzvah trips to Israel can help make all necessary arrangements.

Preparing for Bar and Bat Mitzvah Getting ready for a bar/bat mitzvah is a challenge, both intellectually and developmentally. Children must learn enough Hebrew to read from the Torah and *Haftarah* and in some cases lead the congregation through parts of the liturgy. The speech, or *d'rash,* is a test of intelligence, thoughtfulness, and discipline. It takes a lot of self-confidence and poise to stand in front of a room full of friends, relatives, and strangers and give what for most kids is the biggest performance of their lives.

Children need time to acquire the knowledge and skills that make bar and bat mitzvah meaningful. Synagogue schools start gearing up in fourth or fifth grade, teaching the Torah blessings, studying the *siddur* (prayer book), and mastering Hebrew reading. In the final months, students are privately tutored, either by a cantor, rabbi, or Hebrew teacher.

Thoughtfully run synagogue schools also devote at least a year's worth of special programming for children studying for bar/bat mitzvah. Many schools require some form of public service such as doing volunteer work, as well as discussion and practice of *tzedakah* (righteous giving). The bar/bat mitzvah curriculum may include a series of family study sessions and/or a Shabbat retreat for parents and children.

Parents also have a great deal of preparing to do. There are so many details to work out: choosing who gets honors at services (*aliyot*), the guest list, hotel reservations, meals, transportation. Throughout this process, every choice—even apparently trivial ones, such as the size of the invitation—can be a lesson for your son or daughter.

Many parents read from the Torah as part of the bar/bat mitzvah service and have a speech to write—both of which responsibilities require a great deal of preparation and forethought.

Since every synagogue has its own bar/bat mitzvah customs and culture, be sure to attend services in the year preceding your event to see how they are conducted and to become comfortable with the service. Some temples have a bar/bat mitzvah every Shabbat during the school year; for others, they are a rare event. In some temples, congregants attend Shabbat morning services regularly; in others, only invited guests show up on Saturday morning. Some communities permit the family to personalize the service, others expect the bar/bat mitzvah family to conform to the *minhag* (custom) of the congregation. Talk to the rabbi if you have special requests or concerns, such as the role of non-Jewish relatives at bar/bat mitzvah.

One way to prepare your guests for the event is to send a pamphlet that explains the service for people who may never have attended a bar/bat mitzvah before.

Making It Meaningful   The bar/bat mitzvah season is a pivotal time for parents to teach values through their own choices. Will you spend more time and money on the cake than on your child's prayer shawl? Will you be inviting all the cousins? Do you permit your child to attend her friends' bar/bat mitzvah parties even if she missed the service in order to attend soccer practice? Do you go to the services yourself? However you choose, your children will be watching and learning from you.

One way to send a powerful message about values during a bar/bat mitzvah season is by making *tzedakah* a key element in the celebration. Many families now donate 3 percent of all monies spent on food for the bar or bat mitzvah to Mazon: A Jewish Response to Hunger, which funds soup kitchens, food pantries, and other feeding programs in the United States and around the world.[4] Other ways of putting *tzedakah* at the top of the bar/bat mitzvah agenda include: bringing floral centerpieces to a local nursing home after the party; delivering leftover food to a shelter; including a note on the bar/bat mitzvah invitation asking guests to bring canned goods for donation to a local food pantry; using baskets full of toiletries for centerpieces, with a note explaining they will be donated to a shelter.

Unfortunately, bar and bat mitzvah celebrations tend to be associated less with *tzedakah* than with conspicuous consumption, bad taste, and religious shallowness. To help avoid the pitfalls of life in a consumer culture, consider the following questions while planning for the big day:

Who Really Cares about the Canapés? If everyone in your congregation hosts a lavish party, you will doubtless feel pressured to do the same. Given the tribal mentality of young teens, it's easy to understand where they get the idea that three disc jockeys and endless party favors are mandatory if they have been so entertained by "everyone else."

The level of wealth in the American Jewish community has led to legendary examples of ostentation and poor judgment: absurd and wasteful quantities of food, roller-skating chimpanzees, roulette tables, re-creations of the *Titanic*. But the tendency to over-do the celebration is nothing new. During the Middle Ages, rabbis decreed limits on the number of guests and even the kind of clothing worn at bar mitzvah celebrations. In part those laws were an attempt to avert anti-Semitic resentment about Jewish wealth; however, the rabbis also wanted to allay pressure on poorer Jews, who might incur debts or suffer embarrassment by comparison with the well-to-do.

Today, there is a healthy backlash against excessive spending. In an effort to keep the focus on the *mitzvah* in bar/bat mitzvah, synagogue curricula stress community service and *tzedakah*, and many congregations strongly encourage all families to donate to Mazon. Families have even chosen to hold *mitzvah* parties (helping restore a crumbling synagogue, visiting seniors) in lieu of dance parties.

Who's in Charge? Your son or daughter should be a junior partner in his/her own bar/bat mitzvah; after all, this ritual calls forth and acknowledges growing maturity and responsibility. Nevertheless, thirteen-year-olds are not grown-up enough to make all the decisions by themselves. Parents have to balance a child's maturity and the social pressures s/he faces while remaining firm about the bottom line—not only financially, but also in terms of values, common sense, and good taste.

For example, parents should guide their child about cash gifts. After all, you wouldn't hand over $500 (or $2,000 or $10,000) to a thirteen-year-old without setting some limits. You might tell your child that he or she can keep some amount for personal use, but that a set percentage will be sent to a charity of his/her choosing; some parents feel it's appropriate to designate the lion's share of money for college or for a high school trip to Israel.

Before you sit down to talk about any aspect of the ceremony or celebration with your thirteen-year old, make sure you are clear and in agreement about what you hope to accomplish. Then make out two lists: one of nonnegotiable items—the budget, for example, or your intention to put Hebrew on the invitation as a way of stressing the religious nature of the event. But there are other items where compromise is appropriate. Remember your child's developmental need to be accepted by peers as you discuss aspects of the celebration that are cosmetic or mostly child-focused: color schemes and dance music, for instance.

Who Is It For? Take a step back and ask yourself why you are spending so much money and expending so much energy on the bar or bat mitzvah celebration. What does this ceremony mean for you? What do you want it to mean for your child? Are you clear about the difference?

If you want the ritual to be meaningful to your child, it must be independently meaningful to you, on your own terms. One way to forge your own, grown-up connection to the event is to study during the year leading up to bar and bat mitzvah, something many synagogues facilitate through family classes and retreats. Another option is to accept an *aliyah* for yourself, and prepare to read from the Torah at the service. It may prove to be far more difficult for you than for your child. The shared effort may put you on a newly equal footing, especially if you've never done it before.

After the Party's Over   For a bar or bat mitzvah to be something more than a great big party, parents need to communicate their belief that the ritual is no more a graduation from Jewish learning than the ceremony that ends junior high school is the end of English and math studies. Bar/bat mitzvah marks the *start* of a new, more mature stage in Jewish education, which includes junior and senior high school programs, youth groups, camping, reading from the Torah on holidays, teaching younger children in the synagogue school, volunteering in the synagogue food drive, etc. To turn this expectation into reality, parents have to locate and encourage challenging, meaningful experiences—both in and out of classrooms—for their young teens in peer-based settings where they can practice learning, working, and playing as Jews.

CHOICES

FORMAL EDUCATION, INFORMAL LEARNING

The two main options for formal Jewish learning in early adolescence are the same as for school-age children: supplementary schools, mostly associated with synagogues, and full-time private day schools (see Chapter 7).

While there are substantial differences between supplementary and day schools, either one can provide children with a Jewish peer group, which is crucial at this stage. Both can provide tools for life-long Jewish learning, including Hebrew skills, a critical approach to texts, and a more sophisticated Jewish vocabulary including: Midrash, Mishnah, tractate, Hillel, Maimonides, Rashi, Hasidism, etc.

Supplementary Schools   The years just prior to bar and bat mitzvah represent the biggest bulge in supplementary school enrollment. Most Jewish eleven-, twelve-, and thirteen-year-olds attend classes preparing for the big day. Supplementary schools invariably focus on Hebrew reading and prayer-book skills in class.

Other coursework covers a wide range, which, depending on the school, may include a more in-depth study of the life cycle (some visit a Jewish funeral home and/or cemetery), immigration and *shtetl* life (family-history projects may be assigned), a unit on contemporary Israel (some teachers team kids with Israeli e-mail pals), comparative religions (with speakers from and visits to area churches and mosques), personal ethics (perhaps focusing on what Judaism has to say about cliques and gossip), and the Holocaust.[5] Some schools give older students electives, with courses in Jewish arts, personal concepts of God and spirituality, and ethics among the choices. Text study (Bible, Talmud, Midrash, etc.) may be incorporated in almost any subject.

Given the developmental importance of peer groups at this stage, schools may start the year with team-building activities, such as a day at a ropes course, or participating in a pledge walk to raise money for *tzedakah*. Socializing is sometimes built into the middle school program, with time for eating and hanging out.

As students face increasingly demanding work in their regular classrooms, Jewish educators often try to avoid "frontal" classes, in which the teacher talks "at" kids arrayed in rows. Discussion formats are favored, with students encouraged to connect their own concerns to Jewish sources. Some programs incorporate pressing life-style topics (body image, drug use, sexual ethics) into junior and senior high school curricula to get across the message that Jewish tradition addresses everything—that Judaism is not a once-a-week or twice-a-year religion, but a way of life. (See the discussion about supplementary school curriculum in Chapter 9.)

If you are shopping for a supplementary school with bar/bat mitzvah in mind, remember that the best predictor of "success" in terms of your child's on-going Jewish education and identity is a high proportion of students continuing their Jewish studies after bar and bat mitzvah. If significant numbers of eighth- and ninth-graders continue to attend religious school, either in the synagogue's program or as part of a community consortium, the school is doing a good job.

Problems and Concerns　Time constraints become even more pressing as homework expectations grow and children commit to particular sports or arts. The physical, emotional, and intellectual stresses of the age make it difficult for many kids to focus later in the day.

By this age, moreover, the students are more sophisticated learners and are far less tolerant of bad teaching and weak curricula. They are also into testing limits at home and at school. These are tricky times that call for both creative programming and a renewed commitment to making Jewish learning as creative and sophisticated as possible.

One of the biggest problems for supplementary programming is the parental message that post–bar/bat mitzvah Jewish education is entirely optional. Whether parents come right out and say, "It's up to you," or simply permit absences on any pretext, the implicit message, "We think Jewish learning is not as important as math, or even soccer," is devastatingly clear.

Day School   Full-time Jewish middle schools enjoy a reputation for academic excellence. Classes are small, and it is common for every teacher in a school to know every child by name—a kind of intimacy that educators consider beneficial for learning and development.

The curriculum in Jewish middle schools is demanding. In addition to the full complement of general studies (math, science, English, and social studies), there is coursework in Jewish studies, including Hebrew language, Jewish history, Bible, rabbinic texts, and Israel. Students who graduate from Jewish middle schools excel in the high schools they attend—public or private—and have no problem gaining entrance to the colleges and universities of their choice.

Socially, day schools reinforce and foster Jewish identity both formally and informally, by providing Jewish content in class and Jewish role models and peers in and out of class. At the same time, there tends to be less pressure on kids to hurry up and become full-fledged teenagers, a slowing down of the transition from childhood to adulthood in matters ranging from dating to wardrobe. Although the sartorial differences between Jewish day school students and the public middle school kids down the block might be invisible to an untrained eye, dress in Jewish schools is generally a bit more modest. And indeed, the mandate to talk about an issue such as modesty is one of the benefits that parents find appealing.

Although day school students participate in sports and take all kinds of private lessons, there are fewer competing pressures. For one thing, bar and bat mitzvah preparation requires far fewer after-school hours. Day school students may also participate in a synagogue bar/bat mitzvah program and be privately tutored, but with their daily Hebrew studies and regular worship services, during which they have the opportunity to practice the Torah portion, the process requires considerably less extracurricular time.

Jewish middle schools also reinforce a comprehensive Jewish lifestyle. School performances and dances are never scheduled on Friday nights, and most of the other kids will be going to Jewish summer camps.

When considering a Jewish middle school, be sure to ask the principal or headmaster, during your visit, about social realities at the school as well as about curriculum and test scores. In small schools, cliques can be especially brutal. In addition to the questions suggested in Chapter 7, more age-specific queries might include:

Has the school developed age-appropriate ways to foster spirituality? Do teachers encourage diversity of opinion and critical thinking? Are there family education programs (for example, sessions about the bar/bat mitzvah year)? Does the school offer sex education or classes on substance abuse and violence?

When you visit the school, observe informal interactions as well as formal classrooms. Studying values in the classroom is not enough; hopefully, you will see them being lived out in the school. Watch the kids at lunch, in the halls, at an assembly. Are children respectful but at ease with teachers and each other? Do the adults seem to enjoy being with teenagers?

Talk to parents of students already enrolled in the school and ask about the social scene, academic pressures, etc.

Transfers Students do transfer from public or secular independent schools to Jewish day schools at this stage and most are successful. Ask how the school helps transferring students and families through the transition. Some schools run a special Hebrew language class to bring newcomers up to speed, and also recommend a tutor. Some schools will customize the curriculum for the first semester or year until students are able to keep up in all their classes.

Problems and Concerns As with elementary day school education, Jewish middle school is very costly. Alienation from synagogue life may be even more of a problem if young teens feel alienated from students in their temple's supplementary school. Supportive clergy and synagogue educators can help find ways to integrate day school students, and youth groups can go a long way to help forge connections. (See the discussion in Chapter 7.)

Parents should be sensitive to the stresses of day school education. The additional classes mean a longer school day and more homework than in public or nonsectarian private schools. A typical school week for Jewish middle-schoolers, including homework, can amount to sixty hours.

Although many Jewish kids enjoy the extra challenge, it can be overwhelming for others, particularly transfers who are unaccustomed to the double load. Parents must assess each child as an individual and make choices based on his or her abilities, interests, and temperament.

Informal Learning   The division between informal learning and formal education is a bit artificial since young teens will socialize and learn from each other at school, just as they may study Jewish texts in camp and youth group. The point is to provide as many opportunities for contact with Jewish peers as possible. Even children enrolled in successful supplementary programs or at Jewish day school benefit from being part of additional informal Jewish peer groups. School-based groups tend to be relatively small and nearly familial; the same tight-knit cadre may have known each other since preschool, which can become an issue as kids start thinking about dating.

Jewish youth groups, Jewish community center activities (from athletics to arts), and Jewish summer camps all provide kids with ways to expand their Jewish lives beyond their families. In general, the more options and choices that put your child in touch with Jewish peers, friends, and role models, the better.

Some congregations run junior youth groups for middle school kids, sometimes in conjunction with other temples. Activities may include *tzedakah* projects, youth congregations, and synagogue service work, but the main point is to foster a Jewish-identified social life and give Jewish young people the chance to hang out together, forge friendships, have fun, and make meaningful contributions to the community. Junior youth group activities (outings, trips, parties) keep kids connected to each other and to the temple until they can join a senior high school youth group (described in Chapter 9). Some Jewish community centers and large synagogues even run a youth lounge staffed by a youth worker.

Summer camps are a great resource for children at this age. Indeed, Jewish camping becomes even more important as children start to define themselves apart from their families, fall in (and out) of love, and explore the larger world. Camps often gear special programs for young teens that might include more challenging camping experiences (backpacking, white-water rafting, and longer overnights, for example), or more off-site field trips. Some camps provide leadership training and counselor-in-training programs. For long-time campers, becoming a "senior" or counselor-in-training carries enormous cachet and status. It's a chance to be a role model to younger kids, and to forge a more egalitarian relationship with other staff members who are models of committed—and cool—Jewish young adulthood (see Chapter 7).

BOOKS FOR CHILDREN

For Kids: Putting God on the Guest List: A Guide for How to Claim the Spiritual Meaning of Your Bar/Bat Mitzvah, by Rabbi Jeffrey K. Salkin (Jewish Lights Publishing, 1998).

BOOKS FOR PARENTS

Whose Bar/Bat Mitzvah Is This, Anyway? A Guide for Parents Through a Family Rite of Passage, by Judith Davis, Ed.D. (St. Martin's Press, 1998).

Putting God on the Guest List: How to Reclaim the Spiritual Meaning of Your Child's Bar or Bat Mitzvah, by Rabbi Jeffrey K. Salkin (Jewish Lights Publishing, 1992).

Get Out of My Life: But First Could You Drive Me and Cheryl to the Mall? by Anthony E. Wolf, Ph.D. (The Noonday Press, 1991).

Chapter 9

Ages Fifteen to Eighteen: Learning to Make Jewish Choices

Adolescence is an intense period of expanding horizons, self-discovery, and emerging independence. In order to create a unique, authentic identity, teenagers experiment with ideas, beliefs, and their own self-image, checking out every nuance with their friends. Peer relationships are primary during these years when, paradoxically, self-definition is a group activity.

This is a notoriously tricky stage for parents. Relationships between teenagers and parents can be strained and at times even combative as you try to figure out how to get along with and love your self-reinventing daughter or son. Parents need to remember that whatever you do and say matters a great deal: when asked, most teens report that the most important people in their lives are their parents.

Teenagers tend to seek out environments where they can be moved, inspired, and challenged together with a group of their peers. Thus, the task for Jewish parents is to channel this need toward Jewish venues where deep, meaning-filled moments can blossom.

The most indelible memories for many Jewish teenagers take place not in classrooms, but in unplanned, serendipitous moments: sitting on a log by the lake with a college-age summer camp counselor; taking a late-night walk with the rabbi during the confirmation class trip to New York; a chance encounter with an Israeli teenager on a trip to Tel Aviv; falling in love during a youth group convention. Although parents are pointedly not part of these moments, you are the ones who make them happen by affiliating with synagogues, suggesting programs, driving to conventions, paying for camp, and so on.

In a way, your input at this stage hearkens back to the days when your six-foot son was an infant. Although you didn't really expect the baby to understand the Shabbat blessings, the exposure to the sounds, smells, and rhythms of your observance laid down a permanent substrate of sweet memories and soothing expectations. Even for teenagers who stalk out of the room while you are lighting candles, the simple fact that you are an engaged, practicing Jew—because it matters to you—remains the most effective Jewish example of all.

Teenagers may pretend not to listen, but they do hear when their parents discuss Israeli politics, the weekly Torah portion, or synagogue life. Teens register the fact that Mom and Dad are taking adult education courses, or participating in a Jewish book group, or going to services. The fact that parental hypocrisy is a cardinal sin for teens demonstrates that, as much as they want and need to separate, they nevertheless keep a keen eye on the grown-ups close to them.

Parents can still act as teachers to their adolescent children, although lecturing a teenager is almost never successful. On the other hand, asking for their opinion sometimes is. At this stage, when money is often an issue (as in "What happened to the twenty dollars I gave you yesterday?"), soliciting your teen's input on family *tzedakah* decisions, and following his/her suggestion, demonstrates that you take him/her seriously. Which increases the chance that your opinions, in turn, will be taken seriously.

Another way to demonstrate respect for an adolescent's voice is by sharing some of your own Jewish dilemmas. In the car on the way home from holiday services, for example, you might ask, "What do you think about that prayer that asks God to raise the dead? That idea has always bothered me so much, I can't say it out loud." Airing doubts about the wisdom of Israeli foreign policy, or some aspect of Jewish thought or practice shows that you think your son or daughter is old enough for a serious conversation.

Planned conversations with teenagers may seem artificial or forced. Still, parents should try to broach ethical questions (using Jewish values and terms wherever possible) that are relevant to their children's lives—

such as the tension between loyalty to a friend and needing to protect a friend's health or welfare—issues that arise around drinking and other risky behaviors.

Take advantage of natural settings for serious Jewish talk; watch TV with your teen. Go to movies or plays that raise important questions and discuss the merits of the production over a quick cappuccino afterwards.

If possible, connect significant moments in your teen's life to his/her Jewishness. For example, on the day he gets his driver's license, take a moment to sit in the front seat together and say *Shehechiyanu.*

Articulate and applaud your child's Jewish choices: "I would never have had the nerve to get up and lead a service at your age." "It's great to see you get so passionate about Israeli dance; I have two left feet."

Arguing and nagging are as much a part of adolescence as learning to walk is part of toddlerhood. Pick your Jewish arguments carefully, and start by letting your teen know what you expect of her. Some items may be nonnegotiable ("Attending Hebrew high school is not up for discussion any more than attending regular high school; you will continue through confirmation"). But others should be stated in the form of personal wishes. At some point when you are *not* arguing, talk to your child about other hopes and wishes:

"Mom and I would really like you to have Jewish friends as well as non-Jewish friends in your life."

"I want us to celebrate some part of Shabbat together every week."

"We expect you to go on an Israel trip during the summer before your senior year in high school, but you can choose which program to go on."

"Now that we're looking at colleges, I would like you to attend a school where there is a Jewish community with a campus Hillel."[1]

By the time children are in high school, parents cannot dictate their adolescents' behavior or choices in all things, nor should they. After all, you want your teenager to practice real decision-making while s/he is still living in the relative safety of home.

Listen to your teenager's views on Jewish life whenever they are volunteered. While these may be stated in the extreme, there may be a reasonable argument or proposal in what s/he says. Be prepared to negotiate—especially if your teen is willing to make Jewish choices:

"Hebrew school is the pits. We're doing the same stuff in ninth grade that we did in sixth grade. Besides, none of my friends are there, and it's boring. Why can't I go to Josh's Hebrew school? It's really cool. They eat pizza and the teachers are all college students."

"I'm going to Jewish day school, for crying out loud! I do Jewish stuff all week long, including more praying than you ever did in your whole life. I want to sleep on Saturday mornings."

Parenting experts agree that changing your position from time to time is not a sign of weakness if the change will accomplish your fundamental goals. Try working out a compromise:

"I'll ask to have you transferred out of Mr. Cohen's class, and if you still aren't getting anything out of it after another month, we'll look into the other temple's high school."

"Our family has always celebrated Shabbat together, and that is still my wish. I won't give up on Friday-night dinner—you have to be home for that—but we won't expect you to join us for services on Saturday morning."

Dating remains a hot-button topic for many Jewish parents, but the fact is that "interdating" (dating non-Jews) is a complicated subject in the liberal Jewish community. Most liberal Jewish teens know families where one parent converted to Judaism, and many know intermarried but Jewish-identified families. Besides, as your teen will tell you, "I'm not going to marry her. I'm only fifteen years old!"

Forbidding interdating, especially without explaining your reasoning, is sure to backfire. Kids hear the caveat "I want you to date Jews only," as a form of elitism or racism, and, just as bad, as an attempt at controlling their behavior. When you say, "I don't want you to date Chris," Chris instantly becomes much more attractive.

Be honest in telling your teenager why you prefer s/he date Jews: "Look, my dream is that you have a Jewish home someday. This is what I chose for myself and for our family: I think Judaism provides a wonderful way to live and to raise kids and I think it would be best for you, too. Although marriage is still far off in the future, all dating is a way to practice choosing a life-partner. Of course, ultimately, I know you'll make a good decision for yourself."

You can be sure that even a short, honest speech will be met by much eye-rolling, but at least you will have made your point openly and honestly.

With teenagers, trying to win each and every battle is a costly strategy. It's best to take the long view and have faith; if you love your children and love your own Jewishness, the fundamental structures you have modeled over the long haul will, in all likelihood, become an essential part of their lives as well.

LIFE CYCLE

CONFIRMATION, GRADUATION

The only public ceremony associated with the teen years is graduation from formal Jewish schooling.

Confirmation is nearly universal in Reform synagogues and a feature of many Conservative congregations as well. Often an impressive ceremony held during the holiday of Shavuot, it celebrates the receiving of the Torah with a ritual reenactment of the moment when the Hebrew tribe became the Jewish people—the people of the book. On a flower-covered *bimah*, the confirmands, boys and girls, act as prayer leaders and Torah readers, and read as well from personal reflections on their Jewish learning and on their visions for themselves as Jewish adults. In many congregations, the year preceding confirmation is an academically and socially rich experience, with special courses taught by the rabbi and a class trip.

An innovation of the Reform movement in the nineteenth century, confirmation was instituted as a replacement for the ritual of bar mitzvah, which many believed occurred when children were too young to appreciate its meaning. The change was also meant to remove the social and financial pressure on individual families and to extend the years for supplementary religious education. The Reform movement long ago reclaimed bar mitzvah and added bat mitzvah, while continuing to confirm students after tenth grade.

However, because confirmation looks and feels so much like a graduation, it has tended to function as an exit point—the end of formal Jewish learning in the temple. Many synagogues now schedule confirmation for the end of eleventh or twelfth grade.

Liberal Jewish high school graduations are a recent phenomenon because liberal Jewish high schools are themselves of recent vintage. (See the discussion on "Education," below, pp. 222–27.) These ceremonies are as moving and meaningful to family and friends as any high school graduation, with the additional emotional wallop that attends a powerful affirmation of Jewish life, learning, and continuity.

Whatever the setting (synagogue confirmation or day school graduation), family and friends can endorse the content of the event with meaningful gifts—for example, a subscription to the *Jerusalem Report*, a backpack for an up-coming Israel trip, tickets to see a play with Jewish content, Hebrew software, and the like.

CHOICES

Except for students enrolled in full-time Jewish day school, Jewish teens inhabit various worlds that rarely interact and generally skew to the non-Jewish. The more time kids spend at the synagogue, in youth group activities, in Israel, and at camp, the more Judaism will be a part of who they are. If teenagers are part of a Jewish peer group for only ninety minutes a week, it only makes sense that they will shape a sense of self from the non-Jewish culture of the high school, sports team, drama club, etc.

Providing Jewish peers for your teen may mean reassessing old choices: Is it time to move to a community where the public high school has a sizeable percentage of Jewish students? Do you want to explore the option of a Jewish high school?

Look around your own congregation: Does the temple employ a youth worker to help implement the community's goals for its teens? How are young adults encouraged to take part in the life of the community? Are there teenagers on the board of directors or school committee? Are teens invited to read Torah on Shabbat and during holidays?[2]

Parents should check their own attitudes and priorities, too. Parenting a Jewish teen means being cheerful while driving kids to Hebrew high and youth group events, and finding ways to finance Jewish education, summer camp, or a trip to Israel.

Finding the right match in a Jewish school, camp, youth group, or Israel trip may require getting involved in your local Jewish community and synagogue.[3]

However, remember that despite all your good intentions and best efforts, your teenager may refuse to attend a Jewish high school or temple youth group. By the time they reach high school, teenagers will insist on being included in decisions that affect them. Jewish tradition respects this reality by making young people over the age of thirteen responsible members of the community. Although not full adults, they can play important and meaningful roles, such as participating in a *minyan* (prayer quorum) or acting as a witness before a religious court (*bet din*). When you give your teenager the chance to make some of his/her own Jewish choices (for example, choosing Israel programs to research, or deciding how much of his/her allowance to give to *tzedakah*), you communicate confidence, faith, and pride in him/her as a *mensch*—a person worthy of trust and respect.

EDUCATION

Although 75 percent of thirteen-year-olds participate in some formal Jewish educational program, by the age of eighteen, fewer than one-quarter of those young people are enrolled in Jewish learning, or indeed, any organized Jewish activity.[4]

This means that a majority of Jews "graduate" from Jewish education with only an elementary level of learning. This is a great shame. If they were to quit their secular studies at the same point, they would be leaving school without ever having read Shakespeare or dissecting a frog.

Jewish high school programs can tackle the complexity of Jewish history, thought, literature, and ethics, and introduce teens to the lively give-and-take of Jewish text study. Jewish schools can also meet the adolescent's desire and need for serious conversations about personal responsibility, ethics, God, spirituality, and the problem of evil in the world. Jewish high school programs can connect Jewishness with teenagers' eagerness to participate in the hands-on work of *tikkun olam* through social justice projects (for example, by tutoring children who need help with reading) and *tzedakah* projects (by raising money for a local homeless shelter or working in a soup kitchen). And of course, Jewish high schools provide the ideal setting for socializing with a Jewish peer group.

Much of the information about schools in Chapters 7 and 8 also applies to high school programs, the basic choice being between supplementary schooling and full-time day school.

Teenagers enrolled in either kind of Jewish educational program deserve the following:

- Inspiring, high-powered Jewish teachers who walk their talk. Teenagers need adult models (including college students) who are connected and committed to living a Jewish life.
- A chance to make Jewish choices, to explore and focus on areas that interest and appeal to them; many high school programs do this by providing a selection of elective courses.
- Ways to connect Jewish concepts, values, and texts with things that are already critically important to them: from concerns about the state of the environment to sexuality and underage drinking.
- Ways to channel their idealism into action.
- Settings in which creativity can flourish, where teens can create Jewish music, art, drama, literature, dance.
- A culture where individual differences are respected and accepted, where nonconformists, geniuses, and jocks know they will not be teased or shunned by their peers.
- Honest conversations about living as a Jew in the non-Jewish world.
- Room for intellectual freedom and curiosity. Teens need to know they can say whatever they really think and that Judaism is a tradition of individuals and iconoclasts. You want your kid to go to the rabbi's class and say, "I don't believe in God," knowing she won't be shot down. You want her to learn that Judaism is full of doubters, that being Jewish is about arguing with other Jews, about intellectual sharpness, about mining Jewish texts for inconsistencies and different ways of understanding.

Jewish high school programs should empower their students as creative thinkers. Adolescents are not interested in hearing only about the received wisdom of the past; they want opportunities to "think outside the box," to see how their ideas can make a difference.

This is best accomplished through the ancient yet lively process of Jewish text study. For Jews, sacred texts are not one-dimensional but textured and complex. The Bible is a collection of diverse voices; the Talmud records some very idiosyncratic voices and is full of minority opinions.

Our tradition invites every Jew to engage, interpret, and debate the nuances and meanings of these texts. According to Jewish tradition, anyone can make an important contribution to the long, unfolding debate, and this can be a powerful message to young teens, who enjoy exercising their emerging voices and often feel unheard and disenfranchised.

When a teacher asks a class, "What do you think of this passage in the

Bible?" she is doing more than asking them to exercise critical thinking skills; she is inviting them to participate in a conversation that transcends time and space. A roomful of kids trying to imagine the conversation between Cain and Abel before the murder, or to conjure Isaac's thoughts as he silently goes up the mountain with Abraham, can find themselves "arguing with" rabbis who died 1,500 years ago as well as contemporary thinkers.

When text study is done right, teenagers discover that they are part of an ancient, ongoing, sacred conversation. They also find out that this stuff is fun.

Supplementary Schools Supplementary high school programs vary from synagogue to synagogue; some conclude formal education for teens after tenth-grade confirmation; the trend, however, is to offer postconfirmation courses through twelfth grade. Some congregations run their own "Hebrew High," while others join together to form a community school.

The supplementary high school curriculum is usually a combination of electives and a core curriculum that includes such areas as the Bible, rabbinics (Talmud and Midrash), Jewish history, literature, and philosophy.

Elective offerings in high school run a wide gamut: modern Jewish thought; the writings of Martin Buber; the prophets; why Jews don't believe in Jesus; Jewish views of the after-life; Jews in film; where was God during the Holocaust?; prayer for doubters; Jewish meditation; Judaism and sexuality; Jewish feminism.

Conversational Hebrew and courses on Israel are sometimes specifically geared to prepare students for trips to Israel.

Most supplementary programs try to link adolescent concerns to Jewish sources, texts, and values. The goal is to get the message across that Jewish tradition addresses everything, from headline issues in the daily newspaper to their own personal dilemmas about sex, dating, violence, stress, gossip, eating disorders, tattooing—whatever comes up.

Most programs meet weekly,[5] and many begin with a dinner hour to allow time for socializing. Retreats, class trips (to the Lower East Side in New York, the Skirball Museum in Los Angeles), and hands-on *tzedakah* projects linked to the study of Jewish texts on repairing the world, may be part of the curriculum. Another highlight in some programs is the chance to study with the rabbi(s) and cantor.

Jewish educators in supplementary schools have been accused of offering too many cooking classes and too little Talmud study. Although "lightweight" sessions are defended as ways to avoid further stress in the already pressured lives of high school students and to keep kids from dropping out, a curriculum that does not demand effort and intelligence will not be taken seriously. Whatever the content of supplementary programs, the curriculum should be sophisticated enough to appeal to Jewish teens who are used to rigorous coursework and Advanced Placement expectations. One solution is to demand serious reflection and engagement in class but avoid homework.

Parents who are shopping for a supplementary program should look for a well-considered curriculum, a principal who can express his goals, and classrooms where kids seem engaged by their teachers and comfortable with one another. Also, find out whether the high school and the youth group are part of a coordinated effort on behalf of teens. The best supplementary programs work in tandem with the youth group.

Day Schools   Liberal and interdenominational high schools are a new development in Jewish education.[6] Until the 1990s, nearly all were run by and for the Orthodox community, however, between 1992 and 1998, forty new non-Orthodox schools opened in cities from Boston to Los Angeles.[7]

Families select Jewish high schools for the same reasons they choose day schools for their younger children (see Chapters 7 and 8). In high school, a time when teens shape their identities, a Jewish setting further reinforces a strong and relatively unconflicted identity at an especially critical period.

This is not to say that teenagers who attend Jewish high schools are less contentious; they are still adolescents. However, conflicts with parents about dating non-Jews or participating in events on Shabbat or holidays are less common, especially compared with the experiences of Jewish teens attending secular schools.

Jewish high schools provide a relatively sheltered environment. Since the institutions are fairly small, it's nearly impossible for students to hide or fall through the cracks. Administrators and teachers get to know each student as an individual and have an easier time fostering a sense of community and accountability.

Jewish high schools are not insular ivory towers, however. One principal describes his goal as providing "semipermeable walls" between the Jewish world and the larger community. Some form working partnerships with non-Jewish schools, and teachers constantly help kids frame the question of Jewish identity in relation to the broader world. Jewish high schools certainly prepare students for full participation in secular society, providing a general education on a par with the best public and independent schools. Graduates are generally accepted by colleges and universities of their choice.

Jewish high schools run on two simultaneous, intersecting tracks. The Jewish-studies track includes Hebrew, Bible, and rabbinics (Talmud), with a variety of other courses in Jewish history, Jewish living, and Israel. The secular-studies track includes college-preparatory coursework in mathematics, English, history, science, and modern languages, with offerings in fine arts and physical education. *Tikkun olam*—community service—is also a requirement. Extracurricular activities include the usual gamut of clubs, student government, sports, music, theater, and the like.

Liberal Jewish high schools stress the notion of integration in every possible setting: connecting Jewish texts to *tzedakah* projects; connecting Jewish history and world history; demonstrating the ways Jewish music and Western music intersect; developing medically sound health/wellness/sexuality curricula that use Jewish sources and express Jewish values.

Critical thinking skills are taught and prized. Founded on principles basic to classical Jewish text study, students are encouraged to interpret what they study, find inconsistencies as well as connections, and creatively solve problems.

The typical course load at a Jewish high school is demanding—as many as ten courses, as compared to five at a secular school. This kind of challenge cannot be forced on a teenager, and indeed, most schools will not admit students who are dead set against attending. Prospective students should get the opportunity to meet with the principal; they should also spend a day in the school independent of their parents, paired up with a student to attend class, eat lunch, and talk with other kids.

Parents who are considering a Jewish high school for their teenager will be invited to attend an informational meeting with the principal. They should also attend classes, meet teachers, and talk to other parents and students of different ages and backgrounds.

The student body at all the liberal Jewish high schools include graduates of both Jewish and non-Jewish elementary and middle schools. High schools sometimes offer a dual-track program to provide extra help in Hebrew and Jewish-living classes for students from non–day school backgrounds. Families have to be prepared to help, too, with understanding and patience as well as tutoring.

INFORMAL LEARNING

The division between formal school-based education and informal learning is artificial; teenagers also learn about Judaism in camp and youth group, just as they socialize at school. In addition to the youth groups, summer programs (including camp), and Israel trips described below, some Jewish community centers run excellent programs for adolescents, with a teen lounge, youth workers, sporting programs and volunteer options.

Youth Groups Jewish youth groups can provide a cool-enough alternative to the allure and demands of secular teen culture, a social context in which adolescents can forge an independent Jewish identity with peers from around the country, and even from around the world.

There are four national youth organizations that serve the liberal Jewish community and operate on regional, local, and chapter (synagogue) levels: the North American Federation of Temple Youth (NFTY), the youth program of the Reform movement; United Synagogue Youth (USY), run by the Conservative Movement; B'nai B'rith Youth Organization (BBYO), which consists of B'nai B'rith Girls (BBG) and Aleph Tzadi Aleph (AZA), for boys, which is nondenominational and sponsored by local B'nai B'rith chapters[8]; and Young Judaea, also nondenominational and sponsored by Hadassah, the Women's Zionist Organization. (B'nai B'rith and Hadassah have chapters overseas as well.)

There are also international Zionist youth organizations that promote interest in and support for Israel through summer camps, year-round youth group activities, and programs in Israel. They include: Hashomer Hatzair, the Socialist Zionist Youth Movement; Hashachar, run under the auspices of Hadassah; and Habonim Dror, the youth agency of the United Kibbutz movement, and historically part of the Labor Zionist movement.

Youth group chapters are run under the direction of an adult adviser, either paid or volunteer. However, since one of the mandates of youth groups is leadership development, many decisions are made by members and their own elected officials.

Youth group activities include: parties and dances; retreats and "institutes" that feature classes and seminars with rabbis and other teachers; the writing and leading of creative Shabbat and holiday worship services; and the running and staffing of social action projects. NFTY, USY, BBYO, and Young Judaea all maintain summer camps, youth leadership training programs, and a wide range of Israel tours.

On the local level, youth groups often create new communities of Jewish teens who attend different high schools and might not otherwise meet, in a place that is separate from the stresses and hierarchies of school. One of the great attractions of youth groups is the chance to travel to other cities and states for weekend or week-long meetings. The dances, religious services, first loves, late-night conversations, study sessions, and soup-kitchen rotations that are the mainstay of youth activities, yield life-long Jewish memories. Having Jewish friends in Alabama and Alaska connects teenagers to a larger Jewish teenage world.

For information about the youth groups discussed above, contact them at:

North American Federation of Temple Youth (NFTY)
c/o Union of American Hebrew Congregations
633 Third Avenue
New York, NY 10017
212-650-4000
www.uahc.org

United Synagogue Youth (USY)
c/o United Synagogue of Conservative Judaism
155 Fifth Avenue
New York, NY 10010
212-544-7800
www.uscj.org

B'nai B'rith Youth Organization
26001 S. Woodland Road
Beachwood, OH 44122
www.bbyo.org

Young Judaea
50 W. Fifty-eighth Street
New York, NY 10019
www.youngjudaea.org

⬧

SUMMER PROGRAMS

Many teens who attended Jewish camps during grade school are eager to move up through the ranks to become counselors-in-training (CITs) or junior counselors. In these positions—part camper, part staff—teens assume some responsibilities for the younger children and serve as important role models. There are also leadership training programs in camps around the United States, where the weeks are filled with singing, outdoor challenges, and intense socializing as well as Jewish study.

Non-camp summer programs for Jewish teens include the Conservative movement's USY on Wheels, a bus tour of North America. Genesis, a month-long residential program at Brandeis University, is a cross between summer camp and summer school, with learning opportunities that integrate humanities, arts, Jewish studies, and community service. For more information, write to them at Genesis at Brandeis University, MSO85, Brandeis University, Waltham, MA 02454-9110, www.brandeis.edu/genesis.

For information about other alternatives such as internships and volunteer opportunities, ask your youth group advisor, rabbis, or staff at your local Board of Jewish Education and/or Jewish federation.

⬧

ISRAEL TRIPS

A summer tour of Israel in the company of other Jewish adolescents can be a life-transforming experience. Many teens return with an indelible sense of their connection to Judaism and to *eretz Yisrael*—the land of Israel.

Israel summer programs last from four to six weeks. Nearly all trips include visits to important historical sites and cover such themes and issues as Jewish identity and Jewish sovereignty in Israel, Israeli-Arab relations, the Holocaust, Shabbat, Hebrew language, Jerusalem, the relationship between Diaspora and Israeli youth. While many tours are "general interest," others are tailored for special interests such as politics, kibbutz life, the arts, archaeology, the environment, Jewish studies, outdoor challenge, and *tikkun olam* (repairing the world.) Typically, youth tours include interaction with other Jewish teens from around the world as well as contact with Israeli teenagers.

To get a sense of real life in Israel, teen visitors usually go to malls as well as religious and historical sites. There may be visits to the theater and a rock concert, dinner in a Bedouin or Druse community.

The summer after eleventh grade is generally considered an optimal time to send teens, since seventeen-year-olds generally get a wider range of choices and are mature enough to appreciate the breadth of the experience.

A trip to Israel is not a panacea or a substitute for a Jewish education. Kids who go to Israel with no Jewish background tend to experience it as "foreign travel." For an Israel trip to be a transforming experience or a "homecoming," teens need context. They also need to be in a program that matches their needs, personality, and interests.

While the content or itinerary of the Israel trip is a key consideration, teenagers who have been to Israel report that the two factors that can make or break a trip are group dynamics and religious expectations. Although some teens look forward to meeting a whole new group on this trip, others feel it crucial to go with friends or acquaintances from synagogue, school, or youth group. Be sure to explore the level of religious observance for any trip; either too much or too little can turn kids off.

Israel trips are costly, but financial aid is available from a variety of congregational and communal sources. For information about scholarships ask your rabbi, call the local Jewish federation and Board of Jewish Education, and contact the Israeli consulate or your national youth group organization.

The Israel Experience Program, run by the Jewish Agency for Israel, works with a wide range of organizations; contact them at 1-888-99ISRAEL or www.israelexperience.org.

Some teens who visit Israel and want more than a few weeks' experience may opt for a semester there as an exchange student. Others choose to return after high school graduation for a ten-month experience called the Year Course; it is sponsored by Young Judaea (see the listing above).

✡

SELECTING A COLLEGE

Decisions about college start taking shape almost from the beginning of high school. Parents who want their teenagers to continue to make meaningful Jewish choices should be clear about their expectations: "It's important to us that there be a Jewish community on whatever campus you choose, whether or not you think you'll get involved in it." Fortunately, there is a great variety and range of private and public colleges and universities that offer interesting opportunities for Jewish living and learning.

Most communal Jewish college programming is run by Hillel: The Foundation for Jewish Campus Life,[9] a nondenominational, international organization. Every Hillel center provides a different mix of programs and services. Hillels are often social centers that sponsor dances and mixers, and many are renowned for lecture series and Israeli folk-dance evenings. Most sponsor social action and community service programs. Some Hillels run kosher kitchens and as many as four separate worship services every Shabbat, to accommodate students who affiliate as Reform, Conservative, "egalitarian-traditional," and Orthodox. Hillel offices can also help students arrange a junior year abroad in Israel. For more information:

Hillel
1640 Rhode Island Avenue, NW
Washington, DC 20036
202-857-6560
www.hillel.org

There are many ways college students can continue their formal Jewish education while attending secular institutions. Jewish studies departments have proliferated and most colleges offer classes with specifically Jewish content. A look at the course catalogue might reveal "The Literature of the Holocaust," in the English department, plus offerings on Jewish thought in the religion and/or philosophy department.

There are many options for students interested in pursuing Jewish studies: both the Reform and Conservative seminaries (Hebrew Union College-Jewish Institute of Religion, and Jewish Theological Seminary, respectively) offer joint undergraduate degree programs affiliated with local secular universities, as does the Conservative-affiliated University of Judaism in Los Angeles. Independent colleges of Judaica that offer joint degree programs with other institutions of higher education include Hebrew College, in Brookline, Massachusetts, Spertus College of Judaica, in Chicago, and Gratz College, in Philadelphia.

At Brandeis University, the private nonsectarian school founded by the American Jewish community in 1948, undergraduates can major in Near Eastern Judaic studies, and take courses in Hebrew, Yiddish, and other courses with Jewish content. Yeshiva University in New York, the oldest and largest independent Jewish university in the United States, is run under Orthodox auspices and offers a wide range of Jewish undergraduate and graduate programs.

Books for Teenagers and Parents
Hillel Guide to Jewish Life on Campus (a Princeton Review Publication, updated regularly).

For campus-by-campus information about Jewish community, social, cultural, and religious programs, some listings are available on the Hillel Web site (see address, listed above).

PART III

Modern Life

Throughout its long history, the Jewish family has always taken a variety of shapes, sizes, colors, and constellations. This has never been more evident than today. Single parents, gay and lesbian parents, and stepparents are visible and active members of the Jewish community. Adoptive parents and parents with special-needs children seek the best for their children and add strength through their participation.

Although nontraditional households of all kinds still face barriers and isolation, the walls are coming down. Through informal and formal support groups, books and magazine articles, and the ever-expanding reach of the Internet, Jewish parents of every description are finding meaningful ways to connect themselves and their children to Jewish life.

Chapters 10 and 11 focus on two kinds of Jewish families that are changing the face of the community through their growing and increasingly organized presence—those with special needs and with adopted children. Chapter 12, "Talking to Children about Death," provides help in addressing a topic that has long been off limits.

Chapter 10

Special-Needs Families

For parents of children with physical, mental, developmental, or learning disabilities, there is great resonance in the Talmudic injunction "The parent should teach the child on the level of the child's understanding."[1]

However, the Jewish mandate for treating all human beings with respect and honor is incumbent not only on parents, but upon the entire community. It is embedded in the Torah ("You shall not curse a person who is deaf and you will not put a stumbling block in front of a person who is blind"[2]) and elaborated in other Jewish writings ("Do not look at the container, but what is in it"[3]).

The Jewish community is mobilized today as never before to meet the needs of its members, of whom at least 17 percent are physically or mentally disabled.[4] Synagogues, schools, Jewish community centers, day camps, and overnight camps provide a wide range of opportunities and services from early childhood through adulthood. Of course, access and sensitivity vary from temple to camp, from teacher to administrator. As in the secular world, Jewish parents need to be advocates, working with rabbis, youth group directors, and camp counselors to insure that institutions are as inclusive as possible.

It is not easy being an advocate in any setting, but within the Jewish world your family's needs have a different status; your requests for access and inclusion are a sacred opportunity for the community. Within a Jewish framework, providing material assistance and a sense of belonging is not "doing you a favor" but doing *mitzvot*—the good and holy things that define Jews as Jews. Special-needs families provide the opportunity for members of the community to do more than talk about Jewish values[5] but to act on them.

In order to give your child the best that is available to him or her, it is important to define your Jewish goals and commitments as honestly and concretely as possible. What do you want from the Jewish community—not only for your special-needs child, but for the whole family? How much of a commitment to Jewish living and Jewish institutions are you willing to make? What Jewish goals are appropriate for your child?

Like all Jewish parents, Jewish parents of special children should model Jewish behaviors at home. For a child who needs more explanations and opportunities to learn, explaining and duplicating lessons at home and in the synagogue helps special-needs learners to process new information, rituals, and prayers.

Consistency in what you say and what you do is probably even more important for your child's development. If you send a child to a Jewish school but do not reinforce and reflect its content or values at home, you may be placing an additional "stumbling block" in front of your son or daughter.

Your example and commitment are the key to your child's finding a place within the Jewish world. But you need not feel alone in this. Enlist the rabbi and cantor, Hebrew school teachers, and camp counselors to help formulate a Jewish "individualized education plan" with reasonable goals based on a realistic assessment of your child's abilities. (Can your child sit still for three hours of Hebrew school? Would it help to have an aide in the classroom?)

Set long-term goals as well as short-term goals. Many special-needs children become bar and bat mitzvah in beautiful ceremonies tailored to their individual capabilities. This milestone may take your child extra years to achieve, requiring practice in skills that are usually taken for granted—for example, standing before a group of people, wearing unfamiliar clothes, including a *tallit* (prayer shawl) and *kippah* (head covering), and behaving appropriately in class.

Fortunately, there is no need to reinvent the wheel while helping your child find his or her place in the Jewish world. There are national committees on special education and accessibility that can provide resources, teaching tools, workshops, and consultation to member congregations. Some federations (umbrella fund-raising organizations) also sponsor committees on Jews with disabilities and/or provide a Jewish information and referral service that can direct families to appropriate agencies and welcoming congregations. Local boards of Jewish education and Jewish family and children's agencies may also be able to provide referrals and other forms of assistance.

Congregations   The heart and hub of Jewish communal life is the synagogue. The most inclusive congregations generally reflect their rabbis' personal commitment and leadership, and their attitude toward—and comfort level with—atypical Jews will tell you a great deal. When shopping for a temple, be sure to meet with the rabbi and share your hopes and dreams for your child. Ask if there are other families like yours in the congregation and speak with them. If you plan to use the synagogue's supplementary school, inquire about class size, tutoring, and other issues that have an impact on how your child learns. (See also the discussion on "Education," below.)

Remember that educational resources in your synagogue include more than the staff. Every temple's membership includes people in the helping professions—physicians, psychologists, social workers, occupational and speech therapists. Invite them to become part of the team creating a Jewish special education plan for your child.

Parents sometimes initiate partnerships between their synagogue and local agencies that can provide extra services. If your congregation isn't as inclusive or helpful as you think it should be, seek help from Jewish agencies and organizations with a track record on disability. (Start with the list at the end of this chapter.) A well-run disability awareness workshop for your synagogue's staff and membership can go a long way in raising comfort levels.

Education   Finding a Jewish match for your son's or daughter's learning style involves many of the same questions and concerns discussed in Chapters 6 through 9. First, it is crucial to know as much as you can about how your child learns: have him/her tested by a skilled educational professional, observe him/her in class, and ask teachers for their insights. Then find out as much as you can about classroom environments and strategies that have been shown to be effective for children like yours.

The specific decisions you make when looking for a Jewish day or supplementary school will depend on your child's abilities and on the school's commitment to inclusion. Jewish day schools feature small classes, which allow teachers to get to know each child and give special students the added attention they need. But even a master teacher in a relatively small classroom may not be able to give the special-needs student the one-on-one attention that she needs to learn how to read, write, and comprehend Hebrew. Thus, resource rooms for Hebrew and Judaica as well as secular studies are crucial. Parents may need to provide additional private tutoring. And even with lots of help, some children are simply overwhelmed by the demanding curriculum of day schools.

If supplementary school is better suited to your child's learning abilities, try to find a program with small class sizes and extra help for kids with learning needs. (Many synagogues provide tutors to help children learn Hebrew.) And look for a focused curriculum that builds on skills and knowledge from year to year; when schools try to teach too many different skills and subjects in a limited amount of time, children get easily frustrated.[6]

Recreation   Children who have difficulty in academic settings may be able to learn a great deal in recreational settings. Enroll your son or daughter in activities at the Jewish community center, in day camp or sleep-away camp. Encourage them to participate in youth group activities. Any and all of these settings can provide Jewish peers, teach social skills, and give your child an independent place within the Jewish community.

Jewish community centers are increasingly accessible, with architectural amenities (ramps, chair access to the swimming pool, etc.), signing for the deaf, and inclusion in classes of all sorts. JCCs often run day camps where special-needs children are mainstreamed and/or provided for in self-contained groups. In the process of participating in JCC activities, you may meet other families with special-needs children.

There are many options for summer camps (detailed above, in Chapter 7). Check the Internet links to "special needs" on the Web sites for the American Camping Association and the Association of Jewish Sponsored Camps (on page 200).

BOOKS FOR CHILDREN

My Special Friend, by Floreva Cohen (BJE of Greater NY, 1986). A boy
and his special-needs friend participate in Shabbat services.

Jeremy's Dreidel, by Ellie Gellman (Kar-Ben Copies, 1992). Jeremy makes a
Braille *draydl* in a Hanukkah crafts workshop for his father, who is
blind.

A Turn for Noah: A Hanukkah Story, by Susan Remick Topek (Kar-Ben
Copies, 1992). Noah has trouble spinning the *draydl* but eventually
succeeds.

RESOURCES FOR PARENTS

The Consortium of Special Educators in Central Agencies for Jewish
Education builds special education options through central agencies for
Jewish education (such as boards of Jewish education) and sponsors a
professional network for special educators around the country. Consortium
activities include a resource database, newsletter, and an annual collo-
quium. The consortium is also affiliated with JESNA (Jewish Education
Service of North America), whose Web site is loaded with links to organizations and educational materials.

> JESNA
> 111 Eighth Avenue
> New York, NY 10011
> www.jesna.org/networks/networks.htm

The religious movements all sponsor programs of interest to special
needs families. The Conservative movement runs a special education committee; the Reconstructionist group is called the Kol Echad Task Force.

Lehiyot: Jews with Special Needs is a program of the Department of
Jewish Family Concerns of the Union of American Hebrew Congregations (Reform movement). (See the listings on page 38.)

The National Jewish Council for the Disabled (Yahad) is a project of
the Union of Orthodox Jewish Congregations of America, which also runs
programs for the deaf (Our Way). It can be reached at:

> 11 Broadway
> New York, NY 10004
> 212-563-4000
> www.ou.org

The Religion and Disability Program of the National Organization on Disability is the sponsor of the "Accessible Congregations Campaign." This interfaith organization seeks to remove all barriers of architecture, communication, and attitude that exclude people with disabilities from full and active participation in congregational life.

National Organization on Disability
910 16th Street, NW, Suite 600
Washington, DC 20006
www.nod.org

Chapter 11

Adoptive Families

E very adoption is a kind of miracle. Every adoption also represents a loss. Your adopted child has this mysterious duality at the core of his/ her life; the great miracle of becoming part of your family and the pro- found loss of his/her birth parents. And yet, in terms of the everyday experience of loving and raising your child, Jewish parenting is Jewish parenting as described in this book and expressed by you. While adoption should not be overemphasized (it was *an* event in your child's life, not *the* most important characteristic of it), it is a mistake to ignore the differences it does make. Adoption experts agree that honesty and openness about the lows as well as the highs of adoption are crucial.

And adoptive parents do face a unique set of questions about fostering a sense of Jewish identity and authenticity: How could this dark-skinned (or towheaded) baby "look Jewish"? Will my parents ever accept my Chinese daughter as their Jewish grandchild? What right have I to choose a religious identity—and a minority status—for a child who was born into another faith or culture? Will my child ever feel authentically Jewish? Should we look for a synagogue where there are other international adopted children? How do I react if my child someday declares herself "part Christian" and thus entitled to a Christmas tree? What happens when he starts dating?

You are not alone with these questions. A 1990 survey estimated that there are approximately 60,000 adopted children under the age of eighteen in the American Jewish population,[1] which means that the community is full of families with stories, resources, and strategies like yours. Virtually every synagogue includes adoptive families; many local Jewish Family and Children's Services offices offer support groups and help; and there is Stars of David.

A nonprofit, national support network for Jewish adoptive parents, Stars of David provides an invaluable link to other families and professionals. Founded in 1984, it has active chapters in cities around the country that publish newsletters and meet for holiday celebrations, arrange speakers and social events. Local support groups often function as extended families, providing the comfort of a common identity, the realization that other families are living through similar situations, and the collective wisdom of people who have already faced the unique challenges of adoptive parenting.[2]

For more information:

Stars of David
3175 Connecticut Avenue
Suite 100
Northbrook, IL 60062
800-STAR-349
www.starsofdavid.org

ADOPTION IN JEWISH HISTORY

Although adoption has probably never been as common as it is today, it is an honored part of Jewish history. Your family is connected to Moses' family—which included a loving adoptive mother, Pharaoh's daughter.

Jews have always considered it a *mitzvah*—a holy act—to take in orphaned children. According to Jewish law, foster or adoptive parents assume all the responsibilities of biological parents, and the rabbinic opinion favored the role of "nurture" over "nature." The Talmud states, "Those who raise a child are called its parents, and not the ones who conceived it."[3]

During the Second Commonwealth (586 B.C.E.–70 C.E.), Jews were known to rescue gentile children who were orphaned or outcast and rear them as Jews.[4] But that was before Christian and Muslim laws made converting to Judaism a capital crime. Since then, Judaism has concerned itself, for the most part, with the needs of orphans born of Jewish parents.

Nevertheless, the adoption of non-Jewish children happened often enough that Jewish law made the conversion of minors provisional until a child reached maturity. Thus, when a child reared as a Jew but born to a non-Jewish mother reaches the age of thirteen, he or she was given the right to affirm or renounce his or her Jewishness.[5] In this way, Judaism always mandated full disclosure of children's adoptive status—an openness that is fully supported by psychologists and adoption experts today, when nearly all children adopted by Jews are born to non-Jewish parents.

The Jewish community today is increasingly welcoming in its attitudes toward adoption. A large and growing proportion of the population understands the benefits and rewards of the new diversity in the Jewish world; still, some people remain resistant to the changing Jewish family. Which simply means that adoptive parents must act as advocates for their children in Jewish settings as they do in non-Jewish ones.

Adoptive parents act as role models for the whole community as well as for their own children. Putting an adoption announcement in the temple bulletin, for example, signals that your family is proud and open about the process. Even the language you use sends a message: talking to teachers about adoption not as a condition ("Sarah *is* adopted") but as an event ("Sarah *was* adopted"), speaking of birth parents who "chose adoption" rather than "gave the baby up."

Advocating for your child means checking the temple library to make sure there are books showing Jews of many colors, backgrounds, and traditions in the children's collection. It means talking to your child's day school or supplementary school teachers to sensitize them to the pain caused by "family tree" assignments, and to alert them to the potential for teasing. It may mean starting a Stars of David chapter in your town or suggesting a support group for adoptive families within your congregation, or running a panel discussion about different kinds of families for the preschool staff.

CONVERSION

The increase of adoption, intermarriage, and stepfamilies in the Jewish community has made the conversion of children a fairly common event (see Chapter 6 for descriptions of ceremonies and rituals). Jewish tradition does not make much of a legal or ritual distinction between the conversion of children and adults; there are, however, real emotional and logistical differences.

The fundamental difference is that children do not ask to convert, nor are they capable of making a decision of this magnitude. The choice and the responsibility rests with parents, who formally and ritually commit themselves to the task of raising a child as a Jew. That commitment includes providing a Jewish education and fostering a Jewish identity. Parents who convert a child make an implicit promise to act as Jewish role models—to live a Jewish life.

Choosing Judaism for a child raises many questions, none of which come with one-size-fits all answers. Issues and solutions vary according to each child's age, health, developmental stage, family constellation, and synagogue affiliation. Even so, there are a few basic ground rules.

First, it is crucial that parents agree with each other about this decision—the hows as well as the whys. Second, the child deserves the fullest explanation he or she can understand, and if the child is old and mature enough to participate in the conversation, his or her wishes must be taken into consideration. Find a rabbi you respect to facilitate the process and guide you through the rituals of conversion.

You may find that the most helpful information and advice comes from other parents who have been down this road before you. Contact Stars of David for help in finding a sympathetic rabbi and for general guidance and support. If you are already a synagogue member, ask your rabbi whether there are families in the congregation who have adopted and converted a child.

Conversion of children, like conversion of adults, inevitably raises the thorny question of Jewish status, the "Who is a Jew?" debate. The Jewish world is deeply divided on this subject because conversions supervised by non-Orthodox rabbis will not be acceptable to much of the Orthodox community.[6] Since the Orthodox rabbinate exercises legal control over issues of personal status in Israel, this may become an issue if your child decides to move there. Families with concerns about acceptance in Israel or challenges to the Jewishness of their child should speak with their rabbi.

AGES AND STAGES

As children grow, reactions to the fact of being adopted tend to follow a fairly predictable pattern. The more you know about the "unique developmental challenges" on your child's path, the better you can prepare for them.[7]

Ages 1 to 3   Babies and toddlers are unaware of adoption or the difference it makes in their lives. This is a great time for parents to create a scrapbook with pictures and stories about the first time you saw each other, information about birth parents, details and photographs of any conversion rituals, essays read at the baby-naming, a letter from you to the baby, and so on.

Ages 4 to 6   Preschoolers are fascinated with pictures and stories from their babyhood. Your child will want to hear you tell their adoption story over and over again, and they will pore over the scrapbook you created. There are many published children's books that speak to this curiosity, some which are listed at the end of this chapter.

Your answers to your child's questions should be honest and positive, but careful. Adoption experts warn against saying things like "Your birth mother chose adoption because she loved you so much." For children at this very literal-minded stage, such a statement may suggest that you, too, will give them away.

This is also an age when children start to sort the world into categories: puppies and kitties, boys and girls, Jewish kids and kids who celebrate Christmas. This is also when children begin to notice whether their skin is darker than the other kids' at temple. Do not try to pretend differences do not exist or "don't matter." Acknowledge them and ask your child to say more.

Ages 7 to 11   By now, children begin to understand the loss of their birth family and to grieve. Birthdays, Mother's Day, and Father's Day may become painful reminders to your child. Some children withdraw, others "act out"—testing to see if you will reject them. Children who stop asking about their birth parents altogether may actually be wondering what they did to "cause" their abandonment. If your child never mentions his birth parents, give him permission to speak about them by bringing the subject up yourself: "Are you wondering about your birth mother today?"

By the time children are in school, they will also be facing the fact of their minority status: as a Jew in America, as an Asian-born Jew, as an adoptee. Since children generally want to blend in, they may be upset or angry about their differentness.

Do not minimize or ignore these feelings and try to avoid being defensive. Complaints about being left out of the Christmas festivities are not limited to adopted children; however, an adopted child who wants to celebrate the holiday may be looking for a way to deal with the loss of birth parents and of figuring out who they are. It may also be an early act of rebellion.

Still, it is difficult to hear your child declare, "My real mother was Christian, so I can have a Christmas tree." Remember that adopted children often feel a divided loyalty. If you do not honor the birth family's culture, your child may overcompensate by seeking it out and embracing it.

Try to validate your child's feelings, but without denying your own beliefs or violating your own traditions and standards. Parents handle Christmas demands in a variety of ways: some permit their child a string of lights or a small tree in her room; others will not let Christmas into their home but encourage children to celebrate at a friend's house.

Remember, this is part of your child's search for him- or herself. Invite your child's questions and be ready to answer honestly. Kids of this age may be getting teased at school. Or perhaps they are being asked to explain about their background. Help them figure out how to respond when asked, "Where did you come from?"

Adolescence   Rarely an easy time for parents or teenagers, these years can be even more complicated for adopted children.

Adopted teens may have an extra share of anger: at the early loss of birth parents, at being different in a variety of ways, at feeling a lack of control over their own lives. One way they might attempt to assert control is to declare, "I'm not going to go to Hebrew school (or have a bat mitzvah, or be part of the youth group, or go to the seder) because I'm not really Jewish anyway."

Adopted or biological, when Jewish teens say things like this, they are announcing, "I'm not like you."[8] The challenge for parents is to try not to get angry or to act out of fear of rejection. Acknowledge the partial truth in what they are saying. In the long run, most teenagers ultimately become adults who make choices that are remarkably similar to the ones their parents made.

If you model a full, active, meaning-filled Jewish life, your example will be an indelible part of your children's identity. After that, the choice belongs to your children—regardless of how you became their parent.

There is no guarantee that an adopted child will embrace Judaism as an adult, but the same can be said of children who are born to Jewish parents. Ultimately, all Jewish children grow up to make their own Jewish choices. And so, like all other parents who want their children to embrace Judaism, your job is to demonstrate, in what you do and what you say, that Judaism is an irresistible choice.

BOOKS FOR CHILDREN

The Day We Met You, by Phoebe Kohler (Aladdin Paperbacks, 1997). Up to age 3.

Horace, by Holly Keller (Greenwillow, 1991). A leopard cub is adopted by tigers. Ages 4 to 8.

Let's Talk about It: Adoption, by Fred Rogers (1998). Ages 4 to 8.

A Mother for Choco, by Keiko Kasza (Paperstar, 1996). Choco the bird finds out that Mrs. Bear can be the perfect mother for him. Ages 4 to 8.

BOOKS FOR PARENTS

Adoption and the Jewish Family: Contemporary Perspectives, by Shelly Kapnek Rosenberg (Jewish Publication Society, 1998). A thorough and thoughtful treatment of the subject, with excellent bibliographies and resource lists.

Choosing a Jewish Life: A Handbook for People Converting to Judaism and for Their Families and Friends, by Anita Diamant (Schocken Books, 1997). For more information about conversion of children.

Talking to Children
about Death

The impulse to shield children from death is so strong, it feels instinctive. But as much as we try to protect them, children often have cause to grieve.

The family cat is found dead. A schoolmate's cousin is killed in a car accident. A beloved grandparent dies.

Even in the face of a loss, some parents avoid talking about death by taking refuge in the notion that youngsters can't understand. But child psychologists, grief experts, and rabbis agree that children need to hear the truth. They also need and deserve to be included—in developmentally appropriate ways—in mourning rituals that can help give shape and meaning to their grief.

Caring for bereaved children can be confusing. It is difficult for adults, often in pain themselves, to explain what has happened. But without honest explanations children are left to fend for themselves in "the valley of the shadow of death." Instead of being protected from the pain of grief, they are left without the comfort they desperately need.

Although every child and every loss is different, there are some general guidelines that are useful in comforting bereaved children:

Don't Delay   News of a death should be delivered by a parent or other trusted adult as soon as possible. Waiting will not soften the blow and only increases the chance that a child will learn what happened in an inappropriate setting. Even the best of intentions can backfire. You may think: "If we wait until after camp to tell Ruth about Grandma's death, we won't ruin her summer." But then Ruth will be mourning all by herself when she learns the news.

Avoid Euphemisms   Use the words "dead" and "death." Terms like "passed away" or "eternal rest" are confusing to children, who are grappling with the finality of what has happened. A young child who hears the words "We lost Grandma," may believe that Grandma will be found.

Explain what happened to the person who died, being careful how you answer questions. Children are literal-minded and can easily draw the wrong conclusion. Saying, "Grandpa died because he was very sick," or "Grandma died in the hospital," can create the impression that all illness leads to death or all hospital stays are fatal. For a child under the age of eight, even a term like "heart attack" may be confusing or even fearful.

Invite Questions   Some children will be able to express their curiosity and ask about everything from bodily decomposition to the existence of heaven. But don't assume that silence means a lack of interest. Some children do not ask because they lack the words, or are confused, or fear upsetting adults.

Make time for children when they know they have your undivided attention and solicit their questions in specific terms.

Not all questions are easy to answer. "What happens to your eyeballs after you die?" "Why can't I have my birthday party this week?" "Is Susan going to be an angel?"

A good response to any perplexing question is, "That's a very good question. What do you think?" Very often, children may need this kind of opening to express what's really on their minds.

One difficult question children sometimes ask is, "Why did God let this happen?" First, provide validation for what the child is feeling ("It is so hard to lose someone you love"). As for the question itself, be honest and say, "I don't know."

Remember That Children Grieve in Their Own Ways   Some will weep and cling, others will run outside to play with friends, and still others will go back and forth between sorrow and apparent indifference. Some children regress to earlier stages of development, becoming hostile or demanding or timid.

Whether or not children can express their feelings, death is profoundly disturbing to them. Whatever they say or do, children need to know that their feelings and moods are normal, and that even grown-ups feel the same things.

Give Children Ways to Say Goodbye   Funerals are for everyone who cared about the deceased. Children who are not permitted to go to the funeral may feel that their grief is being ignored. They may also imagine scenes far more gruesome than the real thing, especially since caskets are almost always closed at Jewish funerals.

Parents should describe what is going to happen at a funeral or *shiva* visit—who will be there, the fact that some people may be weeping, how long the service or visit will last.

Share Your Feelings   Children watch adults for cues about how to manage their emotions. If adults cry and console one another, children learn that it's normal and safe to express emotion. However, since children can be frightened by the sight of weeping adults, they also need specific reassurance. "Daddy is very sad, but crying is just part of what happens when someone you love dies." If a child wants to comfort you, let him. There is comfort in helping others.

Accept Help from Others   Bereaved children benefit just as much as bereaved adults from being part of a community of comforters. Since parents and other close relatives are usually suffering from the same loss, they may be less able to focus on the needs of each child. Friends and neighbors, baby-sitters and teachers, cousins and in-laws can help by sitting with children, encouraging their questions, or giving them breaks from the rest of the family's grief.

A bereaved child's teachers should be fully informed of any loss in his or her life, so they can sympathize, inform classmates, and be alert to changes in behavior.

Books   Reading aloud to prereaders is a good way to start conversations and keep track of a child's understanding of what happened. Children old enough to read on their own can look at books that speak to their interests and anxieties. There are titles for children of all ages, some of which focus on specific kinds of losses, including the death of a grandparent, parent, or sibling.

Your rabbi or child's teacher may have some titles to recommend. Children's librarians will be able to direct you to new releases as well as classics, and can tailor their suggestions to a child's reading level. Many funeral homes provide pamphlets or books for parents and children. Parents or guardians should read any book before giving it to a child, to make sure it is age-appropriate and reflects the family's values and beliefs.

Another kind of book to give a bereaved child is a memory book. Published memory workbooks include questions and places for photographs and drawings, but any notebook or diary can fulfill the same purpose. Some children want to share what they write in these books, others do not. That decision should be left to the child.

Seek Professional Help   Some children are overwhelmed by grief. Adults should consider making at least one appointment with a therapist for any child who has suffered a loss within his nuclear family.

Be alert to signs of depression such as sleep disorders, listlessness, and uncontrollable tears. Children or teens may have panic attacks, show a decline in their attention to schoolwork, or continue to deny that the death ever happened. Sometimes symptoms are delayed, making it harder for parents and other adults to connect behavior changes to the loss.

School counselors are generally the first line of professional assistance. Just knowing there is another concerned but dispassionate adult to talk to can be enormously comforting for a bereaved child. If problems persist, the school counselor may provide a referral to a specialist.

Referrals can also come from your rabbi or pediatrician, the local Jewish chaplaincy organization, a healing center, or a hospice rabbi.

Young mourners need specialized care and treatment. When interviewing counselors, ask about their experience working with bereaved children. Have they taken courses in the field? Are they members of the Association for Death Education and Counseling? Listen to what your child has to say, too. If after two or three sessions, he or she puts up a fight over going, it might be worth considering another counselor.

Children at *Shiva*

Most rabbis encourage parents to let children participate in the funeral and/or some part of *shiva*. The days of visiting and comforting at home can be very reassuring. Seeing bereaved parents, grandparents, or friends smile and even laugh as memories surface shows them that the terrible sadness in the air will eventually lift. *Shiva* also provides a great lesson about how families fit into communities, and how communities can care for families.

Older children may want to participate in *shiva* services, both to express their own sorrow and as a way to maintain connections with family members who have been too preoccupied to pay attention to them. School-age children can be invited (without any pressure) to share memories of the deceased along with the adults during the time set aside for public reminiscence. These options should never be forced upon children, simply offered.

Any child who seems frightened or overwhelmed should be allowed to withdraw. A child who clearly states she doesn't want to go to a funeral, to the cemetery, or to pay a *shiva* visit shouldn't be dragged along or made to feel ashamed of her choice.

AGES AND STAGES

Under Three   Infants and toddlers do not understand death, but they are sensitive to disruptions in routines and changes in the emotional climate. The absence of a beloved care-giver will certainly be missed, and a house full of strangers may be upsetting. When death is in the house, little ones need even more attention than usual and lots of physical affection.

Infants and toddlers can light up the room when people are in mourning; their presence is a reminder of why life must go on. However, fussy or rambunctious babies should be taken out of the room during a funeral or *shiva* call.

Ages Three to Six   Children vary enormously at this age both in terms of what they understand and how they respond. Some young children react to news of a death by crying and clinging, which is perfectly normal. Others appear unaffected and ask if they can go back outside and play, and this is perfectly normal, too.

Some will not be able to focus on the idea of death, which is just too frightening. Others will be fascinated and ask uninhibited questions. The idea of permanence is virtually incomprehensible at this age. Children sometimes appear to deny or forget that the dead person is really dead, and may need several gentle reminders.

A death may raise the terrible fear in young children of losing other adults—especially their own parents. "Are you going to die?" is a common question. One way to answer with honesty and reassurance is, "Most people live to be old before they die. I expect to be alive for a long, long time."

Whether or not they explicitly give voice to their fears, young children need verbal reassurance that they are safe and that things will be okay. Although it's not necessary to go into great detail, they also need simple but honest explanations about illness and death.

Ages Seven to Eleven   Children at this stage start to understand that death is final, with the result that their fears may come into sharper focus. Questions about the mechanics of illness can become more pointed. Some want to hear all the gory details about what happens to the body after death. This may be a way of gaining a sense of control over their fear of death.

The imagination is still a powerful force in children of this age, who might envision death as a kind of scary bogeyman, or worry that death is somehow contagious. While they may consciously "know" that their own words or wishes did not really cause a death, school-age children may not fully believe this and feel miserably guilty about something they said or thought. Some suffer over unkindness shown to the deceased. Parents and guardians need to offer reassurance and absolve them of any guilt.

Adolescents   Death hits teenagers very hard. Cognitively, adolescents understand the finality of death, but few teens are able to tolerate the intensity of their feelings. In addition, adolescents, unlike younger kids, have begun to move out from under the emotional umbrella of their parents and can feel dramatically alone with their grief.

Loss poses a developmental quandary for teens by shattering their new and still-fragile sense of independence. Sometimes it's easier if an adult other than a parent acts as a sounding board in the aftermath of a death.

Peer relationships, which are crucial to teenagers, should also be understood as a source of comfort. Yet adolescents often find themselves cut off from their friends at precisely the time they need them the most. A few close friends should be made welcome whenever a grieving adolescent says he wants them around, including at the funeral and during *shiva*.

Developmental Grief As children mature, they grow into new levels of understanding about death and their connections to loved ones who died. At every stage, new questions and feelings may surface. Bereaved children, especially those who have lost a parent or sibling, encounter the hole in their lives on every birthday and holiday. This may be true even if they have no memory of the deceased.

Family members and other adults should demonstrate their willingness to talk about the deceased: "Daddy would have loved seeing you in that dress." "Did I ever tell you the story about when my brother, your Uncle Joe, caught the biggest fish in the lake?"

Participating in Jewish memorial events may help children feel a personal connection to the loved one. Children can be encouraged to collect and arrange photographs around Grandma's *yahrzeit* candle, or to read the letter Uncle Max wrote before he died. Children might be offered the option of standing for the mourner's *Kaddish*, or given the honor of choosing where to send a charitable donation in memory of the deceased.

As children grow, these acts take on deeper meaning. And as time passes, the candles and the stories themselves fulfill the hope of the *Yizkor* prayer, "May his/her memory be bound up in the bonds of life."

BOOKS FOR CHILDREN
The Keeping Quilt, by Patricia Polacca (Simon and Schuster, 1995). Ages 4 to 8.
When a Grandparent Dies: A Kid's Own Remembering Workbook for Dealing with Shiva and the Years Beyond, by Nechama Liss-Levinson, Ph.D. (Jewish Lights Publishing, 1995). Ages 7 to 12.

Books for Parents

Saying Kaddish: How to Care for the Dying, Bury the Dead, and Mourn as a Jew, by Anita Diamant (Schocken Books, 1998).

Talking About Death: A Dialogue Between Parent and Child, by Earl A. Grollman (Beacon Press, 1990).

Appendix:
Writing a Will

Over 70 percent of Americans do not have a will. Parents with minor children are probably overrepresented in that statistic for understandable reasons: being young and, for the most part healthy, writing a will seems morbid.

However, the most important reason for writing a will is to name guardians for minor children. In the absence of a will, the decision about where your children will reside and who will raise them is left to judges and social service agencies. When someone dies intestate (without a will), their money and property are divided and distributed according to each state's intestate succession laws, which may not be in your child's best interest. If parents are unmarried partners, states may not even recognize the surviving partner's parental rights; and they certainly do not permit property to be inherited by unmarried partners, unless stipulated in a will.

The basic functions of a will all have an impact on minor children:

- to name a guardian to care for minor children and to arrange for management of property left to minors;
- to designate people and/or organizations that will inherit your money and property;
- to cancel debts others owe you;
- to specify how debts and taxes are to be paid;

- to designate an executor—someone who will oversee all the provisions of your will.

To write a will without legal help, check the Yellow Pages for local "legal document preparation services" or consult a guidebook or computer software program. Computer programs for writing wills also include healthcare directives, described below.

If your assets amount to more than $600,000, it's wise to seek the professional services of an attorney, accountant, or financial planner who can help you minimize the impact of estate and inheritance taxes. Making an appointment with a lawyer is the only way many people can force themselves to write a will.

HEALTHCARE DIRECTIVES

While preparing a will, it makes good sense to execute a healthcare directive or living will, and to name a healthcare proxy. Healthcare directives convey your wishes about life-prolonging treatment should you become ill and unable to express yourself. A kind of contract with your physicians, this document binds doctors either to honor your instructions or help transfer your care to others who will. Anyone over the age of eighteen can make a healthcare directive, which, like a will, can be changed or revoked at any time.

All branches of Judaism support and encourage the use of medical directives or living wills that are sensitive to Jewish values.

The organ donor card is the simplest of all medical directives, and one that is supported by rabbinic authorities. The religious precept of *p'kuach nefesh* ("the saving of a life") is fulfilled with this *matan chaim*, gift of life. In the words of Rabbi Isaac Klein, "There can be no greater respect for the dead than to bring healing to the living."[1]

Be sure your physician and rabbi know your status as an organ donor, and note it in all other healthcare directives.

ETHICAL WILL

Leaving a written spiritual legacy to family and friends is a time-honored Jewish custom. For centuries, rabbis wrote instructions to their families and communities about the proper way to live a Jewish life.[2] Since the nineteenth century at least, ordinary people have written about their lives and dreams as a legacy to their own children and grandchildren.[3]

Writing an ethical will challenges you to name what is most important in your life, and to consider how you wish to be remembered. There is no standard form for an ethical will, and most read like personal letters. The following outline is intended as a suggestion only.

Opening   Most people think of ethical wills as a letter and begin with a salutation.

Your Journey   Tell stories about your own parents, siblings, and childhood, a description of the community in which you grew up, and something about events and people that shaped your life, including how Judaism shaped your journey. The more details, the better.

What Counts   What do you believe in? What is most important to you? Why is being Jewish important to you?

Closing Wishes   What is it you wish to bequeath to your children? Be specific in describing your hopes and dreams, and how you want to be remembered. Some end with a hope or prayer for their children.

Keep your will, healthcare directive, and ethical will in a safe location known to your family. Give copies of healthcare directives to your healthcare proxy, close family members, your primary care physician, lawyer, and rabbi.

BOOKS AND OTHER RESOURCES

WillMaker software programs and books (Nolo Press).

United Synagogue Living Will (United Synagogue Book Service, 155 Fifth Avenue, New York, NY 10010).

A Time to Prepare (Union of American Hebrew Congregations, 633 Third Avenue, New York, NY 10017).

Notes

PART I: PROLOGUE

1. According to Jewish law, a person who is born to a Jewish mother is, in fact, considered a Jew. Reform and Reconstructionist Jews have declared the child of a Jewish father who is given a Jewish education and upbringing to be Jewish. But in practice, Jewishness today is increasingly a matter of affiliation. It is a truism that "we are all Jewish-by-choice" rather than law. The authors are talking here (and throughout the book) about the formation of Jewish identity in children who will then choose to be Jews as adults.

CHAPTER ONE

1. *Mishnah Pe'ah* 1.1. Also recited in the morning prayer service.
2. In *S'fas Emes*, a five-volume classic of Hasidic insight. Hasidism was an eighteenth-century revival of Jewish mysticism. (Thanks to Rabbi Nehemia Polen for pointing out this connection.)
3. Merle Feld, *A Spiritual Life—A Jewish Feminist Journey* (Albany: State University of New York Press, 1999), p. 10.
4. *Mishnah Pe'ah* 1.1. Also recited in the morning prayer service. The final line is commonly interpreted to mean "because the study of Torah leads to them all."
5. Proverbs 3:18.
6. Norman F. Cantor, *The Sacred Chain: The History of the Jews* (HarperCollins, 1994), p. 400.
7. Charles Silberman, *A Certain People: American Jews and Their Lives Today* (Summit Books, 1985), p. 145.
8. For more about the subject, see Anita Diamant, *The New Jewish Wedding* (Simon and Schuster, 1985).
9. Genesis 1:28

10. *Zohar* 2:169a
11. *Pirke Avot* 2:21.
12. Talmud: *Baba Batra* 9a.
13. Danny Siegel, *Gym Shoes and Irises* (The Town Mill Press, 1982), pp. 120–24.
14. The words of Isaiah (57:14–58:14) repeated in synagogues throughout the world every Yom Kippur, retain their moral imperative:

> "Behold on the day of your fast you pursue business as usual and oppress your workers. Behold you fast only to quarrel and fight, to deal wicked blows. Such fasting will not make your voice audible on high.
>
> "This is my chosen fast: to loosen all the bonds that bind men unfairly, to let the oppressed go free, to break every yoke. Share your bread with the hungry, take the homeless into your home. Clothe the naked when you see him, do not turn away from people in need. . . . Remove from your midst the yoke of oppression, the finger of scorn, the tongue of malice. . . . Put yourself out for the hungry and relieve the wretched, then shall your light shine in the darkness, and your gloom shall be as noonday."
>
> Translation from the *Mahzor for Rosh Hashanah and Yom Kippur,* edited by Rabbi Jules Harlow (The Rabbinical Assembly, 1972).

CHAPTER TWO

1. Deuteronomy 6:4–9, 11:13–21. Translation from *Vetaher Libeynu* (*Purify Our Hearts*), the prayerbook of Congregation Beth El of the Sudbury River Valley (Sudbury, Massachusetts), p. 35.
2. Genesis 1:29–30.
3. Leviticus 11.
4. The laws of *kashrut* are complex and specific. One of the primary historical functions of rabbis has been to make rulings on what is kosher and what is not. This chapter provides only an overview.
5. Prohibitions against drinking wine made by non-Jews dates back to the Talmud. The rabbis outlawed drinking of wine made by non-Jews for fear it might have been used in idol worship.
6. *Hechshers* appear on a wide variety of products in a variety of forms. Not all of them mean that a rabbi has supervised the preparation of the food. For more information, ask your rabbi or contact the local board that oversees *kashrut,* called a *vaad.*
7. Some people simply wash the offending item in hot water or run it through the dishwasher and return it to its rightful place. If you have specific questions about correcting mistakes, you can ask your rabbi.

CHAPTER THREE

1. *Pirke Avot* 2:5.
2. Mazon: A Jewish Response to Hunger, 12401 Wilshire Boulevard, Suite 303, Los Angeles, CA 90025-1015.

3. For a brief discussion of the history and theology of the three movements, see *Living a Jewish Life* by Anita Diamant and Howard Cooper (HarperCollins, 1991), pp. 118–23.
4. Touro Synagogue in Newport, Rhode Island, and Kahal Kadosh Beth Elohim in Charleston, South Carolina. The oldest synagogue in the Western Hemisphere, however, is on the island of Curaçao, where it was founded in 1651 and is still in use!
5. There are nearly complete Orthodox/Hasidic enclaves in Williamsburg, Brooklyn, for example. Yet while exotic and in some ways attractive, it is a totally separate and in some ways antimodern model.
6. United Jewish Communities, a national umbrella organization, runs this program through local federations. This kind of trip is intended to reinforce Jewish identity and foster support for the philanthropic agency sponsoring the trip, but not to substitute for a congregational ceremony.
7. There are all kinds of alternatives available through local federations, national organizations, and the Israeli government. Check www.shamash.org, a Jewish "consortium" site with links to dozens of organizations and their webpages.
8. See note 2.
9. Danny Siegel's books, listed at the end of the chapter, are a great place to start.
10. For ordering information: The Town House Press, 28 Midway Road, Spring Valley, NY 10977.

1. Abraham Joshua Heschel, *The Sabbath* (Farrar, Straus and Giroux, 1951), p. 10.
2. From the *V'ahavta*, which is the complete first paragraph of the *Shema*, following the familiar one-line statement of God's unity.
3. Translation from *Siddur Birkat Shalom* (Somerville, Mass.: Havurat Shalom Siddur Project, 1991), p. 1. Used with permission.
4. Heschel, *The Sabbath*, p. 8.
5. Ezekiel 20:12.
6. Shabbat 118b.
7. The kinds of work that are forbidden on Shabbat are based on a list of thirty-nine specific jobs listed in the Mishnah, which is part of the Talmud. The rabbis theorized that these tasks, which are largely agricultural in nature, were derived from the work of constructing the portable Tabernacle in the wilderness. Some rabbis based other restrictions, including the modern prohibition against using electricity, both on the Mishnah and on subsequent codes of Jewish law.
8. This translation, and all translations of blessings in this chapter, come from *Vetaher Libeynu* ("Purify Our Hearts"), the prayer book of Congregation Beth El of the Sudbury River Valley, Sudbury, Mass. (1980).
9. Hayyim Schauss, *The Jewish Festivals* (Schocken Books, 1962), p. 33. The blessing dates from the eighth or ninth century.
10. Doing the action before saying the blessing is out of order since, in most cases when a blessing involves an action (such as eating bread or drinking wine) the *b'racha* is recited first. This can't work with candlelighting because once the blessing is recited, Shabbat begins and with it the prohibition against lighting fires.

11. On Friday night, the core *b'racha* is sandwiched between two longer passages, one that speaks of the creation of the world, the other recalling the exodus from Egypt and the sanctity of the Sabbath (see any *siddur* [daily prayerbook] for the Hebrew):

    There was evening and there was morning the sixth day. And the heavens and the earth and all that they contained were completed and on the seventh day God completed the work which God had made and rested on the seventh day from all the work which God had made. And God blessed the seventh day and made it holy, because on it God rested from all the work which God created and made.

    Holy One of Blessing, Your Presence fills Creation, forming the fruit of the vine.

    Holy One of blessing, Your Presence fills Creation, You have made us holy with Your commandments and delighted in us. In love you have favored us with the gift of your holy Shabbat, a heritage that recalls the work of creation. It is the first day among holy days, reminding us of our going out from Egypt. You gave us Your holy Shabbat as a treasure to grace all our generations. Holy One of Blessing, You make Shabbat holy.

12. The process of making challah dates back to ancient Temple days, when Jews ate something much closer to flat pita bread than to our yeasted and braided loaves. The religious definition of challah requires that a piece of dough be broken off during baking and burned as an offering while a blessing is recited (Numbers 15:17–21).

13. Used by permission. Marcia Falk, *The Book of Blessings* (HarperSanFrancisco, 1996), pp. 124–25.

14. Proverbs 31:10–31.

15. Marcia Falk has also written a beautiful "Blessing the Beloved," based on the poetry from Song of Songs, (*Book of Blessings*, pp. 126–27), which is presented in three forms: for use by a woman and a man, by two women, or by two men.

16. Rabbi David A. Teutsch, ed., *Kol Haneshama: Songs, Blessings, and Rituals for the Home* (Reconstructionist Press, 1991), p. 5.

17. Shabbat is the one day that the entire weekly *parasha*, or Torah portion, is traditionally read out loud. Some temples have adopted a triennial Torah reading cycle, so only a third of each *parasha* is read every week.

18. Many congregations have a short additional service, called *Musaf,* after the Torah service.

19. Any bencher will contain the long Shabbat lunch kiddush. Or you can use the short "*borey p'ree hagafen*" version.

20. To observe the *mitzvah* of eating a full meal at lunch, but without breaking the rules against cooking on the Sabbath, Jewish homemakers devised a whole cuisine of slow-cooking casseroles that would simmer overnight on a back burner or in a community oven. This was usually a meat meal: in Eastern Europe, it was called *cholent;* in Morocco, *dafina* stayed warm in Arab bakery ovens; cooks in Iraq made a chicken-and-rice stew called *tbeet.*

21. Samson Raphael Hirsch (1808–1888), one of the founders of modern Orthodoxy in Germany.

22. The tradition of a two-day Rosh Hashanah predates the Diaspora and is still the practice in Israel and in some Reform temples as well.

23. In the Jewish calendar months are made up of either 29 or 30 days, adding up to a 354-day year, 11.25 days short of a solar year. The discrepancy is corrected with the occasional addition of a leap month tucked between the springtime months of Adar and Nisan.

24. In seven out of every nineteen years, the Jewish calendar adds an extra month of Adar, called Adar II.

25. Thus the year 2000 straddles 5760–5761.

26. The *Haftarah* readings are also very powerful: on the first day, 1 Samuel 1:1–2:10 tells the story of Hannah's prayer for a child; the second day's reading is Jeremiah 31:1–19.

27. Not all congregations hold all of the services listed here, nor is the order or content described here universal.

28. The custom about attending *Yizkor* varies, but many people remain superstitious about attending the service if both parents are still alive. Many rabbis and congregations encourage everyone to stay.

29. Over the centuries the four species (three in the *lulav*, the fourth being the *etrog*) have been given many interpretations, symbols of the parts of the human body, of elements of the Jewish people, of the male and female parts of creation.

30. Sh'mini Atzeret, the eighth day of Sukkot, is in fact yet another holiday, but its obscure synagogue observance, which is connected to the rainy season in the land of Israel, was long ago (in the eleventh century) eclipsed by Simchat Torah, celebrated on the ninth day of the Sukkot cycle. That is when the Torah reading cycle was established.

31. There are two other stories of military courage associated with Hanukkah. Found in the Apocrypha, these are tales of heroic women: Judith, a widow who killed a general leading a siege against the land of Judah; and Hannah, the mother of seven sons who died with them rather than bow to a pagan idol.

32. For a fascinating, sophisticated explanation of Hanukkah's historical significance, see "Assimilation, Acculturation, and Jewish Survival: Hanukkah," in *The Jewish Way* by Rabbi Irving Greenberg (Simon and Schuster, 1988), pp. 258–82.

33. Claudia Roden, *The Book of Jewish Food* (Knopf, 1996), p. 33. Cheese and dairy dishes commemorate Judith, another heroine celebrated in the Apocrypha, who fed them to Holofernes, an enemy of the Jews. When he fell asleep, she killed him and saved her people.

34. Intermarried families that celebrate both holidays may be disappointed by this discussion, but the decisions and choices in dual-practice families are beyond the scope of this book. You might want to consult books that deal with making intermarriage work. One of the best of these is *The Intermarriage Handbook: A Guide for Jews and Christians*, by Judy Petsonk and Jim Remsen (William Morrow, 1988).

35. In Israel, Hanukkah was elevated from "minor festival" status for reasons having nothing to do with Christmas. Among Israeli Jews, where the military struggle to establish and maintain the state is part of every family's story, Hanukkah affirms modern victories as well as the ancient one.

36. *Avot de Rabbi Natan* 31b.

37. Deuteronomy 20:19.
38. See Arthur Waskow, *Seasons of Our Joy* (Beacon Press, 1991), for a full discussion of the mystical methodology of the Tu B'Shvat seder.
39. The Talmud says that Purim obliges every Jew to get so drunk that he or she cannot tell the difference between blessing Mordechai and cursing Haman. Megilot 7b.
40. The four other scrolls, or *megillot*, in the Bible include Song of Songs (read at Passover), Ruth (read at Shavuot), Lamentations (read at Tisha B'Av), and Ecclesiastes (read at Sukkot), but the Book of Esther is the one known as "the" *megilla*.
41. Other names for Passover include *Hag ha-Pesach*, Festival of the Passover Offering, and *Hag ha-Matzot*, Festival of Unleavened Bread.
42. The word *pesach* also refers to the lamb that God commanded each Hebrew family to kill, and then mark their doorposts with its blood.
43. Exodus 13:8.
44. For a *matzah* recipe see Joan Nathan, *The Jewish Holiday Kitchen* (Schocken Books, 1998), p. 248.
45. Jews have been celebrating *Pesach* with some kind of seder since the second century c.e., the basic structure having been set by the eleventh century.
46. Actually, Ashkenazic tradition prohibits lamb. Since we no longer observe the biblical practice of sacrificing a lamb, this prohibition acknowledges the dramatic transformation of Judaism after the destruction of the Temple.
47. The Internet is an apparently inexhaustible supply of such. For example:

> There's no seder like our seder,
> Like no seder I know.
> Everything about it is halachic,
> Nothing that the Torah won't allow.
> Listen how we read the whole Haggadah.
> It's all in Hebrew
> 'Cause we know how.
> There's no Seder like our seder,
> We tell a tale that is swell:
> Moses took the people out into the heat,
> They baked the matzah
> While on their feet.
> Now isn't that a story
> That just can't be beat?
> Let's go on with the show!

48. The mandate that Jews relinquish ownership of *hametz* during Passover gave rise to the legal fiction of selling hametz to a non-Jew during the holiday and then buying it back. This practice was instituted to protect the poor and business-owners, for whom this requirement could be an overwhelming hardship.
49. Named to honor Maimon ben Joseph, father of the great twelfth-century rabbi, Maimonides.
50. These holidays were instituted by the Israeli Knesset (parliament) in 1948 (Yom HaAtzma'ut) and 1951 (Yom HaShoah).

51. Genesis 17:8.
52. The biblical references to Shavuot make no mention of Torah or revelation, but describe an agricultural pilgrimage holiday when Jews brought first fruits of the wheat and fruit harvest to the Temple in Jerusalem as an offering to God. After the destruction of the second Temple, in 70 C.E., the day was transformed into a celebration of receiving Torah.

CHAPTER FIVE

1. The Union of American Hebrew Congregations (Reform movement) runs support groups for interfaith families in many cities around the country. Check the listings on page 38 for the national office, which can refer you to regional and local contacts.

CHAPTER SIX

1. Literally, "Blessed is he who comes. Blessed is she who comes."
2. Circumcision is called "the covenant of Abraham," the first man to be circumcised as a Jew. "Such shall be the covenant between Me and you and your offspring to follow which you shall keep: every male among you shall be circumcised. You shall circumcise the flesh of your foreskin, and that shall be the sign of the covenant between Me and you" (Genesis 17:10–11).
3. Rabbi Shimon bar Yochai said, "Behold, a man loves no one better than his son, and yet he circumcises him!" To which Rabbi Nachman bar Shmuel responded, "He rejoices over the *mitzvah* even though he sees his son's blood being shed" (*Midrash Tanchuma* on *Tetzaveh* 1).
4. Task Force on Circumcision, "Circumcision Policy Statement" (RE9850), *Pediatrics*, March 1999, volume 103, number 3. The statement also found no evidence that boys or men suffer psychological damage or harm to sexual function from circumcision.
5. In the words of Maimonides, the great twelfth-century rabbi, philosopher, and physician, "No one should circumcise himself or his sons for any other reasons but for pure faith." *Guide for the Perplexed*, translated by M. Friedlander (Dover, 1956), p. 378.
6. According to one study, there is evidence in favor of waiting the extra few days; in a full-term baby, substances that regulate blood coagulation and facilitate healing are slightly below normal at birth, and one of these actually declines between the second and sixth day of life. But by the eighth day its presence in the body is at above-normal levels (Sheldon B. Korones, M.D., *High Risk Newborn Infants* [C.V. Mosby Co., 1976]).
7. The codified laws and liturgy regarding *brit milah* date from the first century C.E., if not earlier.
8. A *bris* may not be scheduled on a Shabbat or holiday for the purposes of conversion or adoption, or for babies born by Caesarean section, or if the *bris* was delayed for health reasons.
9. Orthodox *mohelim* will not officiate if the baby's mother is not Jewish.
10. The prophet Elijah, who preached about the importance of *brit milah*, is "invited" to every *bris*. The *kisei shel Eliyahu*, the chair of Elijah, has been a custom

since the Middle Ages. Today, a chair is decorated or a special pillow used for this ceremonial gesture.

11. Though not always used at liberal *brises*, the traditional blessing is: "Blessed are You, God, Source of Life, Who sanctifies Your beloved from birth and who has impressed Your decree in his flesh, and marked this offspring with the sign of the holy covenant. Therefore, for the sake of this covenant, O living God, our portion, our rock, protect this child from all misfortune, for the sake of Your covenant that You have placed in our flesh. Blessed are You, Adonai, Who establishes the covenant.

   "Our God and God of our ancestors, sustain this child for his father and mother, and may he be called ____, son of ____ and ____.

   "May his father rejoice in the issue of his loins and may his mother exult in the fruit of her womb, as it is written, 'Your father and mother will rejoice. She who bore you will exult.' "

12. If you are fortunate enough to have more than one grandfather present, they can share the *sandek* honors, one holding the baby during the circumcision, the other holding the baby during the naming.

13. See Anita Diamant, *The New Jewish Baby Book* (Jewish Lights, 1994), pp. 251–56. See the appendices under the heading "What Non-Jews Should Know" that can be used as informational hand-outs at a *bris* ceremony.

14. Ibid., the discussion on "Addressing Your Non-Jewish Family's Concerns," pp. 234–39.

15. The ceremony is known by many names, including *simchat bat* ("joy of the daughter"). It may also be called a "baby naming."

16. In recent Ashkenazic tradition, daughters were named in the synagogue during a Torah service. The new father was called to the Torah, where the *Mi Shebeirach* blessing, an all-purpose healing/special-occasion blessing was recited for the health of mother and baby, and his daughter's name announced for the first time. Often, mother and baby did not attend this service. There may also have been other folk customs for naming, welcoming, and blessing daughters, as evidenced by the archaic term *brisitzeh* (a Yiddish feminine form of *bris*), which suggests some kind of Ashkenazic covenant ceremony.

17. Grandparents are sometimes given special ceremonial roles, called *kvatterin*, *kvatter* (godmother and godfather, respectively), and *sandek* (sponsor). The *sandek* or *sandeket* (the feminine form of *sandek*) may hold the baby during the naming. The *kvatter* and *kvatterin* might bring the baby into the room, hold her during some part of the ceremony, or perform other ceremonial tasks such as candlelighting. Unlike godparents in Christian ceremonies, however, the *kvatter* and *kvatterin* do not assume responsibility for the child's religious upbringing; their roles are strictly honorary and ceremonial. The same holds true for the *sandek*, a word that probably derives from the Greek for "patron."

18. See above, note 10.

19. Courtesy of Rabbi Sandy Eisenberg Sasso, Beth El Zedeck Congregation, Indianapolis, Indiana.

20. Although some people are disconcerted by the similarity between this washing and Christian baptism, water rituals are very much a part of Jewish practice. Observant Jews wash their hands and say a blessing before meals, and the *mikvah* (ritual immersion) marks the cycles of women's lives. The Torah is rich with

water imagery associated with women. Sarah and Abraham welcomed the three guests who brought them news of their son by bringing them water for washing. Rebecca makes her biblical appearance at a well, as does Rachel. Miriam is associated with a well of water that sustained the Hebrews in the wilderness.

21. For Hebrew and transliterations, see Diamant, *The New Jewish Baby Book*.

22. See also Marcia Falk's alternative version in *The Book of Blessings* (Harper SanFrancisco, 1996), pp. 124–25.

23. Christianity acknowledges the purifying, regenerative power of water in the ritual of baptism, which may have been borrowed from Jewish practice. For Jews, the water of the *mikvah* represents beginnings: the primordial waters of Eden, the oceans in which life on earth began, the water of the womb.

24. *Mikvah* is primarily used by Orthodox Jewish women as a precondition for sexual activity, a purification from the *niddah*, or ritual separation of husband and wife during menstruation. While this practice has been abandoned by most liberal Jews, Orthodox women (and men) argue that the laws of family purity (*taharat hamishpachah*) are not demeaning to women, but in fact are spiritually sensitive to women's monthly cycles.

    Liberal Jews have started to reclaim the *mikvah*, which is also used to mark important transitions, such as the change from being an unmarried person to being a bride or groom. Immersing before Shabbat or Yom Kippur bespeaks a desire to start over, do better.

25. Given the right of renunciation (discussed below, in Chapter 11, "Adoptive Families"), some parents and rabbis delay or repeat the conversionary *mikvah* until just prior to *bar* or *bat mitzvah*. However, this is an extremely controversial choice. *Mikvah* for a teenager can be a heavy emotional burden at a vulnerable moment of development, when children are struggling to define themselves. A public challenge to their Jewish identity may be the last thing they need.

26. Not all Reform rabbis require *hatafat dam brit*.

27. For a sample ceremony see *"Ametz HaBrit,* Adopting the Covenant, Jewish Adoption Rituals," in Shelley Kapnek Rosenberg, *Adoption and the Jewish Family* (Jewish Publication Society, 1998), pp. 239–67, and the *brit immuts* ("covenant of adoption") in Diamant's *Choosing a Jewish Life: A Handbook for People Converting to Judaism and for Their Family and Friends* (Schocken Books, 1997).

28. The "generic" convert's name for babies was more common in the past, when adopted children were usually born of a Jewish mother.

29. To find such quotations, consult Alfred J. Kolatch, *The New Name Dictionary: Modern English and Hebrew Names* (Jonathan David Publishers, 1989).

CHAPTER SEVEN

1. Maimonides, *Mishneh Torah, Sefer Mahda*, The Book of Knowledge Hilkot Dayot, translated by Rabbi Lawrence Kushner, 1979.

2. From Martin Buber, *Hasidism and Modern Man* (Horizon Press, 1958).

3. An example of a community-based supplementary school is Kesher Cambridge Community Hebrew School in Cambridge, Mass., which offers up to fifteen hours a week of innovative after-school Jewish programming and is a national model.

4. See page 39 for information about the Society for Humanistic Judaism:
5. For descriptions of eight outstanding synagogue schools in liberal congregations around the country, see, "Supplementary Schools Education," edited by Barry Holtz, project director of the Best Practices Project in Jewish Education, a program of the Council for Initiatives in Jewish Education, (CIJE) 1993. Available on-line at www.jesna.org/publicat/rsrch7.htm.
6. The liberal day school movement began in the 1950s, when the Conservative movement opened its first Solomon Schechter School, named for the first chancellor of the Jewish Theological Seminary. As of 1999, there were sixty-three Schechter schools in North America. The first Reform day schools opened in 1970; their number grew to twenty-one by 1999. New inter- or transdenominational day schools were established in cities throughout the United States in the 1990s, and they continue to expand in order to keep up with demand.
7. There is solid evidence that camping fosters Jewish identity later in life. The National Jewish Population Study of 1990 (Council of Jewish Federations) showed a clear correlation between three particular childhood experiences and later Jewish affiliation and practice: day school attendance, trips to Israel in the teen years, and Jewish summer camp.
8. Camp differences reflect movement differences: Conservative camps keep kosher; most Reform camps do not; services at Conservative camps are traditional, while at Reform camps they tend to be more creative, i.e., written by campers and counselors.
9. According to 1999 figures from the Foundation for Jewish Camping, there are approximately one hundred residential camps in North America sponsored by the Jewish community, serving around 30,000 youngsters, approximately 4 percent of the estimated Jewish population of camp-age kids. These include fifteen Reform movement camps, eight Conservative Ramah camps, twelve religious Zionist and other Orthodox camps, twelve secular Zionist camps (among them Young Judaea and Habonim Dror), twenty-three Jewish community center camps, and another twelve under private-foundation auspices. There are other small programs, mostly run by Orthodox communities.
10. The ACA has given its accreditation to about 25 percent of the camps in the United States and Canada. Although many Jewish camps have ACA accreditation, its absence does not necessarily signal an inferior camp; the process is time-consuming and expensive, so some camps simply forgo it.

CHAPTER EIGHT

1. See Judith Davis's book *Whose Bar/Bat Mitzvah Is This, Anyway? A Guide for Parents Through a Family Rite of Passage* (St. Martin's, 1998) for more about family dynamics at the bar/bat mitzvah.
2. By the first century C.E., adulthood was universally held to begin at thirteen for boys and twelve for girls, a view codified in the Talmud, which states that "At age thirteen, one becomes subject to the commandments." Until the Middle Ages, reaching the age of thirteen was not associated with any particular rituals or celebrations.
3. At first, bar and bat mitzvah were distinctly different: boys were usually expected

to read or chant from the Torah on Saturday morning, while girls read or chanted the weekly *Haftarah* portion at a Friday-night service.

4. Mazon: A Jewish Response to Hunger. 12401 Wilshire Boulevard Suite 303, Los Angeles, CA 90025-1015

5. Facing History and Ourselves, 16 Hurd Road, Brookline, MA 02146; 617-232-1595. A foundation that develops curriculum and trains teachers in Holocaust education for people of all ages and backgrounds.

CHAPTER NINE

1. Check the Hillel website (www.hillel.org) for information on colleges and universities around the world.

2. Serene Victor, Jewish education consultant, summarizes this relationship between teen and institution in the following three questions: Does someone in the congregation strive to know every teen? Do kids make real contributions to the community? Does the community hold them accountable?

3. The current boom in the Jewish teen population, the progeny of the baby boomers, signals a need for more resources—and advocates—devoted to youth.

4. Amy L. Sales, Ph.D., *Jewish Youth Databook* (CMJS/ICR Brandeis University, 1996, p. i).

5. Some communities are experimenting with a series of weekend retreats instead of weekly classes.

6. While there are some single-movement high schools run by the Reform and Conservative denominations, the interdenominational or "transdenominational" community Jewish schools accept students from a wide range of Jewish families, from secular to modern Orthodox. These programs are models of cooperation and respect in the often fractious Jewish world.

7. *Education Week,* vol. XVII, no. 27, March 18, 1998.

8. B'nai B'rith (whose name means "sons of the covenant") is an international service organization with programs in social action and public affairs.

9. Hillel is named for one of Judaism's most beloved teachers, Hillel the Elder, who lived toward the end of the first century B.C.E.

CHAPTER TEN

1. Talmud: *Pesahim* 116a.
2. Leviticus 19:14.
3. *Pirke Avot* 4:27.
4. The figure 17 percent reflects the national estimate that 17 percent of the general U.S. population have a disability that falls under the protections of the Americans with Disabilities Act. Given the genetic diseases to which the Jewish community is prone, that figure may even be a bit low.
5. *Gemilut hassadim* (lovingkindness), *rachamim* (mercy), and *tikkun olam* (repair of the world).
6. Miriam Hyman, "Choosing a Jewish School for Your Learning-Disabled Child," www.Jewishfamily.com (April 20, 1999).

CHAPTER ELEVEN

1. The Jewish Population Survey estimates some 3 percent of all Jewish children are adopted, and the trend seems to be growing.
2. Rita J. Simon, Ph.D., and Howard Altstein, Ph.D., note that "What seems to be universally agreed upon is the importance of linking with an adoptive parent support group such as the Stars of David. This connection appears critical for all concerned. We recommend that social workers actively encourage adoptive families to join local branches of this organization" ("Jewish Families Adopt Children from Abroad," *Journal of Jewish Communal Service*, Spring 1991, vol. 67, no. 3).
3. *Sanhedrin* 19b.
4. Lawrence J. Epstein, *The Theory and Practice of Welcoming Converts to Judaism* (Edwin Mellen Press, 1992) p. 66.
5. There is no drama or ceremony to this "right"; a person who knows but makes no reference to her origin has accepted the decision and the conversion is final. Today, the ceremony of bar or bat mitzvah is seen as a formal affirmation of Jewish identity.
6. The Conservative movement requires that all adoptive children go to the *mikvah* and that boys also undergo *brit milah* or *hatafat dam brit*. The Reconstructionist and Reform movements accept converts without *milah* or *mikvah*, and, according to the doctrine of patrilineal descent, also accept the children of Jewish fathers as Jews without conversion ritual. However, since many individual Reconstructionist and Reform rabbis also strongly suggest full ritual observance, be sure to consult with your rabbi as you make these choices.
7. Shelly Kapnek Rosenberg, *Adoption and the Jewish Family: Contemporary Perspectives* (Jewish Publication Society, 1998), p. 214.
8. Biological children sometimes make similar, equally painful, statements: "I didn't decide to be Jewish. I was just born into this accidentally and you can't make me be something I don't want to be," etc.

1. Isaac Klein, A Guide to Jewish Religious Practice (Jewish Theological Seminary of America, 1979). pg. 275.
2. Jack Reimer and Nathaniel Stampfer, *So That Your Values Live On: Ethical Wills and How to Prepare Them* (Jewish Lights Publishing, 1991). See the ethical will of Moshe Yehoshua Zelig Hakoen, head of a Latvian rabbinic court, c. 1790–1855, (pp. 10–18).
3. Ibid. See the ethical will of Rose Weiss Baygel, an immigrant from Riga, who worked in a sweatshop, picketed with the Garment Workers Union, and raised three children (pp. xxiv–xxv).

Glossary

Akedah   The story of the binding of Isaac in Genesis 22. Hebrew for "binding."

Aleph-bet   Name of the Hebrew alphabet; from the names of its first two letters.

aliyah   Literally, "to go up." In the synagogue, to be called to the Torah. "Making *aliyah*" refers to moving to the land of Israel.

Apochrypha   Fourteen writings that were not included in the final version of the Bible but which are, nevertheless, important Jewish texts.

Aramaic   Ancient Semitic language closely related to Hebrew. The Talmud was written in Aramaic.

Ashkenazic   Describes the Jews and Jewish culture of Eastern and Central Europe.

Baal Shem Tov   Honorific name of Israel ben Eliezer, the founder of Hasidism, the eighteenth-century mystical revival movement.

Baruch Ata Adonai Eloheynu Melech Ha-Olam . . .   The words that begin Hebrew blessings, commonly rendered in English as "Blessed art Thou, Lord our God. . . ." This book contains a number of alternative translations.

bat   "Daughter"; "daughter of"; as in bat mitzvah, "daughter of the commandment." Pronounced *baht*.

B.C.E.   Abbreviation for: Before the Common Era. Jews generally use this instead of the Christian designation B.C., which stands for "Before Christ."

bet din   A court (literally a "house of law") of three rabbis that is convened to witness and give communal sanction to events such as conversions to Judaism.

bimah   The dais or raised platform in the synagogue where the leader of the prayers stands.

bris   Yiddish for *brit*, the most common way of referring to the covenant of circumcision.

brit   A covenant.

brit milah   The covenant of circumcision.

bubbe   Yiddish word for "grandma."

C.E.   Abbreviation for: Common Era. Jews generally use it instead of the Christian

275

designation A.D., which stands for Anno Domini (Latin for "the year of our lord").

cantor   Leader of synagogue services trained in Jewish liturgical music.

challah   Braided loaf of egg bread, traditional for Shabbat, the holidays, and festive occasions.

chazzan   Hebrew for cantor. *Chazzanit* is the feminine form.

cheder   In Europe, the elementary school where Jewish boys studied Torah and Talmud, later transplanted to the United States.

chutzpah   Yiddish for courage; nerve; brass.

Conservative   A Jewish religious movement developed in the United States during the twentieth century as a more traditional response to modernity than that offered by the Reform movement.

daven   To pray.

Diaspora   Exile; the dwelling of Jews outside the Holy Land.

d'rash   A religious insight, often relating to a text from the Torah.

d'var Torah   Literally, "word of Torah," meaning an explication of a portion of the Torah.

draydl   A spinning top used for playing a child's game of chance during the festival of Hanukkah.

etrog   Citron, a lemon-like fruit, one of the four species used in the observance of Sukkot.

erev   Evening. "The evening before." Used to refer to the hours after sunset when holidays begin. For example, "Erev Rosh Hashanah."

flayshig   Any food containing meat, which according to *kashrut*, the traditional laws governing what Jews eat, may not be mixed with dairy (*milchig*) products.

haggadah   A book containing the liturgy of the Passover seder; similarly, a liturgy of the Tu B'Shvat seder. Hebrew for "a telling."

haimish   Yiddish for "homelike," "giving one a sense of belonging."

hakafot   Hebrew plural of *hakafah*, meaning "procession." There are seven processions, or parades, of the Torah during the Simchat Torah celebration.

halachah   Traditional Jewish law contained in the Talmud and its commentaries.

hamentaschen   A triangular, fruit-filled pastry served on Purim and said to resemble Hamen's hat.

Hamotzi   Blessing over bread recited before meals.

hametz   Leavened foods forbidden during Passover.

Hanukkah   Hebrew for "dedication"; an eight-day winter festival commemorating the victory of the Maccabees over the Syrians in 165 B.C.E., celebrated in part by the lighting of a *hanukkiah*, an eight-branched candelabra.

haroset   A mixture of wine, nuts, and apples or dates used during the Passover seder to symbolize the mortar prepared by the Hebrew slaves.

Hasidism   Eighteenth-century Jewish mystical revival, a movement that stressed God's presence in the world and the idea that joy could be seen as a way of communing with God.

hatafat dam brit   Symbolic circumcision (literally, "the taking of a drop of blood") practiced in the case of a convert to Judaism who is already circumcised.

Havdalah   The Saturday evening ceremony that separates Shabbat from the rest of the week; literally, "separation."

havurah   Fellowship; also small participatory groups that meet for prayer, study, and celebration. The plural is *havurot.*

hechsher   A symbol on food packaging that indicates its contents are kosher and prepared under rabbinical supervision.

hiddur mitzvah   The rabbinic principal of adorning or decorating something used for religious purposes. For example, using a beautiful goblet as opposed to a paper cup to make a blessing over wine. Hebrew for "beautification of a *mitzvah.*"

Hillel   A great Talmudic scholar who lived near the end of the first century B.C.E. Also, the name of the Jewish college campus organization.

huppah   Wedding canopy.

Kaddish   The prayer most associated with mourning, a doxology, or listing, of God's attributes.

kashrut   Traditional system of laws that govern what and how Jews eat.

ketubah   Marriage contract.

kiddush   The blessing over wine; literally, "sanctification."

kippah   Hebrew for "cap"; a skull cap, worn as a sign of reverence for God. The Yiddish term is *yarmulke.*

kittel   A white robe worn by the groom at a wedding and by the leader of the *seder;* also used as a burial shroud.

klezmer   A joyful, soulful form of Jewish music that blends military marches, European folk songs, dance tunes, and, in this century, American jazz.

kosher   Foods deemed fit for consumption according to the laws of *kashrut.*

Lag B'Omer   A minor holiday that falls between Passover and Shavuot, associated with weddings and picnics.

L'Shanah Tovah Tikatevu   The greeting for the Jewish New Year: "May you be inscribed for a good year." (Often shortened to *"Shanah tovah"*—"A good year.")

lulav   A bouquet of palm boughs, myrtle, and willow branches used during the holiday of Sukkot.

Machzor   The special High Holy Day prayer book; Hebrew for "cycle."

matzah   Flat unleavened bread eaten during the holiday of Passover; known as the "bread of affliction" and the "bread of haste."

maven   Yiddish for "expert."

Mazel tov   Literally, "Good luck"; in common use, it means "congratulations."

Megillah   A scroll; the Book of Esther, the text for Purim, is *Megillat Esther,* usually called "the *megillah."* Also a Yiddish term that means "story."

mensch   Literally, a "person"; but often used to denote an honorable, decent person.

mezuzah   The first two paragraphs of the *Shema,* a Jewish prayer, written on a parchment scroll and encased in a small container, traditionally affixed to the doorways of Jewish homes.

midrash   Imaginative exposition of stories based on the Bible.

mikvah   Ritual bath.

milah   Circumcision. *Brit milah* is the covenant of circumcision

milchig   Dairy foods, which, according to *kashrut,* may not be mixed with foods containing meat (*flayshig*).

Minchah   "Afternoon"; the afternoon service is referred to as *Minchah.*

minyan   A prayer quorum of ten adult Jews; for Orthodox Jews, ten men.

Mishna   The first part of the Talmud, comprised of six "orders" of laws regarding everything from agriculture to marriage.

mitzvah   Hebrew for "commandment" or "good deed." "Sacred obligation" or "Jewish obligation" are better translations, but there really is no English term that captures the complexity of this concept.

mohel   A person trained in the rituals and procedures of *brit milah,* circumcision. Pronounced *mo-hail* in Hebrew, *moil* in Yiddish.

Ne'ilah   The final closing service of Yom Kippur; Hebrew for "locking" or "closing."

Oneg Shabbat   Literally, joy of the Sabbath. A gathering, for food and fellowship, after Friday-night synagogue services.

Orthodox   In general usage, the term refers to Jews who follow traditional Jewish law. The modern Orthodox movement developed in the nineteenth century in response to the Enlightenment and Reform Judaism.

parasha   The weekly Torah portion.

Pesach   The holiday of Passover.

Purim   A late-winter festival that celebrates the rescue of the Jews from destruction, as told in the Scroll of Esther.

Rabbi   Teacher. A rabbi is a seminary-ordained member of the clergy. "The rabbis" refers to the men who codified the Talmud.

Reconstructionist   A religious movement begun in the United States in the twentieth century by Mordecai Kaplan, who saw Judaism as an evolving religious civilization.

Reform   A movement begun in nineteenth-century Germany that sought to reconcile Jewish tradition with modernity.

Rosh Hashanah   The fall holiday that marks the beginning of the Jewish year. Literally, "head of the year."

Rosh Hodesh   First day of every lunar month; a semi-holiday.

sandek   Jewish godfather; the one who holds the baby during a circumcision.

s'eudat mitzvah   A commanded meal; the festive celebration of a milestone.

seder   The Passover talking feast. "Seder" (Hebrew for "order") can also be used to describe the order of rituals of other meals; for example, the Tu B'Shvat seder.

Shabbat   Sabbath. In Yiddish, *Shabbes.*

Shacharit   Morning; the morning service is called *Shacharit.*

Shalom   A universal Hebrew greeting that means "hello," "goodbye," and "peace."

shamash   "Helper" or "beadle"; also the helper candle in the Hanukkah menorah.

Shechinah   God's feminine attributes.

Shehechiyanu   A common prayer of thanksgiving for new blessings.

Shema   The Jewish prayer that declares God's unity.

schmooze   A Yiddish word that means "chat."

Shavuot   The late spring harvest festival that commemorates the giving of the Torah to the Jewish people.

sh'chitah   The laws of kosher ritual slaughter, according to which butchers say special prayers when they kill an animal and use methods that were, when instituted, considered the fastest and most humane.

shtetl   A generic term used to describe the small Eastern European towns inhabited by Ashkenazic Jews before the Holocaust.

shul   Synagogue.

siddur   Prayerbook.

simcha Joy, and the celebration of joy.

Simchat Torah The holiday at the end of Sukkot that marks the end and the renewal of the annual Torah-reading cycle; Hebrew for "rejoicing over the Torah."

siyyum Completion; Hebrew term used to describe a graduation ceremony.

shiva The seven-day period of mourning following a funeral.

shochet A kosher butcher.

sukkah A temporary hut or booth erected for the holiday of Sukkot.

Sukkot The fall harvest festival; also the plural of the word *sukkah*.

taharat hamishpachah Laws of family purity prescribing times for a wife's sexual availability and the use of *mikvah*.

tallis; tallit Prayer shawl. *Tallis* is Yiddish, *tallit* Hebrew.

Talmud Library of rabbinic thought and laws, collected over the period 200 B.C.E. to 500 C.E.

Tanach The book that contains the entire Hebrew Bible, including the Torah, the Writings, and the Prophets.

Tashlich The Rosh Hashanah ceremony of "casting out" sins by tossing breadcrumbs into a body of natural water.

teshuvah Repentence; from the Hebrew for "turning."

tikkun olam "Repairing the world"—a fundamental Jewish concept of taking responsibility for the world and trying to improve it.

Tisha B'av The ninth day of the Hebrew month of Av, a date that commemorates the destruction of the First and Second Temples in ancient Jerusalem.

Torah First five books of the Hebrew Bible, divided into portions that are read aloud during worship services.

Tu B'Shvat The fifteenth day of the Hebrew month of Shvat, a festival celebrating the New Year of the Trees.

ushpizin "Guests" in Hebrew; refers to the Sukkot tradition of inviting the patriarchs and matriarchs into the *sukkah*.

tzedakah Righteous giving or action toward the poor; charity.

yarhzeit Yiddish for "a year's time"; the anniversary of a death.

Yiddish Language spoken by Ashkenazic Jews, in Europe, it dates back to the tenth or eleventh century.

Yizkor A memorial prayer.

Yom HaAtzmaut Hebrew for Israel Independence Day.

Yom HaShoah Hebrew for Holocaust Remembrance Day.

Yom Kippur Day of Atonement, the holiest of the High Holy Days.

Index

INDEX

ABOUT THE AUTHORS

Anita Diamant is the author of *Saying Kaddish, Choosing a Jewish Life, The New Jewish Wedding, Living a Jewish Life, The New Jewish Baby Book, Bible Baby Names,* and a novel, *The Red Tent.* Her articles have also appeared in the *Boston Globe Magazine, Parents, McCall's, Reform Judaism,* and *Hadassah Magazine.* She lives in Newton, Massachusetts, with her husband and daughter.

Karen Kushner is a clinical social worker and the coauthor, with her husband, Rabbi Lawrence Kushner, of *Because Nothing Looks Like God.* She is the mother of three adult children and lives in Sudbury, Massachusetts.